THE LOW-CARBON COOKBOOK

THE LOW-CARBON COOKBOOK

REDUCE FOOD WASTE & COMBAT CLIMATE CHANGE WITH 140 SUSTAINABLE PLANT-BASED RECIPES

Alejandra Schrader

Publisher Mike Sanders
Editor Christopher Stolle
Art Director William Thomas
Senior Designer Jessica Lee
Photographer Kelley Jordan Schuyler
Food Stylist Chung Chow
Recipe Tester Irena Kutza
Proofreaders Georgette Beatty & Diane Durrett
Indexer Celia McCoy

First American Edition, 2021
Published in the United States by DK Publishing
6081 E. 82nd St., Suite 400, Indianapolis, IN 46250

ISBN 978-1-6156-4989-1
Library of Congress Catalog Number: 2020950753

Note: This publication contains the opinions and ideas of its author. It is intended to provide helpful and informative
material on the subject matter covered. It is sold with the understanding that the author and publisher are not
engaged in rendering professional services in the book. If the reader requires personal assistance or advice, a
competent professional should be consulted. The author and publisher specifically disclaim any responsibility for
any liability, loss, or risk, personal or otherwise, which is incurred as a consequence, directly or indirectly, of the use
and application of any of the contents of this book.

Trademarks: All terms mentioned in this book that are known to be or are suspected of being trademarks or service
marks have been appropriately capitalized. Alpha Books, DK, and Penguin Random House LLC cannot attest to the
accuracy of this information. Use of a term in this book should not be regarded as affecting the validity of any
trademark or service mark.

DK books are available at special discounts when purchased in bulk for
sales promotions, premiums, fund-raising, or educational use. For details, contact:
DK Publishing Special Markets, 1450 Broadway, Suite 801, New York, NY 10018
SpecialSales@dk.com

Printed and bound in Canada

Photo Credits 6: Jørgen Gomnæs, 7 and 9: David Schrader, 12: Dreamstime.com: Adfoto, 17: Dreamstime.com: Stockr,
18: iStock: piyaset, 22-23: Dorling Kindersley: Peter Anderson, 24: Dreamstime.com: Melanie Hobson, 28: 123RF.com:
Richard Whitcombe 37: Dorling Kindersley: Mark Winwood, 38-39: 123RF.com: kasto, 54: Dorling Kindersley: Will Heap
All other images © Dorling Kindersley Limited
For further information see: www.dkimages.com

For the curious
www.dk.com

CONTENTS

FOREWORD 6

INTRODUCTION 8

01 | CLIMATE & FOOD CRISES 10

02 | OUR CARBON FOOTPRINT 26

03 | THE LOW-CARBON DIET 40

04 | FEEL-GOOD ACTION PLAN 50

05 | BREAKFAST 58

06 | SMALL BITES 74

07 | SALADS 90

08 | SIDES 112

09 | SOUPS & STEWS 130

10 | MAIN DISHES 154

11 | BEVERAGES 180

12 | DESSERTS 196

13 | SAUCES, DIPS, PICKLES & MORE 212

14 | MAKE-AHEAD 228

ENDNOTES 244

REGIONAL & SEASONAL SWAPS 247

INDEX................................... 252

FOREWORD

Talk of planetary emergencies and climate change can be so overwhelming as to scare us into inaction. Who has a budget for solar panels, let alone an electric car? We might want to protect the Amazon and other wild places but feel rather powerless at being able to do anything to protect these faraway places.

Food changes all this. Our food choices have an outsized impact on the future of the planet. Fortunately, we have no shortage of options, no shortage of flavors, and no shortage of diversity to guide this transition. In this beautiful book, Alejandra has assembled amazing recipes with flavors from around the world. What I really like is how these recipes remind us that being climate citizens isn't just urgent and necessary but that it can be enjoyable while also being good for us.

This is a book for the evidence-based, action-oriented eater. For those who want to better understand the challenges we face as a society and who refuse to sit back and watch. Who want to engage, act, and be a part of this decisive decade. There are rich chapters that outline climate, biodiversity, and food challenges. That explain how food can be a major solution. But best of all, it beautifully provides 140 recipes for people and planet.

In 2019, my organization, EAT, brought together a team of 37 scientists from around the world to provide the best available evidence on what are healthy diets and what are the environmental limits of food—the so-called "planetary boundaries"—that define the safe environmental space for all of us and for our children. In conversations with Johan Rockström, one of the world's leading environmental scientists who signaled such guidelines are still missing, we learned that food, our most intimate relationship with our own health, and also our most intimate relationship with nature were failing in both areas. Food has become the leading cause of poor health globally and is the biggest source of environmental destruction and degradation.

However, this doesn't have to be the case. What foods we eat, how we produce them, and how much is lost and wasted can change everything. It also makes food our best bet for restoring the environment as well as regenerating health.

Gunhild Stordalen *focuses on climate, health, and sustainability issues in her work. She was named to a lead role at the UN Food Systems Summit 2021 and she's an influential female leader shaping the climate agenda. In 2019, Gunhild received the UN Foundation's Global Leadership Award for her work transforming the global food system for people and planet.*

As Alejandra suggests, healthful and sustainable eating starts with plant-rich options, putting much more emphasis on fruits, vegetables, beans and pulses, whole grains, seeds, and nuts. This means taking meat completely off the table for those who desire vegetarian or vegan options or for moving it to the side—smaller portions of sustainably produced meat, with a focus on flavor.

This book calls for being smarter about where we source foods and supporting farmers who leave space in their fields for nature. Space for pollinators. Space for pest-controlling ladybugs and wasps as well as insect-eating birds. Space for healthy soils that soak up carbon and water, fighting climate change and helping grow more and better food.

Dig in, explore, adapt, engage! Remember that food is about sharing. Sharing stories, cultures, and time with our loved ones. I encourage you to share these recipes with them but to also take a moment to share a conversation on climate. Our collective future depends on all of us.

Dr. Gunhild Stordalen
Founder and Executive Chair, EAT Foundation

ACKNOWLEDGMENTS

Writing my first book wouldn't have been possible without the loving support of my dear husband, David. From taking last-minute trips to the market to buy missing ingredients while I developed recipes and serving as the designated taste-tester to proofreading entire chapters in the middle of the night and offering unwavering help throughout my high-risk pregnancy, he was the best ally and companion throughout this process. *Muchísimas gracias, Papi.*

Thanks to everyone on the DK Publishing team who helped make this passion project of mine a reality. Special thanks to the ever-patient Christopher Stolle, my wonderful editor, for enriching this experience with knowledge and much encouragement. Grateful for the hard work that art director Bill Thomas, designer Jessica Lee, photographer Kelley Jordan Schuyler, food stylist Chung Chow, photo shoot chef Ashley Brooks, and recipe tester Irena Kutza put in to create a gorgeous book while satisfying my ambitious requests.

I appreciate the support of SDG2 Advocacy Hub Secretariat and the Chefs' Manifesto team. Special thanks to Director Paul Newnham, who for years has backed my passion for sustainable food systems and provided many opportunities for professional development, which have helped me get to where I am today as a chef and environmental steward.

I'm thankful for my "OxFamily"—the entire team at Oxfam America—who continues to give me a platform to fight for the causes I am most passionate about, including food and nutrition equality. I'm so lucky to have the support of Abby Maxman, their CEO and director! Special thanks to Clara Herrero for being such a powerful ally.

Thanks to everyone at the EAT Foundation, an organization that has paved the (scientific) way to understanding the relationship between food and planetary health. They've valued my voice and culinary perspective and have offered numerous opportunities for professional growth. Special thanks to Dr. Gunhild Stordalen and Dr. Fabrice DeClerck.

Writing a cookbook in the middle of a global pandemic was challenging and rewarding. I'm thankful for the love and encouragement from family and friends in Venezuela and the East Coast of the United States. *Si se puede!*

Alejandra Schrader is a plant-based nutrition certified chef, public speaker, and activist based in Los Angeles. Her culinary career was sparked on Fox's MasterChef: Season 2, where she was a top finalist and fan favorite. Alejandra seeks to promote sustainable diets that are good for humans and for the planet; to connect home cooks and chefs to the land that provides us sustenance; and to empower people to do their part in building stronger food systems for everyone.

INTRODUCTION

Earth has more than 30,000 edible plants, and while we rely on only about 30, just 3 make up 60% of humanity's caloric intake: corn, wheat, and soy. With so much to choose from—legumes, grains, fruits, vegetables, nuts, seeds, and more—we need to make a better effort to incorporate a wider variety of plants into our lives.

Just looking out the window or watching the news allows us to see that the worst effects of climate change are already upon us. Our everyday actions—lifestyles, preferred modes of transportation, energy consumption patterns, eating habits, and excessive wasting—have a direct impact on the environment. In the face of a climate emergency, we need to make shifts in the way we live.

Generating a whopping 26% of all human-generated greenhouse gas emissions, food production in the United States is undeniably related to our climate crisis. More than 50% of all food-related emissions are associated with industrialized animal production: livestock and fisheries. Not all foods are created equal! So our choices around food do indeed make a difference.

After I left a career in land development and planning to transition into the culinary world, it was imperative for me to carry over my passion for the environment and focus on sustainability in the food space. A deep awareness of how our food choices and individual actions impact our carbon footprints motivated me to adjust the operating practices in my food business and inspired change in my eating habits.

For nearly three years, I've pursued a plant-based diet and taken a personal responsibility to help alleviate the environmental crisis. I believe individual actions can make a big difference as part of a collective effort! I've acquired a sense of purpose in promoting plant-based eating, educating others about planet-friendly food habits, and motivating people to support small farmers and sustainable agricultural practices.

Whether you're ready to fully commit to a low-carbon diet or determined to take small actions in your kitchen for the sake of your health and that of the environment, this book will give you the tools to minimize your carbon footprint. I've provided 140 plant-based recipes that will inspire you to eat deliciously, diversify your culinary palate, and get adventurous with new and wholesome ingredients.

It's important to focus our attention on the wide variety of foods we get to taste, enjoy, and benefit from as opposed to grieving the ingredients we choose to avoid. Eating the rainbow—savoring foods from all shades of colors—will open the door to many new and exciting flavors and textures. Browse through my book and you'll see there's no sacrifice in eating this way!

I BELIEVE INDIVIDUAL ACTIONS CAN MAKE A BIG DIFFERENCE AS PART OF A COLLECTIVE EFFORT!

In an effort to help you lose waste and make the most of your investment in GOOD FOOD, I've provided tips to upcycle food—to repurpose ingredients traditionally thrown away to create delectable and beautiful dishes full of nourishment—and to shop wisely, cook smarter, and store your food to maximize its shelf life. Some of the tools I've shared throughout the book are meant to help you be a better, more conscientious cook and to motivate you to become a Food Systems Hero!

We've gotten out of balance—our demands have been surpassing Earth's supply. *The Low-Carbon Cookbook* provides science-backed information to motivate you to be part of the solution: to help build a more sustainable future. By eating more plants and cooking more of the foods that help Mama Earth, we can shrink our carbon footprint and help combat climate change from our own kitchens.

The time is NOW!

ALEJANDRA SCHRADER

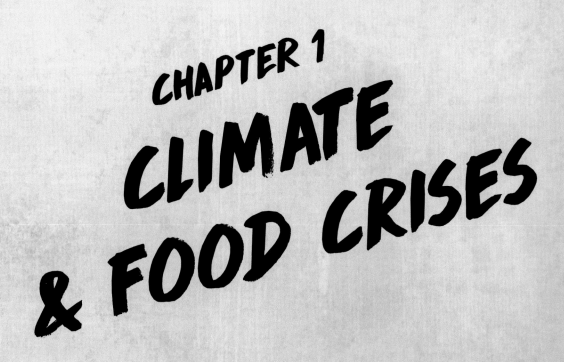

CHAPTER 1
CLIMATE & FOOD CRISES

Our lifestyle choices—from transportation and energy consumption to dietary and wastage patterns—have a direct effect on our health but also on that of the planet. According to Nobel Prize–winning atmospheric chemist Dr. Paul J. Crutzen, a new geological era—the Anthropocene—is demarcated by when human activities started to have a substantial global effect on Earth's systems.[1] This chapter focuses on the extent and significance of the consequences of our actions: to the environment, to our food systems, and to the well-being of humanity. I aim to share with you the science-based facts that originally raised a red flag and pushed me to dig deeper to understand the relationship between food and sustainability.

THE CLIMATE CRISIS

Planet Earth is suffering. Rising global temperatures, natural disasters, and extreme weather events threaten natural ecosystems and humankind as a whole. They've taken a severe toll on food systems, public health, global economies, and even peace. The Alliance of World Scientists has declared a climate emergency[2] and has warned that continuing to live without adjusting our lifestyle choices, such as transportation, energy consumption, diet, and wastage, is no longer an option.

We've taken our planet for granted. We use resources faster than they can be regenerated and stored. Human activities like the combustion of fossil fuels, production of industrialized livestock, deforestation, and degradation of soils have taken a toll on Earth: Land ice sheets are melting, oceans are acidifying, forests are burning, etc.

Human-generated impacts on the environment aren't equally inflicted worldwide. Following only China, the United States is the second-largest contributor of global emissions[3] even though we only represent 4% of the planet's population. Our country takes the lead when accounting for aggregated emissions over the past 150 years.[4] We're undergoing a global crisis that has no borders. Our actions affect others, especially poor and vulnerable countries, and we must take responsibility to make greater efforts to alleviate these impacts.

Climate science has been politicized by many in the United States. But I prefer to accept irrefutable evidence, which demands action at every level—and quickly.[5] Inspired by the mindset of climate activist Greta Thunberg, I'll let my convictions guide my own behavior. I'll lead by example and hope to inspire others to help give Mama Earth a loving hand. In the face of a climate emergency, we need to take a bold and collective action.

"I WONDER WHEN WE WILL MAKE EARTH MORE BEAUTIFUL AGAIN INSTEAD OF DEPLETING EVERYTHING."
— DR. PAUL J. CRUTZEN

DEFINING CLIMATE CHANGE & GLOBAL WARMING

Climate change is large-scale, long-term shifts in average weather conditions, including temperature, precipitation, and wind patterns, which are primarily caused by human activities. These shifts might cause a wide range of effects, such as the increase in temperatures worldwide, the rise in sea levels, the length of droughts, and the severity of tropical storms as well as natural disasters caused by flooding, crop damage, and soil erosion, among others.

Global warming is the rapid rise in our planet's average surface temperature caused by increased concentrations of greenhouse gas (GHG) levels in the atmosphere. According to the National Oceanic and Atmospheric Administration's (NOAA) 2019 Global Climate Summary, "the combined land and ocean temperature has increased at an average rate of 0.07°C (0.13°F) per decade since 1880; however, the average rate of increase since 1981 (0.18°C / 0.32°F) is more than twice as great."[6]

It's alarming that 9 of the 10 warmest years recorded since 1880 have occurred since 2005, and as of 2019, there have been 43 consecutive years where global land and ocean temperatures registered above the 20th century average.[7] I'm quite disappointed to know that our planet has never recorded a decrease in average surface temperature in my lifetime. And I think that should change—pronto! Don't you?

GREENHOUSE GASES

Greenhouse gases are gaseous components of the atmosphere. First identified by Professor Svante Arrhenius in 1896,[8] the *greenhouse effect* occurs when greenhouse gases absorb thermal infrared light emitted by the land, the oceans, and the atmosphere itself. This infrared light is redirected back toward Earth, increasing the average temperatures of the surface and keeping Mama Earth comfortably warm and at a habitable temperature for humans: 59°F (15°C) on average. Without GHG, our planet would be near 0°F (-18°C) and covered with ice. Brrr!

GHG emissions have increased exponentially since the Industrial Revolution. Human activities, such as deforestation and burning fossil fuels for energy, release carbon dioxide into the air. Prior to the mid-1700s, the global concentration of CO_2 in the atmosphere was 280 parts

GLOBAL SURFACE TEMPERATURES (1880 TO PRESENT)

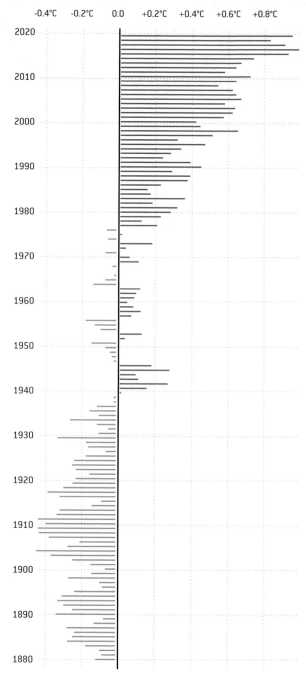

Source: Climate.gov

per million molecules of air (ppm) on average. In 2020, the new record high was determined at 414 ppm. Over two-thirds (65.7%) of the total increase in global greenhouse gases documented in 270 years have taken place in just the last 50.[9] The following sections discuss the most significant gases contributing to the greenhouse effect.

Carbon Dioxide (CO_2)

About three-quarters of global human-generated greenhouse gas emissions come from CO_2. About 40% of carbon dioxide emitted still remains in the atmosphere after 100 years. Although the combustion of fossil fuel use is the primary source of this gas, it can also be released through deforestation, land clearing, and peatland degradation. In addition to contributing to global warming, high CO_2 levels decrease nitrogen content in forest vegetation, increase acidity in ocean waters, and intensify algal blooms in lakes and reservoirs.[10] Decreased nitrogen diminishes soil health and affects plant growth and functions. Ocean acidification affects sea life in general (especially corals, shellfish, and plankton). Algal bloom can produce toxins that affect animals, humans, and the ecosystem as a whole.

Methane (CH_4)

This gas remains in the atmosphere for about a decade after being emitted. However, methane's global warming impact is beyond 25 times greater than CO_2 over 100 years. Of all human-induced global GHG emissions, CH_4 accounts for about 16%. These emissions might come from biomass burning, waste management, and energy use.[11] Livestock supply chains make up 44% of methane emissions generated by human activity.[12]

Nitrous Oxide (N_2O)

This has a global warming potential (GWP)—a unit of how much a given mass of GHG contributes to global warming—300 times higher than CO_2 over 100 years and accounts for approximately 6% of human-caused global emissions. It stays in the atmosphere for more than 100 years after its emission, at which point levels of concentration might still reach 6%. Fertilizer use in agricultural activities is the main source of N_2O emissions.

Fluorinated Gases

Various food manufacturing and industrial processes, such as refrigeration, contribute to the emission of fluorinated gases, which include hydrofluorocarbons (HFCs),

perfluorocarbons (PFCs), and sulfur hexafluoride (SF6). Although they only represent 2% of GHG emissions, these gases have a high GWP—up to tens of thousands—and some of them last tens of thousands of years in the atmosphere. Replacing fluorinated gases is considered to be one of the most important climate actions we can take.

ECOSYSTEMS & BIODIVERSITY

Ecosystems provide essential services for all life—from food and drinkable water to life-supporting atmospheric conditions and materials for basic human needs, such as wood for shelter or cotton and fiber for clothing. Terrestrial, marine, and freshwater ecosystems are affected by climate change and they rapidly modify in response to global warming, precipitation, CO_2 concentration in the atmosphere, ocean acidity, and extreme weather events.[13]

Changes in ecosystems manifest in many different ways, which might affect their physical appearance, the type and number of organisms present, and their functioning, including the cycling of nutrients and productivity. These changes jeopardize *biodiversity*—the vast array of living organisms, ranging from animals and plants to bacteria and the ecological systems of which they're a part[14]—and negatively affect the global food supply and production, among others.

An intricate part of ecosystem structures and functions, biodiversity supports a variety of goods and services derived directly from biological resources. At least 40% of the global economy and a whopping 80% of the economy in developing countries depend on these resources. Climate change has posed a major threat to biodiversity-based ecosystem services, thus affecting the livelihood and well-being of people who rely on these services.[15] Global warming and precipitation are predicted to be the worst drivers of biodiversity loss over the next 50 to 100 years.[16]

Climate change might alter habitats for species by inducing changes in habitat quality and distribution, which, in turn, might force species to move outside of their preferred habitats.[17] The United Nations Intergovernmental Panel on Climate Change (IPCC) has determined that over the next century, climate change will increase the risk of extinction for many species and impair the healthy functioning of ecosystems as a whole.

"Our planet works as a linked biological and physical system (an ecosystem), which is built from the essential element of life: carbon. When ecosystems are destroyed, they release the carbon they are built from into the atmosphere, which contributes to global warming."[18]

While ecosystems are currently susceptible to climate change, they also offer one of the best defenses for our planet and a natural solution to the climate crisis. Just as they're built out of carbon, ecosystems have the ability to store it—in forests, grasslands, coastal wetlands, and agricultural lands.[19] For humans to adapt to climate change, we'll need to depend on our ability to manage the stressors affecting our ecosystems, to change the way in which we live and operate, and to restore damaged biomes.

A coalition of organizations, including the UN Foundation, Environmental Defense Fund, and Conservation International, is urging world leaders to invest in sustainable solutions, such as reforestation, soil regeneration, wetland protection, and ecosystem restoration. These efforts are critical to help limit the rise of global surface temperatures.

BROKEN FOOD SYSTEMS

Scientists say that the effects of climate change—higher temperatures, extreme weather, drought, land degradation, etc.—present significant challenges to global agriculture, food sustainability, and nutrition.[20] Projected environmental changes will likely decrease the yield of important crops for human populations around the world. At a time when one in nine people around the world doesn't get enough food to be healthy and lead an active life, a sharp reduction in staple foods (up to 35% by the year 2100) could be detrimental for humans, especially for those in the poorest communities.

Climate change also affects the quality of our food supply. Elevated levels of CO_2 in the atmosphere are known to reduce concentrations of protein and essential minerals in most plant species, including food staples in American homes, such as wheat, rice, and soybeans.[21] Because about 2 billion people around the world suffer from micronutrient deficiency, diminished nutrients in our food as a result of carbon emissions should be a major public health concern.[22]

At least 80% of the world's cultivated lands are rain-fed and produce about 60% of our food supply.[23] Most farmers rely on predictable weather patterns for their crops. Climate change has altered rainfall patterns globally and intensified precipitation events. Flooding caused by severe storms and sea level rise can damage crops and decrease yields.[24] These extreme conditions might also interrupt efficient food transportation, which would affect accessibility and affordability, and without proper storage conditions, food might become vulnerable to spoilage and contamination.

The remaining 20% of agricultural land relies on groundwater irrigation systems. Climate change—drought and rising temperatures—has been tied to high rates of groundwater depletion around the globe.[25] But nonrenewable irrigation systems are also being drained faster than they can naturally be replenished. The United States ranks within the top 10 countries using unsustainable water in agriculture and in the top 3 of countries exporting the most food grown with such earth-depleting water sources.[26]

Climate change is disrupting agricultural practices and interfering with farmers' ability to raise their traditional crops. Farmers around the United States are trying to keep up. Even those who don't believe in climate change refer to their local weather as extreme or erratic. For example, peach crops in Georgia need a certain amount of cold weather (known as "chill hours"), followed by reliable warm weather. Rising temperatures interfere with chill hours and, therefore, with the yield and quality of the fruit.

When optimal temperature ranges for a specific crop are exceeded, the plant's biological cycles (known as "phenological stages"[27]: pollination, flowering, root development, etc.) are disrupted because of heat stress, ultimately affecting agricultural productivity. Although wheat is one of the earliest plants cultivated by humans, it's been documented as severely affected by current high temperatures and drought, even in its region of origin—the Levant area of the Near East and Ethiopian Highlands. Because wheat is an essential staple for about 2 billion people, a decrease in production severely affects food security and the livelihood of many.[28]

PEOPLE & GLOBAL COMMUNITIES

The environmental crisis affects major global biomes, threatens biodiversity, diminishes agricultural production, and disrupts food supply. This predicament also affects the

lives of those who've caused it: humans. An Oxfam report says this "is a crisis that is driven by the greenhouse gas emissions of the 'haves' that hits the 'have-nots' the hardest." Thus, this *carbon inequality*, as the report labels it, seems to be just another layer of the complex socioeconomic dynamics where the poorest and most vulnerable are most impacted.[29]

Populations including older adults, underprivileged communities, and racial minorities are often disproportionately affected by and less resilient to the health impacts of climate change.[30] Extreme weather events increase the rates of food- and waterborne-related diseases. Higher heat-related deaths are predicted globally given the record-high temperatures registered in recent years and projected for the near future.[31] Poor air quality is also expected to increase vulnerability for those with allergies and respiratory illnesses.

Climate change could impact human health by exacerbating existing health problems caused by climate or weather factors and by producing first-time, unexpected health threats in previously unaffected places.[32] Without the

proper resources or access to healthcare, the vulnerable, low-income communities would be the most affected. These are the very people who suffer the impacts of elevated food prices and lack of accessibility to nutritious, immunity-boosting food.

Besides taking a toll on the health of those who depend on particular ecosystems, global warming and extreme environmental conditions also affect people's mental health. Global communities have strong emotional, cultural, and spiritual connections to the natural habitats they know and the species within each biome. From stress-related to economic instability, uncertainty, and hunger to clinical disorders like anxiety, depression, and suicidality, the intangible impacts of climate change in some communities might be greater than we think.

The concept of planetary health was first coined by the Rockefeller Foundation–Lancet Commission on Planetary Health in 2015. It refers to the "the health of human civilization and the state of the natural systems on which it depends." The report in which the concept first appeared suggests that the global community should recognize that human and planetary health are "two sides of one climate coin" and that together they offer opportunities to alleviate the worst effects of climate change.[33]

The COVID-19 pandemic further revealed the vulnerability of global food systems and the inequalities experienced throughout global communities. Underprivileged people, such as BBIPOC (Brown, Black, Indigenous, and People of Color) in the United States, have been the most affected at every level—from being infected with the virus and lacking job security to not having the means to access basic resources and acquire goods.

Determined to have a zoonotic source, COVID-19 has shown the world the devastating effects of such diseases. The 2015 report on planetary health establishes that "at least half of the world's infectious disease events of zoonotic origin between 1940 and 2005 are estimated to result from changes in land use, in agricultural practices, and in food production practices."[34] In the midst of a climate emergency partly caused by these human practices, we should establish the proper mechanisms to mitigate zoonotic (as well as insect-borne) diseases, including education and sustainable practice standards.

GLOBAL MITIGATION STRATEGIES

The Alliance of World Scientists warning regarding the climate emergency, which has been signed by 13,766 scientists from 156 countries so far, describes "six critical and interrelated steps" that everyone should take to ensure a sustainable future and avoid the worst effects of climate change. In no particular order, they've suggested we make drastic changes in the following areas: energy, short-lived pollutants, nature, food, economy, and population.

Scientists at NASA have set forth a dual approach to respond to climate change. It calls for mitigation by minimizing the amount of greenhouse gases that go into the atmosphere and adaptation by figuring out ways to adjust to climate change. Because I'm generally in favor of action and hands-on tactics, I'll lean into the mitigation approach (while learning to adapt—without giving up!).

In 2015, 196 countries committed to the Paris Agreement— an initiative coordinated by the UN Framework Convention on Climate Change, the primary intergovernmental forum orchestrating the global response for climate change. It aims to secure a sustainable future by limiting the rise of global temperature for this century well below 2°C—preferably 1.5°C— compared with pre-industrial levels.[35]

The Paris Agreement intends to strengthen the ability of countries to deal with the impacts of climate change and to minimize greenhouse emissions in a way that wouldn't harm food production or halt economic development. It proposes a global plan of action while acknowledging the importance of supporting developing nations and vulnerable countries to achieve its ambitious goals.[36]

The original commitment from the United States to the Paris Agreement, as signed in 2015 under President Barack Obama, showed a strong pledge to reducing greenhouse gas emissions. Taking accountability for the magnitude of national emissions—per capita and cumulative—the United States expressed its intent "to achieve an economy-wide target of reducing its greenhouse gas emissions by 26–28 percent below its 2005 level in 2025 and to make best efforts to reduce its emissions by 28%."[37] This Nationally Determined Contribution (NCD) represented our ambitious effort to help combat the climate crisis.

"A CRY OF SURVIVAL COMES FROM THE PLANET ITSELF. A CRY THAT CAN'T BE ANY MORE DESPERATE OR ANY MORE CLEAR."
– PRESIDENT JOE BIDEN

Unfortunately, in 2017, President Donald Trump announced our withdrawal from the Paris Agreement—a decision that left many Americans, me included, concerned about Mama Earth and disappointed about the current state of affairs. I felt a strong sense of relief once I learned that even prior to the beginning of his administration, President Joe Biden had already declared his intention to sign executive orders to rejoin the Paris climate accord. Because of our temporary withdrawal, we might be expected to set new and better targets to meet by 2030 and to introduce a detailed plan of action to accomplish our goals.

At a time when only a collective action will help mitigate the climate crisis, it's important to have global treaties and protocols holding countries accountable, especially developed nations and larger emitters. I believe it's of the utmost importance that an international organization such as the United Nations coordinates not only the Paris Agreement but other important worldwide efforts, such as the Sustainable Development Goals, which I wholeheartedly support in many of my personal and professional endeavors.

Born at the UN Conference on Sustainable Development in Rio de Janeiro in 2012, the Sustainable Development Goals (SDGs) objective was "to produce a set of universal goals that meet the urgent environmental, political and economic challenges facing our world."[38] The 17 goals promote the health of our planet and encourage everyone to build a sustainable and prosperous future for all with a very simple and thorough plan of action: "The Sustainable Development Goals are a call for action by all countries—poor, rich and middle-income—to promote prosperity while protecting the planet. They recognize that ending poverty must go hand-in-hand with strategies that build economic growth and address a range of social needs including education, health, social protection, and job opportunities, while tackling climate change and environmental protection. More important than ever, the goals provide a critical framework for COVID-19 recovery."[39]

Of all SDGs, one specifically addresses the climate crisis: Goal 13. It calls for *Climate Action: Take urgent action to combat climate change and its impacts*. Climate change has been identified by the 2030 Agenda for Sustainable Development as "one of the greatest challenges of our time" and UN member states have expressed concern that climate change's "adverse impacts undermine the ability of all countries to achieve sustainable development."[40] Goal 13 is fundamentally linked to the other 16 for achieving a sustainable future and implies a collective effort across all sectors globally.

It's true that global organizations and governments have to take the lead to establish frameworks to combat climate change, to implement policies and regulations, and to establish mechanisms that monitor greenhouse gas emissions. Businesses must do a better job: Optimize their operations, invest in energy efficiency, and enhance conservation strategies. But we, citizens of the world,

need to do our part and hold ourselves accountable. Individual actions can make a big difference as part of a collective effort. We need to change the way we live.

THE FOOD CRISIS

Food production is intricately associated with our climate crisis. Today's food supply chain—from production and transportation to storage and waste management—generates 26% of all human-generated greenhouse gas emissions. About half the planet's ice-free and desert-free land is occupied by agricultural uses and 87% of that land is used to produce food. It's estimated that 70% of freshwater withdrawals are used for agricultural irrigation.[41, 42]

The negative bearing food production has on our planet goes even deeper. It's responsible for more than 30% of global terrestrial acidification—a phenomenon caused by the atmospheric deposition of acidifying compounds that threatens plant diversity.[43] It also causes 78% of global eutrophication—a process by which runoff fertilizers from food production end up in lakes, rivers, and other bodies of water. The excessive richness of synthetic nutrients in the water causes an extreme algal bloom (such as a dense growth of plant life), which suppresses the availability of oxygen, threatening animal life, aquatic ecosystems, and the environment.[44]

The EAT—Lancet Commission, a collaboration of 37 world-leading scientists, affirms that global food production currently poses a threat to humanity: worsening the climate crisis, deteriorating the environment, diminishing natural ecosystems, and driving the loss of biodiversity.[45] The industrialization of agriculture radically transformed food systems in the United States and globally. It has made production more efficient—in quantitative terms—but it has caused serious consequences to the planet.

INDUSTRIALIZED FOOD PRODUCTION: LIVESTOCK & FISHERIES

Scientists have categorized food emissions based on four major areas: livestock and fisheries, crop production, land use, and supply chain.[46] More than half of all food-related emissions (53% to be precise) are associated with livestock and fisheries. These emissions include land use for livestock, crops for feed, manure and pasture management, and fuel consumption by fishing vessels. This estimate doesn't take into account the share that animal production, wild fish catch, and aquaculture have in the supply chain, which involves processing, transportation, packaging, and retail. Thus, in reality, emissions linked to industrialized animal production are even higher.

The UN Food and Agriculture Organization (FAO) estimates that "about 44 percent of livestock emissions are in the form of Methane (CH_4). The remaining part is almost equally shared between Nitrous Oxide (N_2O, 29 percent) and Carbon Dioxide (CO_2, 27 percent)."[47]

But how exactly are these gases produced? One of the largest sources of greenhouse gases is cattle and other ruminants, such as goats and sheep. As they digest their food, microbes decompose and ferment food (a process called "enteric fermentation"[48]), which produces methane (CH_4) as a by-product. Ruminants belch (er, burp) and the rest is history. Livestock manure, which mostly consists of their feces, contributes to CH_4 emissions as well as nitrous oxide (N_2O). Deforestation and land clearing to make room for industrial livestock production farms release large stores of CO_2 into the atmosphere.[49, 50]

Accountable for approximately 62% of the livestock sector's emissions, cattle are the animal species generating the highest amounts of greenhouse gases. This includes beef and milk but also inedible by-products, such as manure. The products that follow in terms of emissions are pigs, chicken meat and eggs, buffalo meat and milk, and small ruminants' meat and milk. The rest of the emissions pertain to other poultry species, such as turkey and game hen, and nonedible products.[51]

Red meat is favored in North America, where people eat more than six times the recommended amount. In the United States, per capita beef consumption increased by nearly 4% in 2018. Likewise, per capita pork consumption went up by more than 4% in the same year. According to the US Department of Agriculture (USDA), Americans ate 222 pounds of meat and poultry per capita in 2018.

The World Wildlife Fund reported that in 2014, "there were over 23 billion chickens, turkeys, geese, ducks and guinea fowl on the planet—more than three per person."[52] The poultry industry has exploded worldwide in the

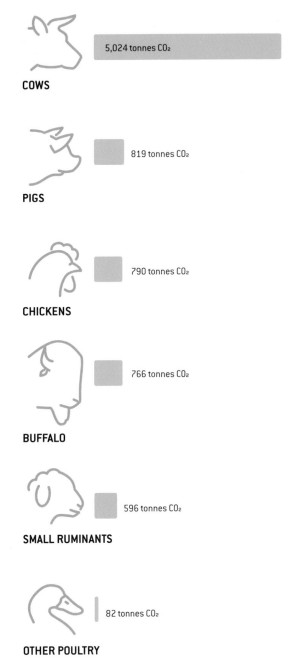

GLOBAL ESTIMATES OF EMISSIONS BY SPECIES

COWS — 5,024 tonnes CO_2

PIGS — 819 tonnes CO_2

CHICKENS — 790 tonnes CO_2

BUFFALO — 766 tonnes CO_2

SMALL RUMINANTS — 596 tonnes CO_2

OTHER POULTRY — 82 tonnes CO_2

Source: Food and Agriculture Organization

last few decades and has become the biggest user of crop-based feed in North America, Europe, and the Asia-Pacific.

The majority of greenhouse gas emissions from the poultry industry—carbon dioxide and nitrous oxide—are mainly associated with on-farm energy consumption but also with the use of fertilizers for feed production.[53] Most emissions are generated during the production stage at the pullet and breeder farms, where propane is used for heating houses and electricity is used for lighting and ventilation. Following the rapid growth of global industrialized poultry production, elevated environmental impacts have been assessed not only near local production settings but also at the regional and global levels—from water pollution and degradation of soils to algal blooms and habitat destruction.[54, 55]

When I first learned these facts about poultry production, I understood that limiting red meat consumption in my diet wasn't enough if I wanted to reduce my carbon footprint and make a real difference for the environment. The same goes for seafood—whether it comes from farms or wild fisheries. More than 155 million tons of seafood are produced globally each year—more than 4 times the amount produced 50 years ago.[56] A spur in overall consumption of fish in developed countries, such as China, the United States, and Japan, created a demand that couldn't be met by fisheries in their national waters. Fish populations declined over time:

The amount we caught exceeded the rate at which it could be reproduced and replenished—a concept known as "overfishing." Our appetite for seafood literally caught up with us.

This global challenge plays an important part in today's industrialized production of fish, crustaceans, and mollusks. Major distant-water fishing companies (which catch in developing countries, often illegally and unreported) rely on more intensive fuel use for their operations. The global fishing industry increased its emissions by 28% in just 20 years despite production staying roughly the same.[57] In 2016, the FAO reported that poorly managed capture fisheries have caused serious environmental implications because of overfishing, pollution, and habitat loss, which generated losses exceeding $50 billion per year.

Aquaculture—aquatic farms for fish and seafood—is growing very rapidly. Where 17 million tons were produced globally 30 years ago, today's production surpasses 100 million tons. Farms rely on crop-based feeds (dry pellets) made with commodity crops, like corn and soy. In 2010 alone, aquatic farms indirectly used more than 26.4 million hectares to produce enough crops to feed farmed fish and seafood. More than 70% of greenhouse gas emissions associated with aquaculture came from feeds: crops (including fertilizers used), fishmeal, and other feeds.[58]

FOOD LOSS & WASTE

About one-third of the global food supply never gets eaten. Food loss occurs during the post-harvest and processing phases of food production, while food waste occurs on the consumption side of the food systems chain when edible and good food go unconsumed.[59] Global GHG emissions from food loss and waste account for 6% of all emissions—more than three times those of global aviation![60] And here's something really alarming: "[I]ntegrated into a country ranking of top emitters, food wastage would appear third, after USA and China."[61]

More than 3 billion tonnes of Carbon Dioxide Equivalents (CO_2eq)—a quarter of the emissions from food production—end up discarded along the supply chain and by consumers. Throwing away food means dumping valuable natural resources (water, energy, and more) as well as wasting/not honoring/not taking advantage of the GHG emissions produced to grow, process, transport, and store the food. Americans throw away about 20% of the food they buy. Food waste is then sent to landfills, where it decomposes and generates substantial amounts of methane.

Sustainable Development Goal 12 calls for *Responsible Consumption and Production*. One of the targets set forth to achieve this goal is to "halve per capita global food waste at the retail and consumer levels and reduce food losses along production and supply chains, including post-harvest losses,"[62] by 2030. Climate scientists have estimated that meeting SDG 12 by 2050 would reduce projected food-related CO_2eq by 22%.[63]

Project Drawdown, an ambitious plan to address the climate crisis proposed by an alliance of environmental experts, indicates that reduced food waste could be among the top 3 solutions (of 80 proposed) to reduce heat-trapping gases. This estimate is based on projected emissions impacts globally. The plan uses two different scenarios that are roughly in line with the goals of the Paris Agreement: to limit global warming to a temperature rise of 2°C by 2100 and 1.5°C by the end of the century. Tackling food waste under these scenarios would reduce/sequester approximately 87 to 94 gigatons of CO_2eq between 2020 and 2050.[64]

Knowing that food waste is such a big contributor to the climate crisis has motivated me to find creative ways to use food and ingredients that traditionally end up in the trash bin. From peels and seeds to stalks and leaves, I use as much of each ingredient I buy as possible. There are many nutrients (and flavor!) to benefit from, but most importantly, I know I'm doing my part to help save the planet!

MONOCROPPING

As the name suggests, *monocropping*, or continuous cropping, is the practice of growing a single crop year after year on the same land.[65] In the United States, the top three crops grown using monocropping techniques are corn, wheat, and soybeans. According to the National Agricultural Statistics Service (NASS), farmers plant 218 million acres with just these three crops.[66] The main problem with using this practice is that it requires intensive fertilizer and pesticide inputs that increase greenhouse gas emissions.[67]

In the midst of a climate crisis and to cope with unpredictable weather conditions, agricultural systems must be resilient. In this context, resilience is highly related to high levels of diversity, self-sufficiency, and soil health, among others. Monocropping eventually removes all nutrients from the soil, leaving it depleted and unable to support healthy plant growth. To continue production in this environment, farmers must rely on fertilizers, herbicides, pesticides, etc.—chemicals that come with severe environmental consequences.

As discussed earlier in this chapter, fertilizer use in farming is the main source of nitrous oxide (a powerful greenhouse gas with a global warming potential 300 times higher than carbon dioxide). Pesticides also disturb *nitrogen fixation*— a process where nitrogen is absorbed from the air and deposited in tiny root nodules underground—which lowers crop yields, stunts plant growth, and perpetuates the need for more chemicals to boost production.[68] To me, this sounds like a horrible, vicious cycle where the biggest victim is our planet. Wouldn't you agree?

CHANGING THE PARADIGM

The worst effects of food production on the environment are deeply connected to the industrialization of agricultural methods, including animal production—terrestrial and aquatic—and crop farming. High productivity and cost efficiency come at the cost of environmental soundness as well as public health. Unsustainable farming practices, such as deforestation, land clearing, monocropping, and tilling, cause the depletion of soils and "lead to the breakdown of soil aggregates, allowing formerly stable soil carbon to be released as a greenhouse gas (CO_2)."[69] Currently, the agriculture sector in the United States is a net emitter, which means our yearly production generates more greenhouse gas emissions than it absorbs. With that said, "agriculture is the ONE sector that has the ability to transform from a net emitter of CO_2 to a net sequesterer of CO_2,"[70] according to the Carbon Cycle Institute.

The FAO defines *carbon sequestration* as the process through which CO_2 is absorbed from the atmosphere and stored (or "sequestered") in terrestrial or aquatic ecosystems.[71] Carbon dioxide is the most predominant greenhouse gas in the atmosphere. Therefore, implementing agricultural practices that enable carbon sequestration (such as crop rotation, cover crops, etc.) would be imperative to tackle the climate crisis. It's estimated that cropland soil worldwide could sequester at about 1 PgC (a unit to measure the amount of carbon dioxide stored in a given reservoir, also known as *carbon stock*) per year, and although I don't *really* know what that means, scientists believe that's a great percentage of emissions caused by human activity.[72] That's good news!

The best agricultural practice to promote carbon sequestration and, therefore, to help mitigate the current climate crisis and reverse climate change is regenerative organic agriculture. Through methods that leverage the process of photosynthesis in plants, this holistic style of agriculture also helps promote soil health, crop resilience, and nutrient density, which in turn build resilient agricultural systems and better food systems for all.

Regeneration International states that regenerative agricultural practices "(i) contribute to generating/building soils and soil fertility and health; (ii) increase water percolation, water retention, and clean and safe water runoff; (iii) increase biodiversity and ecosystem health and resiliency; and (iv) invert the carbon emissions of our current agriculture to one of remarkably significant carbon sequestration thereby cleansing the atmosphere of legacy levels of CO_2."[73]

Sustainable farming practices help combat climate change while improving the quality of our food. When mindfully grown, produce contains higher nutritional density and minimizes our exposure to chemicals, such as harmful toxins present in pesticides and herbicides.

As consumers, we might have little power to control the food supply chain, but we do have the ability to support sustainable practices. When using our purchasing power, we can favor environmentally friendly produced goods and sustainably grown products. Demand drives the market! A collective shift in mindset might create the right buzz to motivate more farmers to implement better and greener growing methods without sacrificing financial gains.

Shopping for more foods like beans and pulses—which are nitrogen-fixing plants that help minimize the use of harming chemicals in agricultural practices—is definitely a way to focus the demand on food that saves the planet. Minimizing food waste at home is a must! I'll share ideas and recipes to help with that throughout this book, but in the meantime, shop only for what you need and avoid throwing food away. Changing our diet might be the biggest contribution we can make to help Mama Earth (and I assume you already knew that because you're reading this book), but I'll get to that in the next chapter.

I understand that organic, sustainable food might not always be within everyone's reach—financially or geographically— but my plea is that to the best of our abilities, we all support the farming practices that might save our planet. The easiest way to start is going to farmers markets, seeking local community-supported agriculture (CSA) co-ops, getting to know your farmers, and, if all else fails, growing your own vegetables at home. Be part of the solution! The planet— as well as future generations—will thank you.

CHAPTER 2
OUR CARBON FOOTPRINT

This chapter discusses the difference between the concepts of *ecological footprint* and *carbon footprint* and explores the environmental impacts of food, also known as *foodprint*. The same science that has warned us about a climate crisis and its daunting effects on the environment and natural resources has also helped us gain a better understanding of its relationship to human activities. We've gotten out of balance—our demands have been surpassing Earth's supply. My intent is to make a strong argument that will motivate you to be part of the solution and help build a more sustainable future.

HUMAN IMPACT ON THE ENVIRONMENT

Our growing population and lifestyle choices—where and how we live, how we move around, how we grow our food, what we eat, and how much we waste—are pushing the planet to a breaking point. The rate at which we're deteriorating Mama Earth's natural resources and exacerbating climate change isn't allowing ecosystems to regenerate, thus creating a global ecological deficit. Continuing to conduct business as usual might result in an environmental bankruptcy.[1]

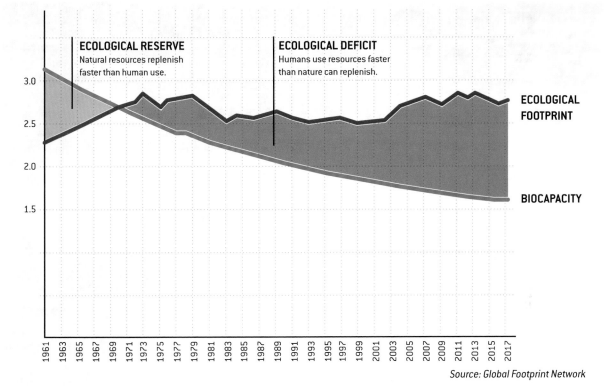

ECOLOGICAL RESERVE
Natural resources replenish
faster than human use.

ECOLOGICAL DEFICIT
Humans use resources faster
than nature can replenish.

ECOLOGICAL
FOOTPRINT

BIOCAPACITY

Source: Global Footprint Network

ECOLOGICAL FOOTPRINT

First coined by doctors William Rees and Mathis Wackernagel, the concept of ecological footprint "enables us to estimate the resource consumption and waste assimilation requirements of a defined human population or economy in terms of a corresponding productive land area."[2] In other words, ecological footprint measures the impact of human activities on the planet's ecosystems. Our demand from nature varies across populations and cultures—it's directly related to our ways of life.

Ecological footprints are determined by such factors as demand for food (plant-based and animal-sourced) for human consumption, timber and other products for shelter, and fibers for human comfort, including cotton and wool for clothing. At a larger level, they're also influenced by our demand for space to build infrastructure; forests and oceans to absorb emissions caused by fossil fuel consumption; and resources to assimilate the waste generated by human activities, including materials sent to landfills, biological waste from agricultural and other activities, and pollutants released from factories and the like.

Biocapacity is the ability of a particular ecosystem to regenerate the natural resources needed to meet human demands for goods and services. An ecosystem might include cropland, grazing land, forest land, built-up land, and fishing grounds.[3] Biocapacity might vary throughout time—even yearly—according to fluctuations in climate, management strategies for each of the aforementioned ecosystems, and other factors.

Ecological footprint and biocapacity are expressed in global hectares (gha), a measuring unit. Comparing these in any given area (city, state, country, etc.) allows us to assess whether it's running an ecologic deficit or surplus (also known as "reserve"). The National Footprint and Biocapacity Accounts 2019 edition confirms that currently, more than 80% of the world's population resides in nations struggling to be self-sustainable and running ecological deficits.

Despite a global increase in biocapacity since 1961, our per capita ecological footprint continues to rise at a faster rate, creating a global overshoot. Per the latest data, Earth's total biocapacity is 1.63 gha per capita, while humanity's ecological footprint is 2.77 gha per capita.[4] This means that our ecological "quota" was surpassed by nearly 70%! We're spending resources faster than Mama Earth is able to replenish them and this leads to the further depletion of natural resources, the exacerbation of climate change, and the accumulation of wastage.

Earth Overshoot Day marks the date "when humanity's demand for ecological resources and services in a given year exceeds what Earth can regenerate in that year."[5] In 2020, Earth Overshoot Day fell on August 22, which basically means we'd have needed 1.6 planets to support that year's demands from human activities on global ecosystems. Going back one decade at a time, Earth Overshoot Day has fallen on the following dates. See a pattern?

YEAR	EARTH OVERSHOOT DAY
2020	August 22*
2010	August 7
2000	September 23
1990	October 11
1980	November 4
1970	December 29

*In 2019, Earth Overshoot Day fell on July 29. An earlier date was expected for July 2020, but measures taken to mitigate the global pandemic caused humanity's ecological footprint to shrink slightly.

A strong correlation exists between income level and ecological footprint.[6] Acquisitive power amplifies access to goods and services and guides lifestyle choices for many. In 2016, the US ecological footprint was 8.1 gha per person and its biocapacity at 3.6 gha per person. If the world's population lived like us, we'd need 5 planets to meet humanity's demands. We're not leading by example— that's for sure!

CARBON FOOTPRINT

Carbon footprint concentrates on our impact on the planet as related to greenhouse gas (GHG) emissions.[7] Carbon footprint accounts for 60% of the global ecological footprint and is considered the fastest-growing component of that footprint. In nearly 60 years, humanity's carbon footprint has increased elevenfold, taking its toll in climate change and global warming. The Global Footprint Network affirms that "reducing humanity's carbon Footprint is the most essential step we can take to end overshoot and live within the means of our planet."

Carbon footprint can be expressed in tonnes of CO_2 emissions, a measurement that might be supplemented by Carbon Dioxide Equivalents (CO_2eq), a metric measure used to compare the emissions from various greenhouse gases, including methane (CH_4) and nitrous oxide (N_2), based on their global warming potential (GWP).[8]

The United States is the second-largest emitter of CO_2, producing 15% of global emissions—a whopping 5.3 billion tonnes of CO_2 per year. Our emissions are 1.5 times greater than the 28 countries of the European Union *combined*.[9] Each person in the United States creates an average of 16.2 tonnes of CO_2 emissions per year. This is more than 3 times the global average, which in 2017 was calculated at 4.7 tonnes of CO_2 emissions per person.[10]

Rises in CO_2 emissions have been proportionately related to improved living conditions throughout history. But to protect the environment and human living conditions for future generations, especially as citizens of a top emitter nation, we must reduce our emissions. The world won't come close to meeting its global targets, such as those set forth by the Paris Agreement, without our commitment.

Our individual carbon footprint is mostly associated with our way of life and dictated by our choices of food, mobility, goods, and services. The World Health Organization estimates that our individual activities contribute to approximately 45% of our carbon footprint, while the rest is our share of emissions linked to public and social services as well as public infrastructure. "While both system-level and individual actions will be required to help reach agreed targets, there is much everyone can do to reduce their own carbon footprints."[11]

To be part of the solution, we must be better informed— we need to calculate our carbon footprint and understand how our lifestyle choices affect our scores. There are many free carbon footprint calculators available online, including those offered by the Environmental Protection Agency (EPA) and the World Wildlife Fund (WWF).

WHICH COUNTRY IS RESPONSIBLE FOR THE HIGHEST CO$_2$ EMISSIONS?

- CHINA (9.8)
- USA (5.3)
- EUROPEAN UNION (3.5)
- INDIA (2.5)
- RUSSIA (1.7)
- JAPAN (1.2)
- INTERNATIONAL AVIATION & SHIPPING (1.15)
- IRAN (0.672)
- SAUDI ARABIA (0.635)
- SOUTH KOREA (0.616)
- CANADA (0.573)
- MEXICO (0.49)
- INDONESIA (0.489)
- BRAZIL (0.476)
- SOUTH AFRICA (0.456)
- TURKEY (0.448)
- AUSTRALIA (0.414)
- THAILAND (0.331)
- KAZAKHSTAN (0.293)
- UNITED ARAB EMIRATES (0.232)

| 2 billion tonnes CO$_2$ | 4 billion tonnes CO$_2$ | 6 billion tonnes CO$_2$ | 8 billion tonnes CO$_2$ | 10 billion tonnes CO$_2$ |

Source: Our World in Data

"THE FIRST STEP TOWARD REDUCING OUR ECOLOGICAL IMPACT IS TO RECOGNIZE THAT THE 'ENVIRONMENTAL CRISIS' IS LESS AN ENVIRONMENTAL AND TECHNICAL PROBLEM THAN IT IS A BEHAVIORAL AND SOCIAL ONE. IT CAN THEREFORE BE RESOLVED ONLY WITH THE HELP OF BEHAVIORAL AND SOCIAL SOLUTIONS."
— DR. WILLIAM REES, CANADIAN PROFESSOR

I use FootPrintCalculator.org, where I'm able to assess my own ecological and carbon footprints. While the calculation takes into account lifestyle choices related to transportation, housing, and energy consumption, it also considers my food choices and my efforts to minimize waste at home. It's encouraging to see that my scores set me slightly under average global figures for ecological footprint (at 2.5 gha) and carbon footprint (at 4.3 CO_2 emissions in tonnes per year). With that said, because my carbon footprint still represents 60% of my ecological footprint, I'll need to make further improvements, especially in relationship to mobility.

As discussed in Chapter 1, today's food supply chain generates 26% of all human-generated greenhouse gas emissions. Food impacts our carbon footprint according to the lifestyle diet we choose. Furthermore, the types of food we purchase and where they're sourced; how much food we buy and how it's stored; and how food is cooked and how much we dispose affect other aspects of our carbon footprint. Food has an impact on our energy consumption, water use, and waste management, among others.

FOODPRINT

The concept of *foodprint*—food's carbon footprint—refers to "the environmental pressures created by the food demands of individuals, organizations, and geopolitical entities."[12] It considers the GHG emissions generated to produce food to get it from the farm to our plate. Many steps involved in the food production side are invisible to consumers, such as growing, rearing, farming, processing, transporting, and storing. On the consumption side, cooking, storing, and food waste (among others) help calculate a foodprint.[13]

The carbon intensity and environmental impacts of food production vary according to food groups. Not all foods are created equal! Animal-sourced products account for 58% of the greenhouse gas emissions. The production of red meat—beef, lamb, and pork—generates 30%, whereas poultry, seafood, eggs, and dairy production account for 28%. Conversely, the production of plant-based ingredients generates 22% of food-related emissions.[14] Finally, beverages, sugars, oils, and snacks account for 21%.

These figures help determine the foodprint of various diets—meat lover, average, no beef, vegetarian, and vegan or plant-based—which are generalized adaptations of the average US diet based on data from the USDA's Economic Research Service. A diet free from all animal-sourced products yields the lowest foodprint—1.5 tonnes of CO_2eq per person per year—while a meat-lover diet more than doubles that figure to 3.3 tonnes of CO_2eq per person per year. The average diet has a foodprint of 2.5 tonnes of CO_2eq per person per year, whereas the no-beef and vegetarian diets yield 1.9 and 1.7 tonnes of CO_2eq per person per year, respectively.

Because the United States is the top emitter of CO_2 with the highest rate of consumption of meat and dairy per person, we must make shifts toward low-carbon diets.[15] However, this might not be feasible for every American because other factors, including affordability and accessibility, help determine people's decisions about food choices. Small shifts in diet choices would help reduce an individual's carbon footprint and, as part of a collective effort, could make a significant impact nationwide and globally.

FOOD & OUR CARBON FOOTPRINT

Per the Food and Agriculture Organization (FAO), sustainable diets refer to "those diets with low environmental impacts that contribute to food and nutritional security and to healthy lives for present and future generations. Sustainable diets are protective and respectful of biodiversity and ecosystems, culturally acceptable, accessible, economically fair and affordable, are nutritionally adequate, safe, and healthy, and optimize natural and human resources."[16]

To shrink my carbon footprint, I focus on whole foods, including fresh and colorful vegetables, fruits, legumes, leafy greens, and herbs as well as diverse grains, seeds, and nuts. I make an effort to support sustainable farming practices, and as much as possible, I try to source food that's seasonal, organic, and mostly local.

FOOD TYPE

The foods we eat could have a significant impact on our carbon footprint. Whether we favor animal-sourced or plant-based ingredients makes a massive difference to the planet. Ruminant meat has up to 100 times the environmental impacts of plant-based foods, which carry the lowest. For example, the production of 100 grams of protein from peas emits 0.4 kilogram of Carbon Dioxide Equivalent (kg CO_2eq). To get the same amount of protein from beef, emissions would be 35 kg CO_2eq, approximately 90 times higher.[17]

Across food production, two stages—land use change and farming—are responsible for more than 80% of the carbon footprint of most foods. They cause the biggest difference in emissions between animal production (ruminant and non-ruminant livestock, farmed fish, and seafood) and that of fruits, vegetables, grains, and nuts.

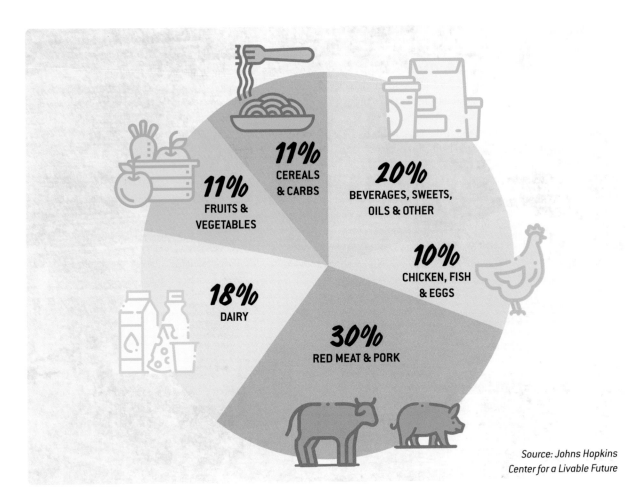

11% CEREALS & CARBS

11% FRUITS & VEGETABLES

20% BEVERAGES, SWEETS, OILS & OTHER

10% CHICKEN, FISH & EGGS

18% DAIRY

30% RED MEAT & PORK

Source: Johns Hopkins Center for a Livable Future

FOODPRINTS BY DIET TYPE

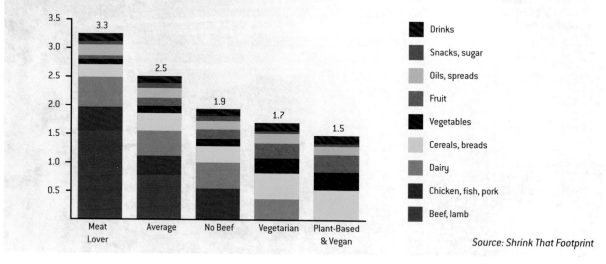

Source: Shrink That Footprint

Science-based evidence suggests that plant-based foods will always have less GHG emissions than meat and dairy, even if these are sourced from low-impact producers.[18] Even considering the highest plant-based GHG emitters, such as chocolate, a plant-based diet has been consistently identified as the most environmentally sustainable. Generally, emissions from plant-based foods are 10 to 50 times lower than animal-sourced foods.[19]

Transitioning to a diet that excludes animal products has such transformative potential for the environment, including but not limited to a reduction by about 76% in food's land use and 49% in food's GHG emissions. Furthermore, "the land no longer required for food production could remove ~8.1 billion metric tons of CO_2 from the atmosphere each year over 100 years as natural vegetation reestablishes and soil carbon re-accumulates."[20]

These were some of the arguments that originally inspired me to transition to a plant-based diet. That was *my* reason—knowing that by merely changing my eating habits, I could lower my carbon footprint and have a positive impact on Mama Earth, the environment, and planetary health. With that said, mine wasn't an instant conversion. My journey started with a pescatarian diet that slowly eliminated animal-sourced products. After roughly six months, I found myself immersed in the plant-based world.

People often ask me whether they have to give up animal-sourced foods "forever." The journey to lower your carbon footprint is your own. My goal is to inspire you to add more plant-based ingredients to your diet and to diversify your palette. I aim to prove there's no sacrifice in eating this way!

SEASONALITY

Seasonal food refers to produce that's consumed at the time of the year it's harvested—when it's at its peak. When sourced locally, seasonal foods are generally tastier and more nutritious. There's nothing like a plump ripe tomato just harvested in the summer, a fiddlehead fern picked during its short harvest season in the spring, or bright and earthy beetroots gathered in autumn. While taste and freshness are probably the best qualities of in-season produce, these foods also have a lower environmental impact,[21] which makes them a big winner in my book.

Out-of-season produce is harvested early—before reaching its optimal flavor and nutritional value—and stored in refrigerated containers for extended periods of time. Fruits and vegetables tend to lose some of their health-promoting properties because certain nutrients, including vitamin C and other water-soluble vitamins, degrade with time. If you're buying off-season food, be mindful of where it's coming from. Despite transportation accounting for low fractions of GHG emissions in global food production,

ANIMAL-SOURCED VS. PLANT-BASED EMISSIONS

LAND USE CHANGE
Aboveground changes
in biomass from
deforestation

FARM
Methane
emissions from
cows and rice

ANIMAL FEED
On-farm
emissions and
its processing

PROCESSING
Emissions
from energy
use in transport

TRANSPORT
Transport of food
items in-country
and internationally

PACKAGING
Package
materials
and disposal

RETAIL
Refrigeration
and other retail
processes

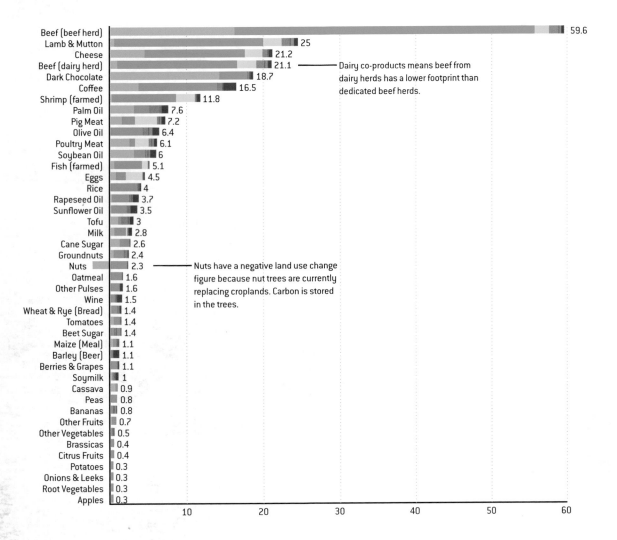

Beef (beef herd) — 59.6
Lamb & Mutton — 25
Cheese — 21.2
Beef (dairy herd) — 21.1 — Dairy co-products means beef from dairy herds has a lower footprint than dedicated beef herds.
Dark Chocolate — 18.7
Coffee — 16.5
Shrimp (farmed) — 11.8
Palm Oil — 7.6
Pig Meat — 7.2
Olive Oil — 6.4
Poultry Meat — 6.1
Soybean Oil — 6
Fish (farmed) — 5.1
Eggs — 4.5
Rice — 4
Rapeseed Oil — 3.7
Sunflower Oil — 3.5
Tofu — 3
Milk — 2.8
Cane Sugar — 2.6
Groundnuts — 2.4
Nuts — 2.3 — Nuts have a negative land use change figure because nut trees are currently replacing croplands. Carbon is stored in the trees.
Oatmeal — 1.6
Other Pulses — 1.6
Wine — 1.5
Wheat & Rye (Bread) — 1.4
Tomatoes — 1.4
Beet Sugar — 1.4
Maize (Meal) — 1.1
Barley (Beer) — 1.1
Berries & Grapes — 1.1
Soymilk — 1
Cassava — 0.9
Peas — 0.8
Bananas — 0.8
Other Fruits — 0.7
Other Vegetables — 0.5
Brassicas — 0.4
Citrus Fruits — 0.4
Potatoes — 0.3
Onions & Leeks — 0.3
Root Vegetables — 0.3
Apples — 0.3

10   20   30   40   50   60

Source: Our World in Data

anything that's shipped by air has a substantial carbon footprint. Buying fresh blackberries or asparagus in the middle of winter is definitely not a good idea.

Growing food out of season and outside its natural climate might require a hothouse, which is heated by artificial sources that generate CO_2 emissions. This practice is highly carbon-intensive: A tomato grown in a hothouse can produce emissions five times higher than one grown in season.[22] Warm-season crops grown in colder climates also require lots of artificial fertilizers, which emit greenhouse gases.

When we buy in-season produce, we can rest assured it was grown within the planet's own system of production. In many cases, eating seasonal produce is more affordable because it's less expensive for farmers to produce at the peak of the harvest. Visiting a nearby farmers market and joining a community-supported agriculture (CSA) network are some of the ways to get access to seasonal produce.

There are free online resources to help you find out what's ready to harvest in your area. I enjoy using the *Seasonal Food Guide*, which also provides a convenient app, as well as the *Seasonal Produce Guide* offered by the US Department of Agriculture (USDA). Having access to information to figure out what's currently in season could help you make the best choices to keep your carbon footprint in check and to avoid high-impact, out-of-season goods at the grocery store (no matter how fresh and tempting they might seem).

GEOGRAPHY

Per the Food, Conservation, and Energy Act of 2008, the term *local food* refers to a "locally or regionally produced agricultural food product" distributed less than 400 miles from its origin or within the state in which it's produced.

For many people, food is considered local when produced within a 100-mile radius—and this reflects my own interpretation. When grown in season, local foods are less energy-intensive and more sustainable.[23]

It's assumed that eating local is crucial to minimize our carbon footprint. However, studies show that transportation-related emissions often account for a small fraction (6%) of global GHG emissions from food production.[24] *What* you eat is significantly more important than *where* your food is grown and *where* it travels from. The biggest factor to lower our individual carbon footprints is to choose plant-based foods (while eliminating or avoiding animal-sourced products, especially meat and dairy) and that's exactly what's promoted in this book.

While it's true that the distance between where food is grown and where it's consumed (often referred to as "food miles") is rapidly increasing thanks to international food trade, the mode of transportation involved makes all the difference when considering environmental impact. Transporting the same amount of food by sea and by air would generate 0.023 kg CO_2eq and 1.13 kg CO_2eq per tonne-kilometer, respectively. In simpler terms, transportation-related emissions by air are 50 times higher than by sea.[25] This is because airplanes emit 500 g while ships emit 10 to 40 g of CO_2 per metric ton of freight per kilometer of transportation.[26]

As seen on below, traveled distance does have a large environmental impact when food items are transported by air. Foods that are highly perishable must be eaten soon after they're harvested, which makes air the only feasible mode of transportation. Thankfully, very little food is air-freighted globally—percentage-wise, about 16 hundredths. Common goods shipped by air are berries, cherries, tomatoes, asparagus, and bell peppers. These are some of

FOOD MILE FOOTPRINTS

Source: *Shrink That Footprint*

the fruits and vegetables I suggest sourcing locally while they're in season.

With that said, choosing local foods ultimately has greater benefits than their carbon emissions or lack thereof. Sourcing locally grown, organic, plant-based ingredients directly from small farmers allows me to support my local economy and sustainable farming methods that promote soil health, biodiversity, and environmental soundness. Learning about the process that brings produce to my table and knowing exactly where it comes from allows me to feel connected to Mama Earth. Plus, local, seasonal food tastes better to me!

FARMING PRACTICES

It's true that eating a plant-based diet carries the lowest foodprint of all—what we eat is what matters the most. However, it's important to be mindful of how food is produced and understand how agricultural methods differ from one another. Conventional agriculture depends on fossil fuels and relies heavily on artificial fertilizers, pesticides, and herbicides, which have detrimental effects on ecosystem health, water quality, and soil microbiome. Often involving monocropping and tilling, these traditional farming practices tend to destroy life in the soil and release hefty amounts of CO_2 into the atmosphere. Conventionally grown produce often includes genetically modified organisms (GMOs).

Organic farming methods don't count on chemical-intensive inputs, such as fertilizers, to manage crops, which make them less damaging for local ecosystems, natural water sources, and soils. Organic food doesn't contain GMOs and is widely available in the United States, in grocery stores, and at produce and farmers markets. Organic farming methods are less energy-intensive and inflict a minimal impact on the environment.

As discussed in Chapter 1, regenerative organic agricultural practices have the least environmental impact and the highest benefit for the planet: counteracting resource depletion, contributing to mitigate problems linked to climate change and desertification, and helping maintain and promote biodiversity globally.[27] The holistic farming methods effectively alleviate the worse effects of climate change—they improve soil health and increase ecosystem resilience, which, in turn, create the proper conditions to stimulate carbon sequestration.[28] Regenerative organic food is grown without chemical-intensive inputs and contains higher nutritional density.[29]

Food labeling systems for organic and regenerative crops have been established as a way to safeguard the integrity of produce and to ensure farmers comply with the regulations set forth by the agencies responsible for their management. The National Organic Program (NOP), a federal regulatory program supervised by the USDA's Agricultural Marketing Service, was established in 2000 to develop and enforce uniform standards for organically produced agricultural products in the United States.[30] A new label for Regenerative Organic Certified (ROC) has been available since 2020. It's part of a private certification program, created by the Rodale Institute and overseen by the Regenerative Organic Alliance.

Nowadays, many other food labels issued in the United States are available in grocery stores, including non-GMO project verified as well as certified vegan, gluten-free, keto, and paleo. Although these labels might help guide people with specific lifestyle diets or health concerns, they don't offer any insight into sustainability standards or environmental impacts of their products or ingredients.

Thanks to inequities in food systems in the United States and around the world, produce from organic and/or regenerative farms might not be equally accessible or affordable for everyone. I'll tell you this: It's better to eat a conventionally grown apple than not eating an apple at all. As I stated earlier, the most significant contribution you'll make to the environment is transitioning to a plant-based diet or minimizing your consumption of animal-sourced products, such as ruminant meat (beef, lamb, goat) and dairy products, including cheese.

BIOLOGICAL DIVERSITY

Although Earth has about 30,000 edible plants, we only cultivate approximately 170 crops globally. Humanity relies heavily on about 30 of those crops for needed calories and nutrients. Even more surprisingly, more than 40% of our daily calories come from *three* staple crops: rice, wheat, and corn.[31] We can all do better than that!

A monotonous diet has been linked to the loss of *agrobiodiversity*: the diversity of plants and animals used in and around agriculture. This in turn threatens the resilience of our food systems and limits the range of foods we can eat.[32] Biodiversity, human health, and environmental soundness are intricately related. They overlap in important issues, such as food security, livelihood of underprivileged communities, nutrition and human health, agriculture, and climate change.

A simple way to promote biodiversity is to buy heirloom fruits and vegetables from local producers, such as community-supported agriculture (CSA) networks or farmers markets. "Heirloom varieties are the descendants of seeds grown before about 1950, when hybrids began to dominate the commercial market."[33] These cultivars are mostly grown by regenerative and organic small farmers and typically thrive in the conditions created by sustainable farming practices compared with industrialized farming lands and

agricultural systems. Our purchases help boost the demand for these valuable crops and promote genetic diversity in our plant-based foods.

Diversifying our culinary palette—the variety of plant-based foods we purchase, cook, and enjoy—presents a great opportunity to lower our carbon footprint and boost our good health. When we "eat the rainbow" and enjoy a variety of colorful fruits and vegetables, including heirloom cultivars, we reap the benefits that each unique crop has to offer.

Changing our eating habits and favoring sustainable food choices could have a profound impact on the environment but also on our health—physical and mental—and our wallet. Mama Earth's bounty is endless, and with the right "tools"—recipes and other resources—our journey to a low-carbon way of eating can be delicious, fun, and fulfilling in more ways than one. Wholesome plant-based foods are rich in fiber and other nutrients that help us feel satiated and nourished. Focusing on a diet that minimizes our footprint can also give us a satisfying sense of purpose. We can be sustainability heroes!

"OVERALL, BECOMING A CARBON-NEUTRAL COUNTRY WOULD INVOLVE CHANGES IN OUR BEHAVIOR, BUT THESE ARE MODEST COMPARED WITH THE CHANGES THAT WILL BE FORCED UPON US IF WE DO NOTHING."
— CAROLINE LUCAS, BRITISH POLITICIAN

CHAPTER 3
THE LOW-CARBON DIET

A recent study calculated that if the US population gave up animal products entirely and switched to plant-based foods, the demand for cropland and nitrogen fertilizer as well as the generation of GHG emissions would be reduced by nearly 50%.[1] Although this is highly unlikely (but a chef can dream!), this confirms that our diets could play an important role in mitigating climate change and reaching global environmental goals and targets. In this chapter, you'll learn what it means to follow a low-carbon diet, how to modify your eating habits to be more sustainable, and the various benefits of making these changes in your life. A plant-based diet has the lowest carbon footprint of all lifestyle diets. It's clear that our dietary choices—whether animal or plant—make a massive difference to the planet.

WHAT'S A LOW-CARBON DIET?

A low-carbon diet is a way of eating that aims to reduce GHG. A crucial component of a low-carbon diet is to consume foods that have a low impact on the environment: wholesome and diverse plant-based foods grown in season with sustainable farming methods. Other important components of a low-carbon diet include favoring unprocessed or minimally processed foods, shopping responsibly, cooking smarter, and minimizing food waste.

Adjusting our eating habits and choosing low-carbon foods not only help minimize emissions but also stimulate carbon sequestration and promote soil biomass, biodiversity, and healthy terrestrial, marine, and freshwater ecosystems—all of which are needed to mitigate the climate crisis and lower the average temperature of our planet.

HOW TO EAT A LOW-CARBON DIET

In this section, I provide a dietary roadmap to help you shrink your carbon footprint—an implementation plan to give you tools to pursue the low-carbon diet like a boss! You'll learn about the food groups that will diversify your culinary palette and the nutritional richness that comes with "eating the rainbow." The types of food we consume and when and where they're grown ultimately determine the sustainability of our diets.

A low-carbon diet primarily focuses on plant-based foods; They include a wide variety of groups, which are discussed in greater detail below. Nature's bounty is so rich—approximately 30,000 edible plants are available on Earth. But we rely on about 30 of them—and 3 crops alone provide humanity with nearly 60% of our calories: rice, wheat, and corn. We've been missing out and it's time to incorporate more plants in our lives. Would you join me on this journey?

The idea of switching to a plant-based, low-carbon diet might seem daunting at first to meat-loving omnivores. However, instead of focusing on the foods we must give up to minimize our carbon footprint, why not place the emphasis on the plethora of delicious, colorful, and diverse ingredients we get to incorporate into our culinary palettes?

Legumes

Hands down my favorite food group! Legumes includes pulses—often referred to as beans—such as garbanzo beans (also known as chickpeas), black beans, pinto beans, kidney beans, lentils, split peas, and black-eyed peas, among others. Beans are an excellent source of plant-based protein! Legumes also include soybeans, fresh green beans, sugar snap and snow peas, peanuts, carob (often used as a substitute for chocolate), and tamarind.

Grains

The USDA groups grains, cereals, and pseudo-cereals in this category.[2] Well-known grains include wheat, rice, and corn (although the latter is considered a vegetable when harvested fresh). Whole grains lend fiber and carbs to our diets, which are necessary for our well-being. Some of my favorite grains are quinoa, oats, farro, amaranth, millets, and fonio. Other grains include barley, rye, buckwheat, and spelt.

Fruits

There are many subgroups in this category: pome fruits like apple and pear; stone fruits like peach and cherry; citrus fruits like orange and pomelo; melons like cantaloupe and honeydew; and berries like blackberry and blueberry. Some fruits are considered vegetables, including tomato, bell pepper, cucumber, eggplant, and squash (such as zucchini and pumpkin). Despite their botanical classification, these fruits are often listed as vegetables.

Vegetables

A variety of produce fall under this group! Cruciferous, like broccoli, cauliflower, Brussels sprouts, and cabbage, as well as leafy greens, such as spinach, arugula, chard, and kale. Bulbs (also known as alliums), including onion, garlic,

shallot, scallion, and leek, are often called aromatics. There are root vegetables, like carrot, beet, and radish, but also ginger and turmeric. And finally, there are tubers, which include potato, yam, yuca, and jícama.

Nuts & Seeds

A very important food group because of their nutritional superpowers. Nuts include walnuts, cashews, almonds, pecans, and hazelnuts. Why are peanuts not listed here? Because they're legumes! Some of my favorite seeds are chia, flax, and hemp but also sunflower and pumpkin. In this book, I've included a couple nontraditional seeds, such as papaya and avocado (yay for zero waste!).

Fungi

Mushrooms fall under this category (there are thousands of edible ones!). Technically, fungi aren't a plant because they don't have chlorophyll nor do they make their food through photosynthesis (and they're also not an animal because

they don't ingest their food[3]). They're some of my favorite meat substitutes thanks to their textures and umami flavors.

Cacti

Edible cacti have been showcased in some Latin American cuisines for many generations. The opuntia cactus is featured in my recipes—I use the pads, known as nopal, as well as the fruit, which I grew up calling "tuna" but is better known as prickly pear. Cacti are sustainable and healthy—they deserve to be in our diets.[4]

Algae

What we commonly call seaweed is part of the algae family. An excellent source of antioxidants, seaweed also lends protein and other nutrients to our diet. Pyropia (also known as nori), wakame, and laver are some of the most popular edible varieties of algae and are often used in cuisines from around the world.

EASE YOUR WAY

A slower transition might prove to be the easiest way for some people to make more permanent dietary changes. To start, I suggest trying dense vegetables, such as eggplant or mushrooms, to help avoid ruminant meat, such as beef and lamb. Minimizing the consumption of poultry could follow and replacing that with cruciferous vegetables, such as cauliflower, and dense pulses, such as garbanzo beans. Then shunning highly processed dairy products, such as cheeses, and so forth.

But if giving up meat is out of the question, I suggest looking at the Planetary Health Diet introduced by the EAT–Lancet Commission, which suggests "a consumption level of no more than 98 grams of red meat (pork, beef or lamb), 203 grams of poultry and 196 grams of fish per person per week where possible." As part of a diet rich in plant-based foods, said consumption would stay within planetary boundaries.[5]

From personal experience, I can attest that eating only or mostly plants will become second nature over time. Our taste buds evolve, and by trying new and exciting foods, we learn to appreciate their textures and flavor profiles. You sacrifice nothing by eating a low-carbon diet! As you'll see in my plant-based recipes, I love infusing food with vibrant and mouthwatering flavors by using spices, herbs, and aromatics. I like leading with flavor!

CONSIDER NUTRITION & PROTEIN

Will a plant-based diet provide enough nutrients? Yes indeed. Eating a plant-based, low-carbon diet does provide all the necessary macronutrients—protein, fats, and carbs—as well as vitamins, minerals, fiber, phytonutrients, and powerful antioxidants, which are essential for good health. If you're eating *only* plants, a low-carbon diet should be supplemented with a reliable source of vitamin B_{12}, which physicians affirm can be met with "a daily supplement or fortified foods, such as vitamin B_{12}-fortified breakfast cereals, plant milks, and nutritional yeast."[6]

According to the Dietary Reference Intakes (DRI) suggested by the US Department of Agriculture (USDA), "the desired daily amount of protein is 0.8 grams (g) per kilogram of body weight, which equates to about 0.36 g of protein per pound each day."[7] This is the daily recommended dietary allowance (RDA) for protein. "For a 70 kg (144 lb) adult male, this is

56 gms; for a 60 kg (132 lb) female, 48 gms."[8] More than 90% of people consume substantially more protein than the RDA and most Americans consume double the amount of protein they actually need.

According to FoodData Central, a tool offered by the USDA's Agricultural Research Service, the protein content of various plant-based foods is calculated as follows.*

PLANT-BASED SOURCE	PORTION	AMOUNT OF PROTEIN (in grams)
Cooked soybeans (edamame)	1 cup	31.30
Cooked lentils	1 cup	17.90
Raw walnuts	4 ounces (100 grams)	16.67
Garbanzo beans (chickpeas)	1 cup	14.50
Firm sprouted tofu	4 ounces (100 grams)	13.24
Cooked quinoa	1 cup	8.14
Cooked Brussels sprouts	1 cup	5.44
Cooked corn kernels	1 cup	5.38
Chia seeds	1 ounce (30 grams)	4.69
Cooked broccoli	1 cup	4.54
Fresh avocado	1 cup (1 unit)	3.00

This list isn't limited to the highest sources of plant-based protein but rather showcases an assortment of legumes and pulses, vegetables, fruits, nuts, and seeds in order to demonstrate how easy it is to meet the RDA of protein from a diverse number of plant-based foods.

You might be surprised to learn that 1 cup of cooked soybeans and 1 cup of cooked ground beef contain almost the exact same amount of protein (31.30 grams versus 31.90 grams, respectively). But going beyond nutritional content and looking at the environmental impacts that each of them has provide proof that the two cups aren't alike.

As it turns out, sources of protein aren't created equal! For example, the carbon footprint of lentils is 43 times lower than that of beef.[9]

The bottom line is that a low-carbon diet with the appropriate calorie intake coming from legumes and pulses, vegetables, whole grains, nuts, and fruits will provide not only the daily RDA of protein—up to 70 grams[10]— but also the vast majority of nutrients needed to lead a healthful life. All while shrinking our individual carbon footprint, helping us mitigate the climate crisis, and contributing to build better food systems for all.

CHOOSE SUSTAINABLE FOODS

Highly adaptable and climate friendly, legumes are nitrogen-fixing plants (because they absorb nitrogen from the air and store it underground). These plants "can prevent soil and wind erosion, improve soil's physical and biological properties, supply nutrients, suppress weeds, improve the availability of soil water, and break pest cycles along with various other benefits."[11] Harvesting legumes helps farmers minimize the use of synthetic fertilizers and pesticides while also improving the health of the soil and making their agricultural practices more sustainable.

	FOOD	IMPACT (GHG emissions per gram of protein)	COST (Retail price per gram of protein)
LOW	Wheat		$
	Corn		$
	Beans, chickpeas, lentils		$
	Rice		$
	Fish		$$$
	Soy		$
	Nuts		$$$
	Eggs		$$
MEDIUM	Poultry		$$
	Pork		$$
	Dairy (milk, cheese)		$$
HIGH	Beef		$$$
	Lamb & goat		$$$

Source: World Resources Institute

Their nutrient density and texture make legumes a great meat substitute and a valuable addition to any dish. Wholesome and sustainable, they're some of the biggest stars of the low-carbon diet! You'll find them featured in various forms in many recipes across this book: from soups, salads, and main dishes to dips and even desserts.

Another set of highly sustainable foods to include in a low-carbon diet comes from drought-tolerant edible plants. These highly adaptive species not only just survive but also produce yields in harsh conditions and arid soils. Some of my favorite drought-tolerant foods include nopal cactus, okra, fonio, and quinoa. These nutrition powerhouses have a low-carbon footprint—they're nourishing and sustainable.

Heirloom vegetables and fruits are some of the most colorful and delicious sustainable foods. Mostly produced prior to industrialized agricultural practices, many heritage seeds have been lost and with them some of the biological diversity associated with a healthy planet. Nowadays, most old cultivars are grown by small farms with sustainable agricultural methods. As consumers, we have the opportunity to support planet-friendly practices and to promote biodiversity.

The popularity of heritage produce has grown exponentially in recent years and this, in turn, has led to an increase in demand. Farmers markets and community-supported agriculture programs (CSAs) around the United States are carrying a wider variety of heirloom tomatoes (in all their beautiful colors) as well as rainbow carrots, heritage squashes, cucumbers, beans, a wide variety of leafy greens, and so much more. That speaks volumes about the power on our plates! As I've mentioned before, our purchasing power and demand drives the market—and we should use this clout to help mitigate the global warming and climate crises.

FAVOR SEASONAL/LOCAL INGREDIENTS

Seasonal foods offer fresher, more flavorful, and often more nutritious options to savor, especially when sourced locally. Contrary to produce grown out of season, which has high energy intensity and emissions (because of the resources needed to adjust temperatures in hothouses and indoor facilities as well as the reliance on artificial fertilizers), seasonal produce has a lower environmental impact and is therefore at the core of a low-carbon diet.

Collected at the peak of the harvest, in-season produce is less expensive for farmers to grow, and because those savings are generally passed on to consumers, such produce is often the most affordable option. Although sourcing from small local farmers is probably the best way to gain access to seasonal foods, requesting local grocery stores and food markets to carry more seasonal items is another great way to use our purchasing power to help build better food systems for all.

Making the most of inexpensive finds from a local farmers market or produce included in a CSA box might be the best way to try to get acquainted with seasonal ingredients we might not otherwise be exposed to. This is a fun (and delectable) way to diversify our culinary palettes and expand our food horizons. When you're not sure how to cook something, farmers are always happy to answer questions! It's in their best interests that consumers become familiar with the produce they harvest each season.

Use the seasonal calendar on the following page to learn the time of year that certain ingredients are generally available and make an effort to incorporate those foods into your dishes. There are local and regional variations to consider as well as year-round availability for other areas with minimal climatic and seasonal changes. The best seasonal calendar is the one you get to see "live" from your local farmers or, better yet, the one you have in or on your own patio, garden, or balcony when you grow your own food.

As discussed in Chapter 2, scientific studies back the argument that what we eat is more important than where our food is grown. With animal-source products being the biggest offenders, choosing a plant-based diet assures that we're already adopting the most sustainable eating habits with the lowest carbon footprint. Locally grown, in-season produce is less energy intensive and more sustainable compared with food being transported from somewhere else, despite the negligible environmental impacts of ground and maritime transportation. (This fact doesn't apply to air-freighted food.)

To make the most of seasonal produce, I suggest sourcing fruits and vegetables locally and storing them safely for later use. This might be particularly helpful in regions with extreme weather. Food preservation methods for the long-term storage of plant-based ingredients include canning, preserving, fermenting, pickling, freezing, and drying.

SPRING	Apples Apricots Asparagus Avocados Bananas Broccoli Cabbage	Carrots Celery Collard greens Garlic Kale Kiwi Lemons	Lettuce Limes Mushrooms Onions Peas Pineapples Radishes	Rhubarb Spinach Strawberries Swiss chard Turnips
SUMMER	Apples Apricots Avocados Bananas Beets Bell peppers Blackberries Blueberries	Cantaloupe Carrots Celery Cherries Corn Cucumbers Eggplant Garlic	Green beans Honeydew melon Lemons Lima beans Limes Mangoes Okra Peaches	Plums Raspberries Strawberries Summer squash Tomatillos Tomatoes Watermelon Zucchini
FALL	Apples Bananas Beets Bell peppers Broccoli Brussels sprouts Cabbage Carrots Cauliflower Celery	Collard greens Cranberries Garlic Ginger Grapes Green beans Kale Kiwi Lemons Lettuce	Limes Mangoes Mushrooms Onions Parsnips Pears Peas Pineapples Potatoes Pumpkin	Radishes Raspberries Rutabagas Spinach Sweet potatoes & yams Swiss chard Turnips Winter squash
WINTER	Apples Avocados Bananas Beets Brussels sprouts Cabbage Carrots	Celery Collard greens Grapefruit Kale Kiwi Leeks Lemons	Limes Onions Oranges Parsnips Pears Pineapples Potatoes	Pumpkin Rutabagas Sweet potatoes & yams Swiss chard Turnips Winter squash

Source: USDA Supplemental Nutrition Assistance Program Education Connection. "Seasonal Produce Guide."

There are many resources available to help us execute these methods at home. Although nowadays you're just a Google search away from step-by-step information and videos, I find the Library of Congress's selection of titles under Food Preservation[12] quite fascinating!

Every season offers new opportunities! In the summer: ripe tomatoes, bell peppers, cherries, and all types of berries—strawberries, blackberries, blueberries, and raspberries. (When not in season, these are some of the ingredients most commonly transported by air, which *seriously* increases their foodprint.) Some of my favorite ingredients to ferment and preserve in the springtime are asparagus and rhubarb. In the colder months, I love to can or freeze various types of winter squash. Preserving food might seem like extra work, but Mama Earth totally deserves that small sacrifice.

FOCUS ON WHOLE FOODS

Especially when transitioning from the standard American diet (SAD), you might feel inconvenienced (and perhaps a bit overwhelmed) to have to concentrate on whole foods and to avoid processed foods. However, the "convenience" of buying and consuming processed foods isn't worth the negative effects they have on human health or the damage they cause to our environment.

The very additives (sweeteners, artificial colors, and emulsifiers, to mention a few) and preservatives that make processed foods unhealthy also increase their environmental impact and carbon footprint. Additionally, many more greenhouse gas emissions are produced across the food supply chain to prepare, package, store, and transport processed foods, especially when compared with fresh and minimally processed foods.

Cooking from scratch using wholesome ingredients is the best way to avoid highly processed foods. By preparing your own food using fresh vegetables, fruits, legumes, grains, seeds, and nuts, you know exactly what's in your food—you're able to enjoy a wide variety of plant-based ingredients and to reap all their health benefits, to save money, to reduce food waste, and, most importantly, to reduce your emissions.

To best benefit from a low-carbon diet, choose the least processed alternatives for shelf-stable products: whole wheat flour instead of refined white flour; dry pulses instead of canned beans; and brown and wild rice instead of white rice; and nutrient-dense grains, pseudo-cereals, and seeds, such as fonio, farro, quinoa, and amaranth. To replace high-fructose corn syrup and refined cane sugar, try minimally processed sweeteners, such as maple syrup and coconut palm sugar—both of which come from the sap of trees that can produce for up to 100 years.[13]

Another minimally processed ingredient included in this book is organic sprouted tofu, which requires only three ingredients to prepare: soybeans, water, and nigari. The high levels of plant-based protein it provides, along with minerals like calcium and selenium as well as B vitamins, plus a low carbon footprint (0.9 CO_2eq per pound produced)[14] make organic sprouted tofu a friendly low-carbon diet food.

While eating plants—lots of them!—is the most important factor to cut down our emissions and choosing foods that are sustainable, seasonal, local, and wholesome is also vital, there are other actions involved in following a low-carbon diet. These include shopping wisely, cooking smart, and (this one is huge) cutting down on the amount of food waste produced at home.

BENEFITS

Being conscious about our food intake and embracing sustainable consumption habits are just a couple actions we can take to help mitigate the worst effects of climate change and to meet the goals of the Paris Agreement. The most significant benefit of following a low-carbon diet is our contribution to the environment—a step in the right direction to save the planet. The time to tackle the climate crisis is *now* and only a collective action can truly make a difference for the sake of humanity and future generations.

Reducing global temperatures and the amount of carbon dioxide and other greenhouse gases in the atmosphere, regenerating broken ecosystems, improving soil health, rebuilding biological biodiversity, and strengthening global food systems for all are possible if we commit to doing our part. No action is too small.

As illustrated on the next page, foods that include fruits, vegetables, legumes, and nuts are able to simultaneously provide benefits for the planet and human health. These are precisely the types of foods embraced in the low-carbon diet. Conversely, animal-sourced foods prove to be a detriment for environmental soundness and human well-being. "A large body of evidence has demonstrated that overconsumption of red and processed meat, saturated fats, and (to a lesser degree) dairy products, are linked to increased risk for certain types of preventable diseases" (such as cancers and heart disease).[15]

Noncommunicable diseases (NCDs)—health conditions that can't be spread from one person to another—include cardiovascular and respiratory disease as well as cancer and diabetes, among others. These chronic diseases kill more than 40 million people globally each year. Although alcohol abuse, drug addiction, and unsafe sex have been coined as risk factors for NCDs, scientists have identified unhealthy

HEALTH & ENVIRONMENTAL IMPACTS OF VARIOUS FOODS

Note: The x-axis is the relative risk of mortality. A relative risk greater than 1 means consuming another daily serving of a food group has an increased mortality risk. A relative risk less than 1 means this consumption has a lowered mortality risk.

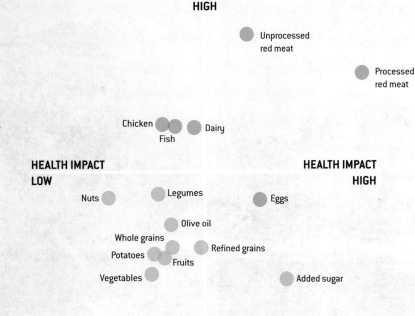

Source: Proceedings of the National Academy of Sciences

diets as a greater threat than these three risks combined.[16] Unhealthy diets are characterized by the overconsumption of animal-sourced products, such as red meat and dairy, as well as sugar and highly processed foods—the antithesis of a low-carbon diet. Healthy foods are linked to wholesome, plant-based ingredients that generally include legumes, fruits, vegetables, whole grains, nuts, and seeds. They've been shown to reduce the risk of noncommunicable diseases and even some mental-health illnesses.[17]

A recent scientific study concluded that "[t]he same dietary changes that could help reduce the risk of diet-related noncommunicable diseases could also help meet international sustainability goals. Focusing diets on foods consistently associated with decreased disease risk would likely also reduce diet-related environmental impacts."[18] It's very encouraging to know that the same foods that benefit our well-being could also help us combat climate change!

Other benefits of choosing sustainable and nutrient-dense plant-based foods go beyond planetary and human health. They have to do with socioeconomic benefits for individuals and communities. Avoiding animal-sourced and processed products, which are generally more expensive than fresh fruits and vegetables and bulk legumes and grains, while cooking from scratch and minimizing food waste might help individuals save money and maximize the investments made to buy good, nutritious food.

Buying seasonal food from farmers markets and CSA networks might benefit not only the consumer but also spur local economic development. When we support small farmers, we help them fund their sustainable agricultural practices, which, in turn, benefit Mama Earth. Sourcing the types of foods that reduce our carbon footprints also helps create local jobs at farms and small food businesses as well as food processing and distribution networks that form part of local food systems.

CHAPTER 4
FEEL-GOOD ACTION PLAN

What we eat matters—it impacts our environmental and carbon footprints. Our food consumption habits—how we shop for food and how we cook it—also have repercussions on climate change. These habits play an important role in the amount of food waste we produce, which, as discussed in previous chapters, has a significant impact on our greenhouse gas emissions. This chapter describes simple actions and adjustments for pursuing a low-carbon diet.

SHOP WISELY

Where you source your food from is a key aspect of the climate change equation. How that food ended up at that source is also important. Keep the following in mind when making your buying choices.

Buy direct.
Nothing is better than buying your food as close to the source as possible. Cutting out the middle person and supporting local farms have many benefits: getting ingredients grown in line with methods that support a healthy planet; having access to a diversity of high-quality, locally grown, and nutrient-dense seasonal produce; supporting local economies and the livelihoods of underprivileged communities; investing in our well-being; and saving money.

Many online resources can help you connect with small producers and farmers around the country. LocalHarvest.org allows you to search for farmers markets and community-supported agriculture (CSA) networks near you. Another way to gain direct access to seasonally grown food is through CropSwap, a network that connects you with local growers. This app-based service also allows you to trade garden-grown fruits and vegetables if you grow food at home as well as prepared and preserved foods.

Buy from the grocery store.
Buying direct from local farmers is definitely my preferred option, but that's easy for me to say because I live in a big city in Southern California. This is a luxury for many people around the United States depending on geographical location (or even acquisitive power). I've lived in places such as the Midwest, where farm stands or farmers and artisans markets only operate during the summer and, as weather permits, a few months during other seasons.

At times, making our best effort to support farmers markets near us allows us to acquire only a portion of what we need to buy. There might be limited or no availability of bulk items, such as pulses, grains, and seeds, or ingredients like oils, spices, and flours. The reality is that our weekly or monthly market run might have us making a few stops—one of them being at the grocery store.

One of the pros of shopping at supermarkets is convenience: They're generally a reasonable distance from our homes and open almost every day, so we don't have to wait for a specific day to buy what we need. Other advantages include having the option of one-stop shopping (especially these days when supermarkets carry everything from over-the-counter medications to office products) and in some cases more reasonable prices for certain products.

One of the cons of acquiring food products from a grocery store is a lack of transparency. Larger grocers purvey their produce from large-scale distributors: Produce is often conventionally grown and brought in from other parts of the country (and many times imported from overseas). As discussed earlier, the food supply chain generates a lot of emissions at various stages: from production and processing to packaging and transportation. Unfortunately, we have no way to follow the trace and therefore no way to estimate the carbon footprint of what we buy.

Other disadvantages include less availability of organic, biodiverse, and locally grown produce, although this varies according to market chains and their locations. In general, grocery stores display organic fruits and vegetables in a dedicated area of the produce section and the disparity of their prices—compared with conventionally grown—is quite different. (The markups are real!) Unless they're high-end markets, it's rare to find a wide variety of produce (apart from the main staples) or heirloom varieties.

There's a stronger demand for locally grown products across the United States and this has in turn motivated large grocery stores to support farmers and small producers at a local and regional level from areas adjacent to their stores. Even membership-based warehouse stores have been listening to the market's demands and making better efforts to offer a wider variety of local products. This shift is proving to be advantageous to consumers, especially those interested in reducing their carbon footprints.

Let this be a reminder that our purchasing power counts and sends a clear message up and down the food supply chain. Use your voice to ask the management of your go-to grocery store to carry a wider variety of seasonal or locally grown fruits, vegetables, and legumes. Suggest they clearly label those that are already available so you know which farm they come from. Ask that they feature one farmer a month to help spur support from the community. This will benefit the store and the farmers!

Having a plan while visiting the supermarket will always be a useful strategy. The following are things to keep in mind.

Focus on the perimeter of the store.

The fresh produce and bulk sections are generally located in the outer ring of food markets. Mindfully avoiding the center aisles will make it easier to avoid the temptation of buying highly processed foods and ingredients. While navigating the store's perimeter, prioritize sourcing dry and nonrefrigerated ingredients first and picking up chilled items at the very end of your visit.

Buy dry goods in bulk.

When they're available, choose loose pulses, whole grains, nuts, and seeds in bulk. In many stores, cereals, pseudo-cereals (like buckwheat, chia, and quinoa), flours, and dried fruits are also available in this section. You avoid the extra wrapping and save some money—unpackaged goods are more affordable and they naturally have a longer shelf life. Win-win situation! Visit www.thelow-carboncookbook.com for a suggested list of dry goods to buy in bulk.

Bring reusable bags and containers to the market.

For bulk items, use Mason jars, reusable plastic containers, or drawstring canvas bags to tote your dry goods. Bring an extra bag so the cashier can weigh each item at the register.

For fresh produce, avoid using single-use plastic bags to wrap your fruits and vegetables. Instead, use reusable mesh bags, which are washable and quite convenient. Because all produce has to be thoroughly washed, using single-use plastic bags is nothing but extra waste (and resources). For shopping, don't forget your reusable bags and totes. Some states are charging for single-use shopping bags. Saving money can be just as big of a motivation to carry bags with you as it is doing something good for the planet. Every. Bit. Helps.

Be label-savvy.

Date labels aren't federally regulated for food products (aside from baby formula). Sell-by, use-by, and best-by dates aren't indicative of safety. Be an educated consumer and use your own judgment to assess quality and freshness.

Certification labels might provide some insights about the farming practices used to produce food. Labels such as the USDA's Certified Organic, Demeter Certified Biodynamic, and Regenerative Organic Certified attest to sustainable methods that are better for the environment and climate change. Unpackaged produce sourced from supermarkets and food chains usually come with little (somewhat annoying) stickers that contain a small code. The numbers identifying these products fall under 9XXX (for organic), 4XXX (for conventionally grown), and 3XXX (for genetically modified, or GMO).

There are too many labels! Some have been introduced by independent organizations and this, unfortunately, has increased the potential for label "greenwashing." The lack of regulation and biased messaging have created further confusion for consumers. Be a well-informed one!

Don't rule out less-than-perfect produce.

Industrialized food production and monocrop farming culture have "trained" large food retailers and consumers to favor pristine-looking produce that's also consistent in size, color, and overall appearance. Well, that's not how Mama Earth works. One of the beautiful traits about sustainably grown fruits and vegetables is the variety of colors, shades, shapes, and sizes a single harvest might yield. At a time where more than 20% of fruits and vegetable don't meet grocery store standards, be a sustainability hero and buy ugly produce. Too many resources are wasted with food loss.

Choose organic when possible.

Although organic foods aren't available or affordable for many people around the United States, an increase in demand has positively influenced the market, which has been reflected on the supply side. Nowadays, many small farmers are able to grow their produce organically, which has given certified organic farm stands a stronger presence at farmers markets and in small produce shops around the country. Organic produce is grown without artificial fertilizers (which are highly detrimental to the environment) but also without harmful chemicals, such as pesticides.

Some vulnerable fruits and vegetables (like strawberries, peaches, spinach, potatoes, and cucumbers) retain more pesticide residue than others. For suggested produce to buy organic, visit www.thelow-carboncookbook.com.

Be a mindful shopper.

Consider the carbon footprint of the products you choose at the supermarket: Out-of-season, airfreighted food items have a large impact on the environment. Avoid those at all costs. Foods with a high impact on the environment and short shelf life are often packaged to protect them from spoiling. (I'm talking about the clear plastic boxes used for imported berries and "specialty" tomatoes or the cardboard carriers used for asparagus and peppers transported across the ocean.) Take a moment to review packaging and find out where your food is coming from and how it got there.

Educate yourself about foods with high environmental impacts, such as palm oil, chocolate, or coffee. They're plant-based, yes, but their methods of production and lack of regulation make them detrimental to the environment. As a mindful shopper, you can make the right choices that will help keep your carbon footprint at a minimum.

Make meal plans and shopping lists.

Writing shopping lists has numerous benefits: from planning ahead and buying only what's needed to saving you money and decreasing your food waste. Taking a thorough inventory of what's already available at home is very important prior to creating a shopping list. If you already have several pounds of lentils or brown rice in your pantry, you don't need to buy more. However, you might note other bulk items that are running low or decide to try a new pulse or grain (because there's so much to try). Once that list is created, stick to it! It's the most effective way to avoid impulse purchases.

Planning ahead takes the stress out of having to figure out weekly meals and snacks. This will prove helpful whether you live by yourself or with roommates or you're responsible for feeding a family. As part of a low-carbon diet, a meal plan can also assist you in diversifying your culinary palette— to ensure you're "eating the rainbow"—and thus balancing the nutritional density of your spreads.

If you're subscribed to a CSA delivery service, wait until after receiving your produce box to account for what you have before writing a shopping list. Likewise, if you're making weekly visits to a nearby farmers market or farm stand, see what seasonal vegetables and fruits you're able to get prior to assessing what else you might need at the food market or grocery store. Just remember to check the seasonal calendar (page 47) or review the *Seasonal Food Guide* app to make the best food choices.

If writing shopping lists isn't your thing, just try to keep an open mind for the sake of Mama Earth and slowly implement this small action into your routine. Over time, it might become one of your planet-friendly habits! While venturing out to the market "list-less," remember to practice some constraint and not overbuy food (no matter how good it looks) that might end up going bad before you have a chance to enjoy it. There's always next week.

COOK SMART.

Favoring plant-based foods, sourcing sustainable ingredients, and shopping wisely allow us to reduce our carbon footprints. Cooking at home gives you yet another opportunity to use food as a tool to fight climate change. Changing some of our habits can further the positive impact our diets might have on environmental soundness.

An electric oven might be twice as efficient compared with a gas oven, but neither of them is really energy efficient. In general, ovens use less than 15% of their energy to actually cook. So much of the heat that's generated escapes the oven (especially if we open the door to "peek," which makes the temperature drop by 25°F [-4°C]). The bottom line is that cooking consumes a lot of energy and, at times, more than is necessary.

We can make simple changes at home to make our cooking habits more sustainable: keeping pans tightly covered with a lid to retain the heat, simmering food in covered pots over low heat, cooking a couple or a few dishes at the same time in the oven, and repurposing pots with boiling water to cook, blanch, or steam different ingredients. Small efforts to cook smart have the potential to make a significant difference in our kitchens.

Choosing our menus according to the seasons might also help balance our energy consumption. Choosing raw or minimally cooked foods that don't require extensive use of

the stove or cooking equipment in the summer when our homes are hotter helps us avoid the need for fans or air-conditioning. Likewise, roasting vegetables while cooking a casserole in the oven in the middle of the winter will allow us to take advantage of all that extra heat.

Everyday actions add up to big energy savings. Cooking in batches on a single day (having a "meal prepping day") can help us execute our weekly meal plans and maximize the use of resources in the kitchen. Preparing several batches of food at a time helps us save money and keeps us fed for days. (Who needs to eat out with a refrigerator full of yummy homemade food?) As a bonus, this feel-good action might also help us reduce the amount of food waste we produce.

Cooking smart also involves not having to make unnecessary midweek trips to the market to source food ingredients for the sake of one recipe. Shop around your own home! See what you have available in your kitchen—search in the pantry, check the back of your refrigerator, look at the bottom of the fruit bowl or produce basket. Once you've gathered it all, design a special menu to use everything. This reminds me of my days competing on *MasterChef* where we had "Mystery Box Challenges": We didn't know the ingredients we'd have under each box and we had to create a complete dish. It can be fun!

REDUCE FOOD WASTE.

Simple changes toward more sustainable shopping and cooking habits help us lower our carbon emissions. They also make it possible for us to produce less waste at home. Properly storing the food we buy is also a great way to prevent it from spoiling too fast and to extend its life. Taking the time to sort fresh produce as soon as it's in our homes can prove to be of great value. Storing it correctly helps maximize its life and durability—whether in the refrigerator, saved in a basket in a dry place away from direct sunlight, or sealed in an airtight container and stored in the pantry. If you need help figuring out the best place to store various types of food, visit www.thelow-carboncookbook.com for suggested food options.

Prepping food for later use is something we can also do right away to prevent food from sitting for too long and, eventually, spoiling. We can peel and cut a fresh pineapple so it's ready to enjoy as a snack later in the day or week or invest some time in breaking down a butternut squash so it's cubed and ready to cook. Generally, labor-intensive prep work is something I'd rather "get out of the way" and do straight away. It allows me to portion ingredients I might use in several different ways and to store them adequately. Doing this is definitely worth the time!

Passionate about tackling food waste, I've made it a point to include many recipes in this book that use parts of an ingredient that are traditionally thrown away: from seeds and leaves to stalks and peels. Getting creative with food scraps is promoted heavily in this book. Saving vegetable peels, tops, stems, and other snippets in a reusable freezer bag to then make a broth (page 232) is one of my favorites. When we cook to save the planet, we should upcycle—repurpose those undervalued parts of plants in delicious ways—and make the most of our investments in fresh food. Our carbon footprint shrinks as we reap the benefits of the nutrients (fiber, phytochemicals, etc.) inherent in what might otherwise be, literally, waste.

Other ways of not letting food end up in the trash bin involves freezing leftovers and implementing a weekly CORN: Clean Out the Refrigerator Night. I learned this from my mother-in-law, who, having lived through the recession in the 1970s, is very resourceful in the kitchen. Having a CORN "event" gives me a night off from cooking (when you're on a low-carbon diet and cooking everything from scratch, not having to cook is great) and also allows me to free up space in the refrigerator for produce and a new batch of prepped meals.

Because food lasts much longer when frozen, many recipes in this book provide tips on freezing food for long-term storage. Soups, stews, and casseroles freeze (and reheat) very well. When ingredients have a significant yield (like jackfruit), I like to divide and freeze them in a number of smaller reusable bags. Fruits like mango, pineapple, and berries freeze splendidly and make the most delicious instant sorbets and frozen yogurts. (See pages 196–211.)

Take every step to make the most of food, and when all else fails (even using parts to feed your pets), compost it! Many cities provide pickup services for community composting or you can also start composting at home. The Environmental Protection Agency (EPA) offers many online resources to compost at home, along with information on the benefits of composting and its uses. See www.epa.gov to learn more.

CHAPTER 5
BREAKFAST

60 Amaranth Pancakes with Apple Compote

62 Overnight Beet Oats

63 Tofu Perico Scramble

64 Watermelon Pizza

66 Quinoa Porridge with Stewed Bananas & Prunes

67 Avocado Smoothie Bowl with Fresh Fruits

68 Coconut & Chia Bowl with Warm Ancient Grains

70 Mindful Toasts: Avocado / Hummus

71 Mindful Toasts: Pea Purée / Vegetable

72 Oat Waffles with Mango Sauce

AMARANTH PANCAKES
WITH APPLE COMPOTE

These pancakes will get you ready for the day because amaranth is loaded with protein, fiber, minerals, and antioxidants. The compote reminds me of my childhood, when even fruit toppings were made from scratch. Plus, cinnamon and nutmeg are comforting—and they warm my heart.

PREP TIME: 10 TO 15 MINUTES // COOK TIME: 35 TO 36 MINUTES // YIELD: 16 TO 18 MINI PANCAKES

INGREDIENTS

1 tbsp ground flaxseeds

3 tbsp warm water

¾ cup plant-based milk

½ tsp vanilla essence

¾ cup amaranth flour

1 tbsp coconut sugar

1 tsp baking powder

pinch of coarse sea salt

1 to 2 tsp melted coconut oil

FOR THE COMPOTE

2 medium organic Gala apples, peeled, cored, and diced into medium cubes

2 tbsp water

1 tbsp maple syrup

1 tbsp blackstrap molasses

1 tbsp freshly squeezed lemon juice

1 tsp fresh lemon zest

¼ tsp ground cinnamon

pinch of ground nutmeg

1 In a small saucepan on the stovetop over medium heat, make the compote by combining the apples and water. Bring to a boil, then reduce the heat to low. Cover and cook for about 15 minutes, stirring occasionally.

2 Add the maple syrup, blackstrap molasses, lemon juice and zest, cinnamon, and nutmeg. Continue to cook uncovered for 5 minutes. Set aside.

3 In a small bowl, combine the flaxseeds and water, stirring to remove any lumps. Allow to rest until viscous, about 4 to 5 minutes.

4 Add the plant-based milk and vanilla essence. Whisk until all the ingredients have been incorporated.

5 In a large bowl, whisk together the amaranth flour, coconut sugar, baking powder, and salt. Add the wet ingredients to the dry ingredients, whisking gently until uniform. Allow to rest for 5 minutes.

6 Heat a large nonstick skillet on the stovetop over medium-low heat. Brush the bottom of the skillet with a little coconut oil. Working in batches, place the batter by the spoonful and cook until golden brown, about 2 minutes. Flip with a metal spatula and cook the other side for 1 to 2 minutes.

7 Transfer the pancakes to plates and top each with compote before serving.

» QUICK TIPS

Serve with a side of fresh fruit: cantaloupe, strawberries, or your preferred seasonal fruits. Make your own amaranth flour: In a medium skillet on the stovetop over medium heat, toast 1½ cups of amaranth seeds for 5 minutes, stirring often. Allow to cool. Use a high-powered blender to pulverize the seeds into a fine powder. This makes about 2 cups of amaranth flour. Store the remaining flour in an airtight container in your pantry.

OVERNIGHT BEET OATS

Beets lend an earthiness and sweetness to this dish that might surprise you. They're loaded with vitamins, minerals, inorganic nitrates, and pigments. Soaking oats allows them to soften naturally. Make more than one batch on meal-prep day and brighten your mornings all week long!

PREP TIME: **5 TO 10 MINUTES** // COOK TIME: **30 MINUTES** // YIELD: **2 SERVINGS**

INGREDIENTS

1 small beet, thoroughly washed

2 quarts (2 liters) water

1 small Fuji apple, peeled and cored

1 cup old-fashioned rolled oats, divided

1 cup plant-based milk, divided

½ tsp ground cinnamon, divided

OPTIONAL TOPPINGS

3 tbsp diced dried apricots

2 tbsp raw cashews (halves and pieces)

2 tbsp roughly chopped raw walnuts

½ tsp ground flaxseeds

1 In a small saucepan on the stovetop over medium heat, combine the beet and water. Bring to a boil, then reduce the heat to low. Simmer uncovered until fork-tender, about 30 minutes. Remove the saucepan from the heat and allow the beet to cool.

2 Use a box grater to shred the apple and the cooled beet. In each of two glass canning jars or lidded glass containers, mix 2½ tablespoons of apples, ¼ cup of beets, ½ cup of oats, ½ cup of plant-based milk, and ¼ teaspoon of cinnamon. Mix well with a spoon. Cover and refrigerate overnight.

3 Transfer each jar of beet oats to a serving bowl. Top each bowl with 1½ tablespoons of apricots and 1 tablespoon each of cashews and walnuts. Sprinkle ¼ teaspoon of flaxseeds over the top of each bowl. Serve cold or at room temperature.

» QUICK TIPS

Any variety of red or yellow apple will work in this recipe—go for local and seasonal! Cooked beets and raw apples are naturally sweet. This is why I don't call for additional sweeteners. Feel free to add a little maple syrup if desired. Store the jars in the fridge for up to 5 days. Hold the toppings until ready to eat.

TOFU PERICO SCRAMBLE

Perico, which literally translates to "parrot," is a traditional Venezuelan breakfast scramble that owes its name to the bright colors of its ingredients. As a way to bring both of my cultures into one plate, I've paired a plant-based, protein-packed version of perico with fried green tomatoes.

PREP TIME: **5 TO 10 MINUTES** // COOK TIME: **9 TO 12 MINUTES** // YIELD: **2 SERVINGS**

INGREDIENTS

6oz (170g) organic sprouted extra-firm tofu

1 tbsp pure olive oil

3 tbsp small-diced white onions

½ cup small-diced baby bella mushrooms

½ cup small-diced Roma tomatoes

3 tbsp small-diced orange bell peppers

½ tsp ground annatto

½ tsp coarse sea salt, divided

¼ tsp ground black pepper

2 medium green heirloom tomatoes

1 tbsp ground flaxseeds

3 tbsp tapioca flour, divided

¼ cup plant-based milk

½ tsp nutritional yeast, plus more

2 tbsp precooked white corn flour (Harina P.A.N. or arepa flour)

1 to 2 tbsp avocado oil, plus more

1 tbsp finely chopped fresh chives or fresh herbs

1 Place the tofu in a medium bowl and use a fork to finely crumble. Use cheesecloth to press and remove excess liquid. Set aside.

2 In a medium skillet on the stovetop, heat the olive oil over medium heat. Add the onions and mushrooms. Sauté for 2 minutes, stirring often. Add the Roma tomatoes, bell peppers, annatto, ¼ teaspoon of salt, and black pepper. Cook for 1 minute, stirring often.

3 Add the tofu and cook for 2 to 3 minutes, stirring often. Turn the heat off. Cover the skillet and leave on the stovetop to keep warm.

4 Slice the heirloom tomatoes at roughly ⅓ inch (.75cm) thick (about 3 slices per tomato). Place the slices on a clean kitchen towel to remove excess moisture, flipping once.

5 In a small bowl, whisk together the flaxseeds, 1 tablespoon of tapioca flour, plant-based milk, nutritional yeast, and the remaining ¼ teaspoon of salt. Allow to rest for 5 minutes, then whisk again.

6 In a shallow bowl, combine the corn flour and the remaining 2 tablespoons of tapioca flour.

7 Dip each tomato slice in the flaxseed mixture, coating both sides. Transfer the slices to the corn flour mixture and make sure to coat both sides.

8 In a large cast-iron pan on the stovetop, heat the avocado oil over medium-low heat, making sure to coat the entire bottom of the pan.

9 Place the tomato slices in the cast-iron pan and cook until golden brown and crispy, about 2 to 3 minutes per side.

10 Transfer an equal number of tomato slices to 2 plates and spoon half the tofu scramble in the center of each plate. Garnish with chives or fresh herbs. Sprinkle a little nutritional yeast over the top before serving.

WATERMELON PIZZA

This colorful take on pizza uses refreshing watermelon as the base for a ton of goodness: healthy fats, probiotics, protein, antioxidants, vitamins, and much more. Get creative with the toppings by using seasonal fruits and locally sourced nut butters and seeds.

PREP TIME: **5 MINUTES** // COOK TIME: **NONE** // YIELD: **1 PIZZA**

INGREDIENTS

1 watermelon slice from the center of a large watermelon, 1 inch (2.5cm) thick and 8 inches (20cm) wide

2 tbsp nut butter (pecan recommended), room temperature

1 tbsp maple syrup or date syrup

20 thin banana slices

¼ cup blackberries, halved

¼ cup blueberries

1 tbsp **Cultured Cashew Yogurt** (page 235)

¼ tsp chia seeds

1 tsp fresh mint chiffonade (see Quick Tips)

1 Place the watermelon slice on a cutting board. Use a large knife to cut the slice into 4 to 8 wedges, making sure to keep them together.

2 In a small bowl, whisk together the nut butter and maple syrup until consistent. You can add ½ to 1 tablespoon of water to thin out the mixture as needed.

3 Spread the nut butter mixture over the watermelon. Layer the fruit over the top: banana slices, blackberries (cut side down), and blueberries.

4 Use a fork to drizzle the yogurt over the top. Sprinkle the chia seeds evenly over the top and garnish with the mint chiffonade before serving.

> **» QUICK TIPS**
> To make mint chiffonade, roll 2 mint leaves together and cut the leaves into ribbons. You can use peanut butter or hazelnut butter if you prefer those over pecan butter. Use other parts of the watermelon for **Chunky Tropical Fruit Tizana** (page 183), **Watermelon Limeade** (page 193), and **Lime-Pickled Onions & Watermelon Rinds** (page 227).

QUINOA PORRIDGE
WITH STEWED BANANAS & PRUNES

Once called "the mother grain" by the Incas, quinoa is a pseudo-cereal rich in protein and fiber. Its chewy texture and nutty flavor make quinoa the star of this comforting and nutrient-dense porridge. The spices add such a beautiful flavor and aroma to the dish.

PREP TIME: **3 MINUTES** // COOK TIME: **12 TO 14 MINUTES** // YIELD: **2 SERVINGS**

INGREDIENTS

2 cups cooked **Quinoa**
  (page 242)

1 cup plant-based milk

pinch of ground nutmeg

pinch of ground cardamom

2 tbsp **Cashew Cream**
  (page 230)

½ to 1 tbsp shaved toasted
  almonds

FOR THE STEWED FRUIT

1 tsp coconut oil

1 small banana, sliced ½ inch
  (1.25cm) thick

6 pitted prunes, roughly chopped

2 tbsp coconut sugar

1 tsp pure vanilla extract

2 whole star anise pods

¼ cup water

1. In a small saucepan on the stovetop, make the stewed fruit by heating the coconut oil over medium heat. Stir in the banana slices and cook until browned, about 2 minutes, stirring often.

2. Stir in the prunes, coconut sugar, vanilla extract, star anise, and water. Mix well, then reduce the heat to low. Simmer uncovered until the bananas and prunes are soft and cooked through, about 5 minutes. Remove the saucepan from the heat and remove the star anise. Allow the mixture to rest for 5 minutes.

3. In a medium saucepan on the stovetop over medium heat, combine the quinoa, plant-based milk, nutmeg, and cardamom. Bring to a boil, then reduce the heat to low. Cover and simmer for 5 to 7 minutes, stirring occasionally.

4. Add the cashew cream and whisk until fully dissolved into the porridge. Remove the saucepan from the heat.

5. Divide the porridge into 2 bowls and top each with an equal amount of stewed fruit. Garnish with almonds before serving.

» QUICK TIPS

Thoroughly rinse the star anise, air-dry it, and save for a second or even a third use depending on its potency. White quinoa has the most delicate taste and softens up the most in the porridge, but red/brown or black quinoa will work well in this recipe. Choose unsulfured unsweetened prunes for the healthiest choice. I don't sweeten the porridge when topped with the stewed fruit. If you're enjoying the porridge on its own, feel free to add a little maple syrup or coconut sugar. Store the porridge in an airtight container in the fridge for up to 6 days.

AVOCADO SMOOTHIE BOWL
WITH FRESH FRUITS

This smoothie bowl makes me want to get out of bed in the morning! Heart-healthy fats in the avocado make it ever so velvety, while the bananas give it great density and sweetness. The mild tartness in the berries brightens up the flavors (and colors), adding a pop to every spoonful.

PREP TIME: **5 MINUTES** // COOK TIME: **NONE** // YIELD: **1 TO 2 SERVINGS**

INGREDIENTS

½ Hass avocado, peeled and seeded

1 small ripe banana

1 medium kiwi, peeled

1 cup baby spinach

1 cup cold plant-based milk

1 tbsp freshly squeezed lemon juice

½ cup diced pitaya (dragon fruit)

6 to 12 fresh raspberries

6 to 12 fresh goldenberries (Cape gooseberries)

¼ tsp chia seeds (optional)

1 In a blender, combine the avocado, banana, kiwi, spinach, plant-based milk, and lemon juice. Process on high until smooth.

2 Pour the mixture into 1 to 2 bowls. Top with an equal amount of pitaya, raspberries, and goldenberries. Sprinkle the chia seeds over the top (if using) before serving.

» QUICK TIPS

Save the avocado seed for **Avocado Seed Powder** (page 231). To thin out the smoothie, add cold water 1 tablespoon at a time until your desired consistency is reached. Use your favorite fruits or whatever is seasonal to top the smoothie bowl—from diced pineapple and peaches to blackberries and strawberries. This dish is best enjoyed right away because the avocado might oxidize and the color might change. Store the smoothie in an airtight container in the fridge for up to 1 day.

COCONUT & CHIA BOWL
WITH WARM ANCIENT GRAINS

Coconut and chia pudding serves as a creamy base for this warm breakfast. Considered one of the most nutritious foods on Earth, chia seeds are tiny but mighty! The featured grains—fonio, amaranth, and quinoa—are sustainable food choices as well as nutritional powerhouses.

PREP TIME: **5 MINUTES** // COOK TIME: **5 TO 6 MINUTES** // YIELD: **2 SERVINGS**

INGREDIENTS

5oz (150g) **Coconut Cream** (page 230)

2 tbsp chia seeds

1 cup plant-based milk

2 tbsp fonio

¼ cup cooked **Amaranth** (page 243)

¼ cup cooked **Quinoa** (page 242)

pinch of ground cinnamon

½ tbsp maple syrup (optional)

2 to 3 tbsp desiccated coconut

1 to 1½ tbsp shelled hempseeds

2 to 3 tbsp dried cranberries

1 In an airtight container, combine the coconut cream and chia seeds. Refrigerate overnight.

2 In a small saucepan on the stovetop over medium heat, combine the plant-based milk and fonio. Bring to a boil, stirring often. Reduce the heat to low and cook for 3 minutes, stirring occasionally.

3 Add the coconut cream and chia mixture, amaranth, and quinoa. Stir until all the grains are well incorporated and the mixture is warm, about 2 to 3 minutes. Add the cinnamon and maple syrup (if using).

4 Transfer the grain mixture to 2 bowls. Top each with an equal amount of the coconut, hempseeds, and cranberries. Serve immediately.

» QUICK TIPS
You can toast desiccated coconut in a medium-sized pan on the stovetop over medium-low heat for 3 to 5 minutes, stirring often to allow for even browning. Store in an airtight container in the refrigerator for up to 5 days. Hold the toppings until ready to eat.

MINDFUL TOASTS

Many people have jumped on the avocado toast bandwagon, making their own versions and getting creative with the concept. My mindful toasts incorporate ingredients that take advantage of their textures, flavors, and nutritional content. Use these as inspiration to create your own.

AVOCADO

PREP TIME: **5 MINUTES** // COOK TIME: **NONE** // YIELD: **1 SERVING**

INGREDIENTS

1 small Hass avocado, seeded and peeled

2 pinches of coarse sea salt

1 extra-large slice of whole grain sourdough (or 2 regular slices), toasted

2 small Easter egg radishes, thinly sliced

½ tbsp thinly sliced Fresno peppers

1 to 2 tbsp sunflower sprouts

¼ tsp chia seeds

1 Place the avocado in a small bowl and use a fork to mash into a smooth paste. Season with the salt.

2 Spread an equal amount of avocado on each slice of bread. Top each slice with an equal amount of radishes, peppers, and sprouts. Sprinkle ⅛ teaspoon of chia seeds over the top of each slice. Serve immediately.

> » **QUICK TIP**
> I buy sourdough from my local farmers market. It's great to support a local artisan and to know there are no preservatives in my bread!

HUMMUS

PREP TIME: **5 TO 7 MINUTES** // COOK TIME: **NONE** // YIELD: **2 SERVINGS**

INGREDIENTS

¼ cup **Yellow Split Pea Hummus** (page 220)

¼ cup baby spinach

1 tbsp extra-virgin olive oil

2 large slices of sunflower seed bread, toasted

1 to 1½ tbsp thinly sliced red bell pepper

½ tbsp chopped fresh flat-leaf parsley

¼ tsp ground black peppers

1 to 2 pinches of **Avocado Seed Powder** (page 231) (optional)

1 In a tall blending cup or wide-mouthed glass jar, use an immersion blender to process the hummus, spinach, and olive oil until creamy and smooth.

2 Spread an equal amount of hummus on each slice of bread. Top each slice with an equal amount of bell peppers, parsley, black pepper, and avocado seed powder (if using). Serve immediately.

> » **QUICK TIPS**
> Zero-waste tip: Use the base of the bell pepper, which is normally trimmed off. They're the perfect size for toasts! If the spread is too thick to process, add cold water ½ tablespoon at a time until the blades get going easily.

PEA PURÉE

PREP TIME: **5 TO 7 MINUTES** // COOK TIME: **2 MINUTES** // YIELD: **1 SERVING**

INGREDIENTS

1 cup water

½ cup fresh English peas

1 tbsp extra-virgin olive oil

1 tsp chickpea miso paste

¼ tsp coarse sea salt

2 slices of flourless sprouted whole grain bread, toasted

1oz (30g) Persian cucumber, thinly sliced

1 to 2 tsp thinly sliced red onions

1 tbsp microgreens

2 pinches of **Papaya Seed Powder** (page 231)

1 In a small saucepan on the stovetop over medium heat, bring the water to a boil. Add the peas and cook until cooked through, about 2 minutes. Drain and run under cold water in a mesh strainer for about 30 seconds.

2 In a tall blending cup or wide-mouthed glass jar, use an immersion blender to process the peas, olive oil, miso paste, and salt until smooth and consistent.

3 Spread an equal amount of pea purée on each slice of bread. Top each slice with an equal amount of cucumber, red onions, and microgreens. Sprinkle 1 pinch of papaya seed powder over the top of each slice. Serve immediately.

> **» QUICK TIPS**
> I like using Ezekiel bread because it's low-glycemic, fiber- and nutrient-rich, and, of course, delicious. If the purée is too thick to process, add cold water ½ tablespoon at a time until the blades get going easily.

VEGETABLE

PREP TIME: **10 MINUTES** // COOK TIME: **2 MINUTES** // YIELD: **1 SERVING**

INGREDIENTS

½ tbsp pure olive oil

2 tbsp carrot matchsticks

3 tbsp thinly sliced radicchio

4 thin slices of zucchini

1 to 2 pinches of coarse sea salt

2 to 3 tbsp **Cashew Cream** (page 230)

2 slices of gluten-free oat bread, toasted

½ tsp shelled hempseeds

8 small fresh basil leaves

1 In a medium skillet on the stovetop, heat the olive oil over medium heat. Add the carrots and radicchio. Sauté for 1 minute, then transfer to a plate.

2 Add the zucchini and cook for 30 seconds per side, using a spatula to flip. Transfer the zucchini to the plate. Sprinkle the salt over the vegetables.

3 Spread an equal amount of the cashew cream on each slice of bread. Top each slice with an equal amount of carrots, radicchio, and zucchini. Sprinkle ¼ teaspoon of hempseeds over the top of each slice. Garnish with fresh basil before serving.

> **» QUICK TIPS**
> I love using my mandoline to create very thin zucchini slices. They look like ribbons over the toast and nestle the other vegetables perfectly. You can use any variety of summer squash, including white and crookneck squash.

OAT WAFFLES
WITH MANGO SAUCE

I didn't grow up eating waffles, but a deep love sparked once I tried them. Homemade oat flour adds tons of fiber, minerals, vitamins, and antioxidants to this golden bed that perfectly carries fruits and toppings. The mango sauce is dreamy—sweet, lightly tangy, and bright yellow.

PREP TIME: **15 MINUTES**   //   COOK TIME: **24 TO 27 MINUTES**   //   YIELD: **4 WAFFLES**

INGREDIENTS

2 tbsp chia seeds

¼ cup plus 2 tbsp warm water

2 cups homemade oat flour (see Quick Tips)

1 cup gluten-free flour (or whole wheat flour)

1½ tsp baking powder

2 pinches of ground nutmeg

¼ tsp coarse sea salt

¼ cup unsweetened applesauce

3 tbsp maple syrup

2 cups plant-based milk, room temperature

¼ cup melted coconut oil, plus more

½ cup small-diced ripe pineapple

¼ cup roughly chopped toasted walnuts

FOR THE SAUCE

2 pitted dates

½ cup boiling water

½ cup cubed ripe mangoes

1 tbsp freshly squeezed lemon juice

¼ cup water

1 To make the mango sauce, place the dates and hot water in a medium bowl. Soak for 10 minutes. Cover for better results. Allow to cool slightly. Peel and discard the skins.

2 In a blender, combine the dates, mangoes, lemon juice, and water. Process on high until smooth and glossy. Place the mixture in a small saucepan on the stovetop over low heat. Cover and simmer for 12 to 15 minutes. Remove the saucepan from the heat and set aside to cool.

3 In a small bowl, combine the chia seeds and water. Allow to rest until viscous, about 5 minutes.

4 In a large bowl, whisk together the oat flour, gluten-free flour, baking powder, nutmeg, and salt.

5 In a blender, combine the chia mixture, applesauce, maple syrup, plant-based milk, and coconut oil. Process on high until the chia seeds have been slightly ground. Add the wet ingredients to the dry ingredients. Whisk until dense and consistent. Allow to rest for 5 to 7 minutes.

6 Preheat a classic waffle maker to medium heat.

7 Brush the waffle maker with coconut oil and pour one-fourth of the batter into the center. Cook until golden brown, about 3 minutes. Repeat this process with the remaining batter. Transfer the waffles to a platter, making sure not to stack them.

8 Top the waffles with the pineapple and walnuts. Serve immediately with the mango sauce.

> **» QUICK TIPS**
> To make homemade oat flour, in a high-powered blender, pulverize 4 cups of old-fashioned oats. If you use a store-bought oat flour, you might need less milk because it will likely be less coarse.

CHAPTER 6
SMALL BITES

76 Jackfruit Empanaditas

78 Stuffed Squash Blossoms

79 Broccoli Stalk Cakes

80 Plantain Cups

82 Stuffed Shiitake Mushrooms

83 Fava Bean Pod Bollitos

84 Potato & Eggplant Skewers

86 Barbecue Cauliflower

87 Savory Quinoa Beignets

88 Falafel Bites on Endive Boats

JACKFRUIT EMPANADITAS

These little pockets of goodness are great for parties and get-togethers. The savory filling has a hint of spice to perfectly complement the dough's sweetness. The combination of textures—meaty and soft on the inside and crispy on the outside—make empanaditas a huge crowd pleaser.

PREP TIME: **20 TO 25 MINUTES** // COOK TIME: **20 MINUTES** // YIELD: **12 EMPANADITAS**

INGREDIENTS

1 tbsp pure olive oil

¼ cup minced shallots

2 large garlic cloves, minced

1 cup finely shredded **Green Jackfruit** (page 234)

½ tsp smoked paprika

½ tsp ground annatto

¼ tsp ground cumin

1 tsp coarse sea salt, divided, plus more

¼ tsp ground black pepper, plus more

1¼ cups plus 1 to 2 tbsp water

1 tbsp coconut sugar

1 cup plus 2 tbsp whole grain precooked white corn flour

1 to 1½ cups avocado oil

Creamy Garlic Sauce (page 214)

Guasacaca (page 215)

1. Heat a medium skillet on the stovetop over medium heat. Once hot, add the olive oil. As soon as it smokes, add the shallots and sauté for 1 minute. Add the garlic and sauté for 30 seconds.

2. Stir in the jackfruit until fully blended with the aromatics. Add the paprika, annatto, cumin, ½ teaspoon of salt, and pepper. Cook for 2 minutes, stirring often.

3. Add 1 to 2 tablespoons of water and deglaze the bottom of the pan. Turn the heat off. Cover the skillet and allow to rest on the stovetop for at least 5 minutes. Taste and adjust seasoning.

4. In a large bowl, combine the coconut sugar, the remaining 1¼ cups of water, and the remaining ½ teaspoon of salt. Slowly add the corn flour, mixing with a spoon to prevent lumps. Allow to hydrate for 5 minutes. With damp hands, divide the dough into 12 evenly sized balls.

5. Sprinkle a few drops of water on a 6- × 6-inch (15.25 × 15.25cm) piece of sturdy reusable plastic wrap. Place a ball of dough in the center of the plastic, and with damp hands, flatten it into a 4-inch (10cm) circle. The key to working with this dough is keeping your hands slightly wet. This helps the dough stay hydrated.

6. Place 1 tablespoon of the jackfruit mixture in the upper third of the circle. Grab the ends of the plastic square and fold, using your fingers to lightly press the dough and close the circle into a half-moon shape. You can also use a cup with a thin edge to trim the ends of the half-moon. Repeat this process with the remaining balls and place them on parchment paper.

7. In a small saucepan on the stovetop, heat the avocado oil over medium-high heat until it reaches 365°F (185°C). Working in batches, place 2 to 3 empanaditas in the saucepan and fry until crispy and golden brown, about 2½ minutes.

8. Transfer the empanaditas to a platter. Serve immediately with the garlic sauce or the spicy avocado sauce.

> **» QUICK TIPS**
> If you can't find fresh jackfruit, use canned jackfruit (just drain and rinse prior to using). Use Harina P.A.N. or arepa flour. Don't use masa harina because it's not the same product. Using a small saucepan allows you to deep-fry using the least amount of oil.

STUFFED SQUASH BLOSSOMS

Visually appealing and oh so yummy, squash blossoms are worthy of all the praise.
I love baking them "naked" to expose and celebrate their gorgeous color. The butternut squash
filling is comforting and highly nutritious, with vitamins, minerals, and healthy fats.

PREP TIME: **15 MINUTES** // COOK TIME: **19 TO 22 MINUTES** // YIELD: **4 TO 6 SERVINGS (15 STUFFED BLOSSOMS)**

INGREDIENTS

9oz (255g) peeled and seeded butternut squash

2 quarts (2 liters) water

¼ cup raw walnuts (halves and pieces)

2 tbsp finely chopped fresh parsley stems

1 garlic clove, roughly chopped

1 tbsp nutritional yeast

2 tsp freshly squeezed lemon juice

2 tsp extra-virgin olive oil

½ tsp plus 2 pinches of coarse sea salt, divided

¼ tsp plus 2 pinches of ground black pepper, divided

2 pinches of ground nutmeg

15 squash blossoms

1 tbsp avocado oil, plus more

1 Preheat the oven to 400°F (200°C). Line a large baking tray with parchment paper.

2 Cut the squash into ½- to ¾-inch-thick (1.25cm to 2cm) pieces.

3 In a medium saucepan on the stovetop over medium heat, bring the water to a boil. Add the squash and cook until fork-tender, about 7 minutes. Strain and allow to cool slightly.

4 In a food processor, combine the squash, walnuts, parsley stems, garlic, nutritional yeast, lemon juice, olive oil, ½ teaspoon of salt, ¼ teaspoon of pepper, and nutmeg. Pulse 6 to 8 times. Scrape the sides, pushing the mixture down. Process on high until creamy and consistent.

5 Transfer the mixture to a piping bag with a ½-inch (1.25cm) nozzle. Pipe the mixture into the blossoms until they're about three-fourths full. Gently twist the petals together to seal. Place the blossoms on the tray. Make sure to leave some space between them. Lightly drizzle the avocado oil over the top. Sprinkle the remaining 2 pinches of salt and 2 pinches of pepper over the top.

6 Place the tray on the middle rack in the oven and bake for 12 to 15 minutes, rotating the tray halfway through.

7 Remove the tray from the oven and serve the blossoms immediately.

> **» QUICK TIPS**
> You can use a zippered plastic bag to pipe the mixture into the blossoms: Cut the tip of the bag to make a ½-inch (1.25cm) opening. Store the blossoms in an airtight container in the fridge for up to 5 days.

BROCCOLI STALK CAKES

Zero waste meets nutrition powerhouse! Broccoli stalks are often thrown away, but they're as rich in vitamin C and potassium as the florets but even richer in fiber. Delectable and wholesome, these little cakes are the perfect finger food and you can serve them as tapas or snacks.

PREP TIME: **15 MINUTES** // COOK TIME: **18 TO 20 MINUTES** // YIELD: **4 TO 6 SERVINGS (8 CAKES)**

INGREDIENTS

1 tbsp ground flaxseeds

3 tbsp warm water

8oz (225g) broccoli stalks

2oz (60g) scallions, roughly chopped

½ cup panko breadcrumbs

¼ cup amaranth flour (see Quick Tips)

1 tbsp nutritional yeast

½ tsp dried oregano

½ tsp dried basil

½ tsp garlic powder

¼ tsp smoked paprika

½ tsp coarse sea salt

2 to 3 tbsp avocado oil

1 Preheat the oven to 375°F (190°C). Line a large baking tray with parchment paper.

2 In a ramekin or small bowl, combine the flaxseeds and water. Stir until no lumps remain. Allow to rest until viscous, about 4 to 5 minutes. Set aside.

3 Use a potato peeler to remove the outer skin (the darker green layer) of the broccoli stalks to expose the pale green and even white flesh. (If using the thick broccoli stem, cut about 1 to 1½ inches [2.5 to 3.75cm] from the bottom because that can have a woody texture.) Roughly chop the stalks.

4 In a food processor, combine the broccoli stalks, scallions, breadcrumbs, amaranth flour, nutritional yeast, oregano, basil, garlic powder, paprika, salt, and the flaxseed mixture. Process on high until the stalks have been minced and the mixture is consistent, about 30 seconds. Allow to rest for 5 minutes.

5 Transfer the mixture to a working surface and divide into 8 equal portions. Use clean, damp hands to form the mixture into balls and then flatten to make cakes about ¾ inch (2cm) thick and 1½ inches (3.75cm) in diameter.

6 Use 1 to 2 tablespoons of avocado oil to brush 8 circles (to match the diameter of the cakes) on the lined tray. Place each cake on an oiled circle. Brush the top of the cakes with the remaining 1 tablespoon of oil.

7 Place the tray on the bottom rack in the oven and bake until lightly seared on both sides and golden brown, about 18 to 20 minutes, flipping once halfway through.

8 Remove the baking tray from the oven and transfer the cakes to a platter. Serve immediately.

> ### » QUICK TIPS
> You can use rice crumbs or cracker crumbs for the panko. I recommend not using breadcrumbs as a replacement. See Quick Tips on page 63 to learn how to make homemade amaranth flour. These delicious cakes pair well with **Roasted Red Pepper Dip** (page 217) or **Fava Bean Spread** (page 219).

PLANTAIN CUPS

Plantains are related to bananas and they're cooked in a variety of ways in countries like Venezuela, where it's part of the national dish. The cooked pulp is used to create these mildly sweet cups, which are filled with the flavor-packed plantain peels that are high in dietary fiber.

PREP TIME: **10 MINUTES** // COOK TIME: **23 TO 28 MINUTES** // YIELD: **6 TO 8 CUPS**

INGREDIENTS

2 large very ripe plantains

2½ quarts (2½ liters) water

¾ tsp coarse sea salt, divided, plus more

1 to 2 tsp melted coconut oil

1 medium vine-ripened tomato

1 garlic clove

1 tbsp avocado oil

½ cup thinly julienned brown onions

¼ cup thinly julienned red bell peppers

¼ tsp ancho chili powder

¼ tsp ground turmeric

¼ tsp ground black pepper

chopped fresh herbs or microgreens

Cashew Cream (page 230)

» QUICK TIPS

Very ripe plantains have a dark yellow skin with lots of big black spots (half or more of the peel). If the plantains are very ripe and soft, you won't need any water to mash them properly. Expect some texture and small bits to remain after processing. You can also add the tomato and garlic to a tall glass jar and use an immersion blender to purée.

1 Preheat the oven to 425°F (220°C). Remove the tips from the plantains and cut the plantains into 2 even pieces, leaving the skin on.

2 In a medium saucepan on the stovetop over medium-high heat, bring the water to a boil. Add the plantains and cook until soft, about 6 to 8 minutes. Transfer the plantains to a plate to rest for 5 minutes.

3 Peel the plantains and reserve the peels. In a food processor, combine the peeled plantains and ¼ teaspoon of salt. Pulse until fully mashed. If the mixture is too dry, add water ½ tablespoon at a time until softer.

4 Divide the mash into 6 to 8 evenly sized balls. Lightly brush a muffin tray with the coconut oil. Place the balls in the tray and press down with damp fingers to form cups about 1 inch (2.5cm) high and ¼ inch (0.5cm) thick.

5 Place the tray on the top rack in the oven and bake until golden brown and the top edges are crispy, about 10 to 12 minutes. Remove the tray from oven and allow the cups to cool completely.

6 In a blender, combine the tomato and garlic. Process on high until smooth. Set aside.

7 Use the edge of a knife to lightly scrape the interior of the plantain peels to remove the cream-colored membrane. Finely julienne the peels to create shreds about ⅛ inch (3mm) thick.

8 In a sauté pan on the stovetop, heat the avocado oil over medium-high heat. Add the onions and sauté for 1 to 2 minutes. Add the bell peppers and plantain peels. Sauté for 1 minute more.

9 Add the ancho chili powder, turmeric, black pepper, and the remaining ½ teaspoon of salt. Stir until the spices have evenly coated all the ingredients. Stir in the tomato purée and reduce the heat to low. Cover and simmer for at least 5 minutes. Taste and adjust seasoning.

10 Fill the plantain cups evenly with the shredded peel mixture. Top with the cashew cream and fresh herbs or microgreens before serving.

STUFFED SHIITAKE MUSHROOMS

Shiitake mushrooms are loaded with healthful compounds and have an umami flavor. This is because they contain many of the amino acids found in meat. The stuffing features millets— a sustainable ancient grain that's rich in calcium, phosphorous, and magnesium.

PREP TIME: **7 TO 10 MINUTES** // COOK TIME: **18 MINUTES** // YIELD: **12 STUFFED MUSHROOMS**

INGREDIENTS

2 tbsp pure olive oil

2 tbsp **Vegetable Broth** (page 232)

1 tbsp balsamic vinegar

½ tsp plus 3 to 4 pinches of coarse sea salt, plus more

12 shiitake mushrooms (each about 1½ inches [3.75cm] in diameter), cleaned and dried

¼ cup finely shredded carrots

¼ cup finely chopped spinach

½ cup cooked **Millets** (page 243), room temperature

1 tsp onion powder

½ tsp ground black pepper

1 Preheat the oven to 350°F (180°C). Line a medium baking tray with parchment paper.

2 In a ramekin or small bowl, whisk together the olive oil, broth, balsamic vinegar, and 1 to 2 pinches of salt.

3 Use a paring knife to remove the mushroom stems where they attach to the cap. Place the caps cut side down on the tray. Brush the olive oil mixture on the mushrooms. Flip and brush the bottom of the caps. Space them out on the tray.

4 Place the tray on the middle rack in the oven and bake until the mushrooms release some liquid and soften up slightly, about 8 minutes.

5 In a large bowl, combine the carrots, spinach, millets, onion powder, pepper, and the remaining ½ teaspoon plus 2 pinches of salt. Mix well with clean hands and press the mixture while "kneading" to compact all the ingredients.

6 Remove the tray from the oven. Use a small or medium cookie scoop or spoon to stuff each mushroom cap with approximately 1 packed tablespoon of millet mixture. Use any remaining olive oil mixture to gently brush the top of each mound.

7 Return the tray to the oven and bake until the mushrooms are tender and the stuffing is golden brown, about 10 minutes more.

8 Remove the tray from the oven and serve the stuffed mushrooms warm or at room temperature.

» QUICK TIPS

The best way to clean shiitake and other fresh mushrooms is to use a damp, clean cloth to wipe them and remove any dirt. If you'd prefer to wash them, just run them quickly under water and dry them right away with a clean towel. Be aware that the texture of the mushroom might be slightly compromised. Although the stems are tough to eat, don't discard them. They'll add so much flavor (hello, umami!) to **Vegetable Broth** (page 232).

FAVA BEAN POD BOLLITOS

Bollitos (pronounced *boh-jee-tohs*) are a favorite in Venezuela and similar to tamales and humitas. These bundles offer the perfect opportunity to minimize food waste—I use fava bean pods to make the filling. Once cooked in thin strips, the pods are tender and absorb a lot of flavor.

PREP TIME: **15 TO 20 MINUTES** // COOK TIME: **50 TO 52 MINUTES** // YIELD: **15 SERVINGS (15 BOLLITOS)**

INGREDIENTS

6oz (170g) fava bean pods

1 quart (1 liter) plus 1 cup water, divided

2 tbsp coconut oil

½ cup small-diced shallots

⅓ cup small-diced poblanos

½ tsp smoked paprika

½ tsp ground turmeric

¼ tsp ground cumin

¾ tsp coarse sea salt, divided, plus more

¼ tsp ground black pepper

1½ cups fresh corn kernels

1 cup precooked white corn flour

1 tsp ground annatto (or achiote paste)

18 dried corn husks, soaked in hot water for 30 minutes

Creamy Garlic Sauce (page 214)

Guasacaca (page 215)

» QUICK TIPS

The pods should be empty. Hopefully, you've saved these after making one of my fava bean recipes. You can replace the poblanos with green bell peppers. Use Harina P.A.N. or arepa flour. Store the bollitos in a reusable silicone bag in the freezer for up to 6 months.

1 Wash the pods thoroughly. Snap the stem end of the pods and pull down to remove the stringy vein that runs along the inner side of each pod. Slice the pods ¼ inch (0.5cm) thick.

2 In a medium saucepan on the stovetop over medium heat, bring 1 quart (1 liter) of water to a boil. Reduce the heat to low and cook the pods for 3 to 5 minutes uncovered. Use a mesh strainer to remove the pods from the water and set aside.

3 In a medium skillet on the stovetop, heat the coconut oil over medium heat. Add the shallots and sauté for 1 minute. Stir in the poblanos, fava bean pods, paprika, turmeric, cumin, ¼ teaspoon of salt, and pepper. Cook for 2 minutes, stirring often. Remove the skillet from the heat and allow the mixture to cool. Taste and adjust seasoning.

4 In a food processor, combine the corn kernels, corn flour, annatto, the remaining 1 cup of water, and the remaining ½ teaspoon of salt. Pulse until most of the kernels are broken up and the mixture is chunky. Transfer the mixture to a bowl. Add the fava bean pod mixture and use clean hands or a wooden spoon to mix well. Allow to rest for 5 minutes.

5 To assemble the bollitos, place a husk flat on a working surface and spoon 4 tablespoons (about 2 ounces [60 grams]) of the corn and pod mixture in the center of the husk. Fold each of the long sides of the husk toward the center, making sure the ends overlap over each other. Fold the bottom end of the bundle up. Repeat this process with 14 more husks and stack them on top of each other to keep the wraps in place.

6 Fill a large pot with about 1 inch (2.5cm) of water. Place a steamer basket inside the pot and cover the base with the remaining 3 husks. Arrange the bollitos standing upright and tightly leaning on each other to keep them standing. Bring the water to a boil over medium-high heat. Cover, reduce the heat to low, and steam for 45 minutes.

7 Remove the basket from the pot and transfer the bollitos to a platter. Allow them to cool for at least 15 minutes. Serve with the garlic sauce or the spicy avocado sauce.

POTATO & EGGPLANT SKEWERS

Eggplant is one of my favorite plant-based meat substitutes thanks to its texture and ability to carry flavors. Many nutrients found in potatoes—potassium, folate, and vitamin C—are concentrated in the skin, giving you a reason to leave it on (besides avoiding food waste).

PREP TIME: **10 MINUTES** // COOK TIME: **25 TO 27 MINUTES** // YIELD: **12 SKEWERS**

INGREDIENTS

1lb (450g) baby potatoes (about 24 total)

1½ tsp coarse sea salt, divided

2 tbsp freshly squeezed lemon juice

3 tbsp pure olive oil, divided

1 tbsp **Homemade Curry Powder** (see page 240)

1 eggplant (about 1½lb [680g]), cut into 1½-inch (3.75cm) pieces (36 total)

1 large red onion, cut into 1½-inch (3.75cm) pieces

> **» QUICK TIPS**
> I used bite-sized purple potatoes, but peewee or baby Yukon will also work. You can also use 6 medium-sized potatoes and cut them in fourths. I used 7-inch (17.5cm) skewers, but longer ones can also work. Make sure to perforate through the eggplant skin because the flesh softens while grilling and the eggplant might fall off.

1 Place 12 wooden skewers in a large bowl of water for at least 4 hours.

2 Wash and scrub the potatoes thoroughly. Place them in a medium saucepan and add enough cold water to cover by 1 to 2 inches (2.5 to 5cm). Stir in ½ teaspoon of salt until dissolved.

3 Place the saucepan on the stovetop over medium-high heat. Bring to a boil, then reduce the heat to medium. Cook for about 10 to 12 minutes. The potatoes are done when a wooden skewer or a fork slides easily into the center. Start checking them after 6 minutes.

4 Remove the saucepan from the heat and strain the water. Set aside.

5 In a large bowl, whisk together the lemon juice, 2 tablespoons of olive oil, curry powder, and the remaining 1 teaspoon of salt.

6 Add the eggplant and potatoes. Toss until all the ingredients are fully coated. Allow to marinate for 30 minutes to 1 hour.

7 In a small bowl, combine the marinade and the remaining 1 tablespoon of olive oil. Set aside.

8 Assemble the skewers by alternatingly threading 2 potatoes, 3 pieces of eggplant, and 2 to 4 pieces of onion on each skewer.

9 Heat a cast-iron grill until very hot. Place the skewers on the grill and reduce the heat to medium. Cook until the eggplant is soft and cooked through and the vegetables are charred, about 15 minutes, turning the skewers every 3 to 4 minutes. Brush the skewers with the marinade every time they're turned.

10 Transfer the skewers to a platter and serve immediately with a bowl of **Cucumber & Shallot Raita** (page 219).

BARBECUE CAULIFLOWER

Cauliflower is quite the nutrition powerhouse because it contains most vitamins and minerals needed for human health. It's also rich in fiber and antioxidants. Plus, the meaty texture works perfectly with the light crispy coating as well as the sweet and tangy barbecue sauce.

PREP TIME: **7 TO 10 MINUTES** // COOK TIME: **32 MINUTES** // YIELD: **4 TO 6 SERVINGS**

INGREDIENTS

1 medium head of cauliflower
  [1½ to 2lb [690g to 1kg]]

¾ cup plant-based milk

½ cup whole wheat flour
  (or gluten-free flour)

½ tsp smoked paprika

½ tsp ground annatto

½ tsp garlic powder

½ tsp coarse sea salt, plus more

½ tsp ground black pepper

1¼ cup panko breadcrumbs,
  plus more

1 cup **Barbecue Sauce**
  (page 214), plus more

1 Preheat the oven to 450°F (230°C). Line a large baking tray with parchment paper.

2 Cut the cauliflower into medium bite-sized pieces, leaving some of the stem on each piece.

3 In a large bowl, whisk together the plant-based milk, whole wheat flour, paprika, annatto, garlic powder, salt, and pepper until consistent.

4 In a small bowl, place the breadcrumbs.

5 Add the cauliflower to the batter and use a spatula to coat them evenly. Pick out each floret with a fork and let any excess batter drip off. Transfer to the breadcrumbs bowl, lightly coating on all sides. (Add more panko to the bowl if needed.) Evenly space the florets on the tray.

6 Place the tray on the middle rack in the oven and bake until slightly golden and crispy, about 20 minutes, turning halfway through. Remove the tray from the oven.

7 In a large bowl, combine the florets and barbecue sauce until evenly coated. Rearrange the florets on the tray, return the tray to the oven, and bake until the sauce has caramelized, about 12 minutes.

8 Remove the tray from the oven and transfer the florets to a platter. Brush the florets with more barbecue sauce if desired. Serve immediately.

> **» QUICK TIPS**
>
> Don't throw away the thick cauliflower core or leafstalks. Save them to make cauliflower rice or **Spaghetti Squash with Plant-Based Bolognese** (page 165). These crispy florets are best enjoyed right out of the oven. However, you can store leftovers in an airtight container in the fridge for up to 3 days. For best results, reheat in the oven at 450°F (230°C) for 10 minutes.

SAVORY QUINOA BEIGNETS

Referred to by the ancient Inca civilization as *Chisaya Mama*—mother of all grains—quinoa contains lots of protein and all the essential amino acids. Add to that cauliflower, flaxseeds, and nutritional yeast to make these beignets not only crispy and delicious but very nutritious.

PREP TIME: **5 MINUTES** // COOK TIME: **7 TO 10 MINUTES** // YIELD: **12 TO 14 BEIGNETS**

INGREDIENTS

8oz (225g) purple cauliflower (with stems), cut into 1- to 2-inch (2.5 to 5cm) pieces

½ brown onion, peeled and quartered

1 tbsp pure olive oil

½ tsp dried basil

½ tsp dried oregano

½ tsp coarse sea salt, plus more

¼ tsp ground black pepper

1 tbsp plus 1 tsp ground flaxseeds

¼ cup warm water

1 cup cooked **Quinoa** (page 242)

¼ cup amaranth flour (see Quick Tips)

¼ cup rice crumbs

1 tsp nutritional yeast

1 cup avocado oil

Creamy Garlic Sauce (page 214) or **Salsa Verde** (page 215)

1 In a food processor, combine the cauliflower (including the stems) and onion. Pulse until finely minced.

2 In a large skillet on the stovetop, heat the olive oil over medium heat. Once the oil starts to smoke, add the cauliflower and onion. Sauté for 2 minutes, stirring often.

3 Add the basil, oregano, salt, and pepper. Stir until well incorporated. Remove the skillet from the heat and allow the mixture to cool.

4 In a small bowl, combine the flaxseeds and water, stirring to make sure no lumps remain. Allow to rest until viscous, about 4 to 5 minutes.

5 In a large bowl, combine the cauliflower, onion, quinoa, amaranth flour, rice crumbs, nutritional yeast, and flaxseed mixture. Use clean hands to knead the dough until you can form a solid ball by pressing it in your palm.

6 In a small saucepan on the stovetop, heat the avocado oil over medium-high heat until it reaches 365°F (185°C). Use two soup spoons to press the batter into an oval and gently slide it into the hot oil. Working in batches, place 3 to 4 dough balls in the saucepan and fry until crispy and golden brown, about 2½ minutes.

7 Transfer the beignets to a platter. Serve immediately with the garlic sauce or the salsa verde.

> **» QUICK TIPS**
> Any color cauliflower (purple, yellow, or white) will work well with this recipe. See Quick Tips on page 63 for how to make homemade amaranth flour. Substitute the rice crumbs with panko or homemade breadcrumbs. (Save stale bread, then toast and grind them to avoid food waste.)

FALAFEL BITES ON ENDIVE BOATS

Garbanzo beans are the featured ingredient here. These legumes are rich in protein, fiber, and other healthy compounds. The mildly bitter and crisp endive boats contrast beautifully with the crunchiness of the falafel and the creaminess of the tahini sauce.

PREP TIME: **12 TO 15 MINUTES** // COOK TIME: **5 TO 8 MINUTES** // YIELD: **4 TO 6 SERVINGS (12 ENDIVE BOATS)**

INGREDIENTS

2oz (60g) white onion

2 garlic cloves

⅓ cup plus 2 tbsp chopped fresh parsley (curly or flat-leaf), divided

¾ cup cooked **Garbanzo Beans** (page 238)

2 tbsp garbanzo flour

1 tbsp toasted sesame seeds

½ tsp coarse sea salt

¼ tsp ground cumin

⅛ tsp ground cayenne (optional)

2 pinches of ground cardamom

2 to 3 tbsp breadcrumbs, plus more

1 cup avocado oil

12 endive leaves

¼ cup small-diced vine-ripened tomatoes

FOR THE SAUCE

2 tbsp freshly squeezed lemon juice

1 tbsp tahini

1 tbsp **Aquafaba Mayonnaise** (page 235)

pinch of coarse sea salt, plus more

pinch of ground black pepper

1 In a food processor, combine the onion, garlic, ⅓ cup of parsley, garbanzo beans, garbanzo flour, sesame seeds, salt, cumin, cayenne (if using), and cardamom. Pulse 6 to 8 times and scrape the sides of the container, pushing the mixture down. Process on high until consistent and able to form into a ball. Transfer the mixture to a bowl, cover with a towel, and refrigerate for 30 minutes to 1 hour.

2 Place the breadcrumbs on a shallow plate. Divide the bean mixture into 12 evenly sized portions. Roll each portion into a ball. (Keep your hands damp during this process to prevent the mixture from sticking.) Lightly roll each ball in the breadcrumbs until all the sides are coated.

3 In a small saucepan on the stovetop, heat the avocado oil over medium-high heat until it reaches 365°F (185°C). Use a slotted spoon to gently slide the balls into the hot oil. Working in batches, place 4 to 6 balls in the saucepan and fry until crispy and golden brown, about 2 to 2½ minutes. If they're not fully submerged in oil while cooking, flip them halfway through. Transfer the bites to a plate lined with paper towels and briefly allow any excess oil to drain.

4 In a small bowl, make the sauce by whisking together all the ingredients until smooth and creamy.

5 Place each falafel bite on an endive leaf and top each with an equal amount of tomatoes and the remaining 2 tablespoons of parsley. Arrange the leaves on a serving platter and drizzle the sauce over the top. Serve warm or at room temperature.

» QUICK TIPS

To make homemade garbanzo flour, pulverize dry garbanzo beans in a high-powered blender. For the small amount needed in this recipe, I used my spice grinder to process a couple tablespoons of dry garbanzo beans. Store the garbanzo flour in a cool, dry place in a lidded jar. To make homemade breadcrumbs, toast and grind stale bread (to avoid food waste).

CHAPTER 7
SALADS

92   Nopal Cactus Pad & Quinoa Salad

94   Fava Bean & Zucchini Salad with Apple Cider Dressing

95   Jícama & Corn Salad with Aquafaba Mayonnaise Vinaigrette

96   Sweet Potato & Great Northern Bean Salad with Tahini Dressing

98   Mushroom & String Bean Salad with Roasted Heirloom Carrots

99   Asparagus Salad with Avocado & Grape Tomatoes

100   Millet & Okra Salad

102   Shaved Fennel, Celery & Pink Grapefruit Salad with Dill & Yogurt Dressing

104   Chayote & Mango Slaw with English Peas

105   Amaranth Tabbouleh with Cucumber & Pomegranate Seeds

106   Swiss Chard & Lentil Salad with Balsamic Dressing

108   Curried Cauliflower Salad with Apples & Celery

109   Wild Rice & Tomato Salad with Balsamic & Maple Dressing

110   Cucumber, Pea & Daikon Salad with Almond & Ginger Dressing

NOPAL CACTUS PAD & QUINOA SALAD

This features nopal cactus pads and the fruit (also known as prickly pear). I grew up eating the fruit in Venezuela, but I was introduced to the pads in Southern California. The fluffy texture of the quinoa and crispiness of the tomatillo and bell pepper complement the nopal's density.

PREP TIME: **8 MINUTES** // COOK TIME: **18 TO 20 MINUTES** // YIELD: **2 TO 4 SERVINGS**

INGREDIENTS

2 cups water

3 small fresh nopal cactus pads (about 10oz [285g] total), thorns removed

1 cup cooked **Quinoa** (page 242)

½ cup small-diced tomatillos

½ cup minced red bell peppers

½ cup finely sliced scallions

1 tbsp minced jalapeños (optional)

2 to 4 tbsp cilantro leaves

FOR THE DRESSING

1 small red nopal fruit (prickly pear), peeled and chopped

3 tbsp freshly squeezed lime juice

¼ cup extra-virgin olive oil

2 tbsp chopped fresh cilantro stems

¼ tsp coarse sea salt, plus more

¼ tsp ground black pepper

1 In a medium pot on the stovetop over medium-high heat, bring the water to a boil. Add the nopal pads and reduce the heat to medium-low. Cover and cook until the pads are tender, about 18 to 20 minutes. (Nopales will change from bright green to opaque and olive in color while cooking.) Strain and rinse generously under water to wash away as much of the viscous liquid as possible. Pat dry with paper towels and dice. Set aside.

2 In a blender, make the dressing by processing on high all the ingredients until smooth. Strain through a mesh sieve.

3 In a large bowl, combine the nopal pads, quinoa, tomatillos, red peppers, scallions, and jalapeños (if using). Add the dressing and toss to coat. Taste and adjust seasoning.

4 Divide the salad into 2 to 4 bowls. Garnish with the cilantro leaves before serving.

> **» QUICK TIPS**
> If you can't source fresh cactus pads, you can use 8 ounces (225 grams) of diced jarred tender cactus, or "nopalitos." Just drain the brine from the jar and rinse well prior to using. Fresh is always best for the environment and human health. Many markets sell nopal pads with thorns already removed. If found whole, use a paring knife or vegetable peeler to carefully remove the thorns, trying to keep as much of the outer dark green skin. Save cilantro stems for other recipes: Store in a reusable storage bag in the fridge to use in dressings or sauces or to make zero-waste **Vegetable Broth** (page 232).

FAVA BEAN & ZUCCHINI SALAD
WITH APPLE CIDER DRESSING

This simple and elegant salad features a variety of textures and flavors: nuttiness from the fava beans, mild bitterness from the arugula, and sweetness from the peppers. The delicate zucchini ribbons deliver so much flavor from the savory and tangy dressing!

PREP TIME: **7 MINUTES** // COOK TIME: **3 TO 4 MINUTES** // YIELD: **2 TO 4 SERVINGS**

INGREDIENTS

2 cups water

½ cup shelled fava beans (from about 1¼lb [570g] fresh fava bean pods)

1 large zucchini

⅓ cup baby wild arugula

¼ cup thinly sliced yellow bell peppers

FOR THE DRESSING

2 tbsp apple cider vinegar

2 tbsp extra-virgin olive oil

½ tsp yellow mustard

¼ tsp coarse sea salt

2 to 3 pinches of ground black pepper

1 In a small saucepan on the stovetop over medium heat, bring the water to a boil. Add the fava beans. Cover and cook until tender, about 3 to 4 minutes. Drain with a mesh strainer and run under cold water. Transfer to a medium bowl and squeeze to remove the skins (a light-colored membrane surrounding each bean). Set aside.

2 In a small bowl, make the dressing by whisking together all the ingredients until emulsified.

3 Use a vegetable peeler to cut the zucchini lengthwise into thin ribbons. Peel until you reach the core with seeds. Place the ribbons in a large bowl and drizzle 1 tablespoon of dressing over the top. Gently toss with clean hands. Add the fava beans, arugula, and yellow peppers. Gently toss again.

4 Divide the salad onto 2 to 4 plates. Drizzle the remaining dressing over the top. Serve immediately.

» QUICK TIPS

Fresh fava beans are in season from late spring into the summer months. You can find them at farmers markets or from produce vendors. Don't throw away the fava bean pods—they're actually edible and loaded with fiber. Save the zucchini cores for later use: Add them to **Lentil Minestrone** (page 138) or save them in your vegetable scrap bag.

JÍCAMA & CORN SALAD
WITH AQUAFABA MAYONNAISE VINAIGRETTE

Jícama is a popular legume in many Latin American countries. It's a nitrogen-fixing plant and contributes to soil health. Jícama is often eaten raw and has a slightly sweet flavor. Charring the corn develops a delectable bitterness that plays beautifully with the heat of the Fresno pepper.

PREP TIME: **10 MINUTES** // COOK TIME: **2 TO 3 MINUTES** // YIELD: **2 TO 4 SERVINGS**

INGREDIENTS

1 ear of corn, shucked

1 tbsp avocado oil

1 cup small-diced jícama

¼ cup finely chopped fresh cilantro, stems included, plus leaves

3 tbsp minced celery

1 small Fresno pepper, minced

FOR THE DRESSING

1½ tbsp freshly squeezed lime juice

1 tbsp extra-virgin olive oil

1 tbsp **Aquafaba Mayonnaise** (page 235)

¼ tsp coarse sea salt, plus more

1 to 2 pinches of ground black pepper

1 In a small bowl, make the dressing by whisking together all the ingredients until creamy and smooth. Taste and adjust seasoning. Set aside.

2 Use a large knife to cut the kernels from the ear of corn into a shallow bowl. (Make sure to remove any remaining silk.)

3 In a cast-iron skillet on the stovetop, heat the avocado oil over medium heat. Once the oil starts to smoke, add the corn and cook until some kernels are slightly charred, about 2 to 3 minutes, stirring often. Remove the skillet from the heat.

4 In a large bowl, combine the corn, jícama, cilantro, celery, and Fresno pepper. Mix until well incorporated. Add the dressing and toss with a spatula until evenly coated. Serve immediately.

» QUICK TIPS

To reduce the heat level of the Fresno pepper, remove the seeds and scrape the inner membrane using a paring knife. Non-spicy substitutes include red bell pepper and sweet pepper. Be a food waste warrior and save leftover corn cobs for your vegetable scrap bag. Store the salad in an airtight container in the fridge for up to 1 week.

SWEET POTATO & GREAT NORTHERN BEAN SALAD
WITH TAHINI DRESSING

Eat the rainbow—and enjoy the health benefits and nutritional content from diverse foods in nature's color spectrum—with this vibrant and eye-catching salad. It has a variety of textures: crunchy, smooth, dense, leafy, and creamy—a party for your taste buds!

PREP TIME: 5 MINUTES // COOK TIME: 10 TO 11 MINUTES // YIELD: 2 TO 4 SERVINGS

INGREDIENTS

2 medium sweet potatoes, peeled and diced into ½-inch (1.25cm) cubes

1 tbsp pure olive oil

¼ tsp coarse sea salt

¼ tsp ground black pepper

1 cup cooked **Black & White Beans** (Great Northern beans) (page 238)

1 cup baby arugula

¼ cup shaved purple cabbage

2 tbsp fresh pomegranate seeds

FOR THE DRESSING

¼ cup tahini

¼ cup plus 1 tbsp freshly squeezed lemon juice

2 tsp maple syrup

¼ tsp fresh lemon zest

½ tsp coarse sea salt

1 Preheat the oven to 425°F (220°C).

2 In a small bowl, make the dressing by whisking together all the ingredients until smooth. Set aside.

3 On a baking tray, combine the sweet potatoes, olive oil, salt, and pepper. Toss to coat. Evenly space the sweet potatoes on the tray.

4 Place the tray on the bottom rack in the oven and roast for 6 minutes. Turn the sweet potatoes and roast until golden and cooked through, about 4 to 5 minutes more. Remove the tray from the oven and allow the sweet potatoes to cool.

5 In a large bowl, combine the sweet potatoes, beans, arugula, and cabbage. Toss well.

6 Divide the salad into 2 to 4 bowls. Drizzle the dressing over the top and garnish with the pomegranate seeds before serving.

> **» QUICK TIPS**
> If the dressing is too thick, add a little water at a time and whisk to reach your desired consistency. Store the salad undressed in an airtight container in the fridge for up to 2 days. Separately store and refrigerate the dressing in a small lidded jar and add to the salad when ready to serve.

MUSHROOM & STRING BEAN SALAD
WITH ROASTED HEIRLOOM CARROTS

This features Asian flavors that will make your heart smile. The earthiness from the mushrooms pairs well with the grassiness and mild bitterness of the beans and the sweetness of the carrots. A delicious sweet miso–ginger dressing and crunchy furikake turn this salad into a major YUM.

PREP TIME: **5 TO 7 MINUTES** // COOK TIME: **8 TO 10 MINUTES** // YIELD: **2 TO 4 SERVINGS**

INGREDIENTS

7oz (200g) wild brown beech mushrooms, trimmed and separated

7oz (200g) string beans, trimmed and cut into 1- to 1½-inch (2.5 to 3.75cm) pieces

5oz (140g) heirloom carrots, unpeeled and cut into ⅛-inch-thick (3mm) slices

2 tbsp melted coconut oil

½ tsp **Umami Mushroom Powder** (page 240)

¼ tsp coarse sea salt, plus more

¼ tsp ground black pepper

1 to 2 tsp **Furikake Seaweed Seasoning** (page 240)

FOR THE DRESSING

1 tbsp rice vinegar

1 tbsp toasted sesame oil

2 tsp maple syrup

2 tsp chickpea miso paste

1 tsp grated fresh ginger

1 Preheat the oven to 400°F (200°C).

2 On a large baking tray, combine the mushrooms, string beans, and carrots. Drizzle the coconut oil over the top. Sprinkle the mushroom powder, salt, and pepper over the top. Toss and rub with clean hands to make sure the vegetables are evenly coated. Evenly space them out on the tray and make sure to leave space between them.

3 Place the tray on the middle rack in the oven and roast until the mushrooms are soft and the string beans and carrots are cooked but still have a bite to them, about 8 to 10 minutes, tossing halfway through.

4 Remove the tray from the oven and transfer the vegetables to a serving bowl. Taste and adjust seasoning. Set aside.

5 In a small bowl, make the dressing by whisking together all the ingredients until well incorporated and consistent.

6 Drizzle the dressing over the roasted vegetables and toss until evenly coated. Sprinkle the furikake seaweed seasoning over the top. Serve warm, at room temperature, or cold.

> **» QUICK TIPS**
> Alba clamshell and enoki mushrooms are great substitutes for brown beech mushrooms. Sliced cremini or baby bella mushrooms will also work. You can swap the furikake seasoning with toasted and/or black sesame seeds. Store the salad in an airtight container in the fridge for up to 5 days.

ASPARAGUS SALAD
WITH AVOCADO & GRAPE TOMATOES

Asparagus is low in calories and loaded with vitamins, minerals, and antioxidants. Although it's one of my favorite vegetables, I always buy it locally while in season. Asparagus is one of the top air-freighted items and this form of transportation significantly elevates its carbon footprint.

PREP TIME: **5 TO 7 MINUTES** // COOK TIME: **1 MINUTE** // YIELD: **2 TO 4 SERVINGS**

INGREDIENTS

6oz (170g) trimmed asparagus

1½ quarts (1½ liters) water

2 Hass avocados, peeled, seeded, and cut into ½-inch to ¾-inch (1.25 to 2cm) cubes

4oz (110g) grape tomatoes, halved

¼ cup finely chopped fresh cilantro

3 tbsp minced red onions

FOR THE DRESSING

2 tbsp freshly squeezed lime juice, plus more

2 tbsp extra-virgin olive oil

¼ tsp coarse sea salt, plus more

¼ tsp ground black pepper

1 Cut the tips off the asparagus and set aside. Cut the asparagus stalks into 1-inch-long (2.5cm) spears.

2 In a small saucepan on the stovetop over medium-high heat, bring the water to a boil. Add the spears and poach for 1 minute. Drain with a mesh strainer. Run under cold water for 30 seconds to 1 minute. Tap the strainer to remove any excess water. Set aside.

3 In a small bowl, make the dressing by whisking together all the ingredients until emulsified.

4 In a large bowl, combine the asparagus tips and spears, avocados, tomatoes, cilantro, and onions. Drizzle the dressing over the top and toss with a spatula until the salad is well mixed and evenly coated. Taste and adjust seasoning. Serve immediately.

> **» QUICK TIPS**
>
> To properly trim asparagus, take each end of one asparagus in each hand and bend until it breaks. It will break exactly where the woody part ends and the fresh part begins. Use this piece as a guide to line up the rest of the asparagus on a board and trim accordingly. Cut the avocados right before preparing the salad and drizzle a little fresh lime juice over the top to prevent their turning brown. I prefer not to blanch asparagus tips and instead keep them raw and crispy. Feel free to blanch them if that's your preference.

MILLET & OKRA SALAD

Okra is a nutrient-dense fruit rich in antioxidants and vitamins. Because it can withstand drought and heat, okra has a low carbon footprint—quite the star in the low-carbon kitchen! Adding such sustainable ingredients as millets and cauliflower makes this salad delicious and planet-friendly.

PREP TIME: **5 MINUTES** // COOK TIME: **13 TO 14 MINUTES** // YIELD: **2 TO 4 SERVINGS**

INGREDIENTS

6oz (170g) okra (about 12 pods total), cut into ½-inch (1.25cm) pieces

1 tbsp avocado oil

½ tsp coarse sea salt, divided

2 cups water

4oz (120g) purple cauliflower, cut into small florets (about 1 cup)

1½ cups cooked **Millets** (page 243)

¼ cup finely julienned red bell peppers

2 tbsp fresh mint chiffonade (see Quick Tips)

FOR THE DRESSING

¼ cup apple cider vinegar

3½ tbsp extra-virgin olive oil

1 tbsp finely minced shallot

¼ tsp coarse sea salt

¼ tsp ground black pepper

1 Preheat the oven to 425°F (220°C).

2 In a small bowl, make the dressing by whisking together all the ingredients until emulsified. Set aside.

3 On a baking tray, combine the okra, avocado oil, and ¼ teaspoon of salt. Toss to coat and evenly distribute the okra cut side down on the tray.

4 Place the tray on the top rack in the oven and roast for 7 minutes. Turn the okra and roast until golden and crispy, about 4 to 5 minutes more. Remove the tray from the oven and allow the okra to cool.

5 In a small saucepan on the stovetop over medium-high heat, bring the water to a boil. Reduce the heat to low. Add the cauliflower and cook for 2 minutes. Transfer to a plate and allow to rest for 3 minutes.

6 In a large bowl, combine the okra, cauliflower, millets, and bell peppers. Toss well.

7 Divide the salad into 2 to 4 bowls. Drizzle the dressing over the top and garnish with the mint chiffonade before serving.

» QUICK TIPS

To make mint chiffonade, roll 12 mint leaves together and cut the leaves into ribbons. Smart cooking tip: Reuse the boiling water to cook other vegetables or grains. Store the salad in an airtight container in the fridge for up to 3 days.

SHAVED FENNEL, CELERY & PINK GRAPEFRUIT SALAD
WITH DILL & YOGURT DRESSING

With its crunchy texture and licorice-like flavor, fennel is a favorite in my kitchen. It's often praised for its health-promoting qualities, which include anti-inflammatory and anti-bacterial properties. Along with radishes and celery, this salad also bursts with flavors from citrus and herbs.

PREP TIME: **10 MINUTES** // COOK TIME: **NONE** // YIELD: **2 TO 4 SERVINGS**

INGREDIENTS

1 medium fennel bulb (about 7oz [200g])

4 celery stalks

1 small shallot, thinly julienned

1 pink grapefruit, supremed, juice reserved (see Quick Tips)

2 radishes, thinly sliced

1 to 2 tbsp fennel fronds

FOR THE DRESSING

¼ cup **Cultured Cashew Yogurt** (page 235)

3 tbsp extra-virgin olive oil

1 tbsp freshly squeezed lemon juice

1 tbsp reserved grapefruit juice

2 tbsp finely chopped fresh dill

¼ tsp coarse sea salt

¼ tsp ground black pepper

1 In a small bowl, make the dressing by whisking together the ingredients until smooth. Set aside.

2 Use a mandoline to shave the fennel. Set aside.

3 Use a potato peeler to remove the celery's fibrous outer layer. Cut the base off the bottom and cut the stalks into ¼-inch-thick (0.5cm) slices.

4 In a large bowl, combine the fennel, celery, shallot, grapefruit, and radishes. Toss well. Add ¼ cup of the dressing and toss again to coat.

5 Divide the salad into 2 to 4 bowls. Drizzle the remaining dressing over the top. Garnish with the fennel fronds before serving.

> **» QUICK TIPS**
> To supreme the grapefruit (or any citrus fruit), remove the peel and pith, trying not to cut any of the fruit itself. Use a paring knife to slice as close to the membrane as possible of both sides of each segment. Work over a bowl to reserve the juice. You can substitute the pink grapefruit with a blood orange or any other variety of orange. Save the fennel stalks and stems to prepare zero-waste **Vegetable Broth** (page 232). Store the salad in an airtight container in the fridge for up to 1 day.

CHAYOTE & MANGO SLAW
WITH ENGLISH PEAS

This slaw is wholesome and earth-friendly. Chayote squash is widely popular in Venezuela, featuring folate, vitamin C, fiber, and other disease-fighting properties. Magic happens when paired with a tangy green mango, crispy purple cauliflower, and sustainable fresh English peas.

PREP TIME: 5 MINUTES // COOK TIME: 2 MINUTES // YIELD: 2 TO 4 SERVINGS

INGREDIENTS

2 cups water

½ cup fresh English peas

1¼ cups finely shredded purple cabbage

1 cup julienned chayote squash

¾ cup julienned green mangoes

¼ cup diagonally sliced scallions

FOR THE DRESSING

2 tbsp freshly squeezed lemon juice

2 tbsp extra-virgin olive oil

¼ tsp coarse sea salt, plus more

¼ tsp ground black pepper

1 In a small saucepan on the stovetop over medium-high heat, bring the water to a boil. Add the English peas and poach for 1½ minutes. Drain with a mesh strainer. Run the peas under cold water for 30 seconds to 1 minute. Tap the strainer to remove any excess water. Set aside.

2 In a small bowl, make the dressing by whisking together the ingredients until emulsified.

3 In a large serving bowl, layer the cabbage, chayote squash, mangoes, scallions, and peas. Right before serving (or, even better, at the table), drizzle the dressing over the top and toss to coat. Taste and adjust seasoning. Serve immediately.

» QUICK TIPS

You can use frozen peas instead of fresh. Poach for an extra 30 to 45 seconds before running under cold water (or shock in a bowl with iced water for better results). Don't use canned peas. If making ahead, keep the salad undressed and don't toss until time to serve. Upon contact with the dressing, the chayote and mangoes will start to wilt and the cabbage will release some of its color, which will stain the rest of the ingredients. This salad is best enjoyed right away, but you can store it in an airtight container in the fridge for up to 1 day.

AMARANTH TABBOULEH
WITH CUCUMBER & POMEGRANATE SEEDS

Amaranth is known as an ancient grain and its use dates back to Indigenous civilizations in Latin America. It's packed with manganese, magnesium, and fiber. Avoid food waste by using radish greens and add such colorful ingredients as fresh herbs and pomegranate seeds. Tasty!

PREP TIME: **5 TO 7 MINUTES** // COOK TIME: **NONE** // YIELD: **2 TO 4 SERVINGS**

INGREDIENTS

⅔ cup small-diced seeded Persian cucumbers

¼ tsp coarse sea salt

1 cup cooked **Amaranth** (page 243)

½ cup finely chopped radish greens, plus small leaves

⅓ cup pomegranate seeds

¼ cup finely chopped fresh mint, plus small leaves

2 tbsp minced shallots

FOR THE DRESSING

1½ to 2 tbsp freshly squeezed lemon juice

1½ to 2 tbsp extra-virgin olive oil

¼ tsp coarse sea salt

¼ tsp ground black pepper

1 In a small bowl, make the dressing by whisking together all the ingredients until emulsified. Set aside.

2 Layer the cucumbers in the bottom of a colander. Sprinkle the salt over the top and toss well. Allow the cucumbers to sit for 20 to 30 minutes. Use a clean kitchen towel to gently pat any extra salt off the cucumbers.

3 In a large bowl, combine the cucumber, amaranth, radish greens, pomegranate seeds, mint, and shallots. Mix well.

4 Drizzle the dressing over the salad and toss until evenly coated. Garnish with mint and radish greens leaves before serving.

> **» QUICK TIPS**
> This recipe works well with cooked **Millets** (page 243) instead of amaranth.
> Store the salad in an airtight container in the fridge for up to 5 days.

SWISS CHARD & LENTIL SALAD
WITH BALSAMIC DRESSING

Leafy greens offer so much flavor and nourishment. Because colorful stalks have many healthful properties, instead of discarding them, slice thinly and cook along with the leaves. Lentils add wonderful texture to this salad and the dressing has a subtle sweetness that brings it all together.

PREP TIME: **5 MINUTES** // COOK TIME: **17 MINUTES** // YIELD: **2 TO 4 SERVINGS**

INGREDIENTS

4oz (120g) leeks, white and light green parts only

1 tbsp pure olive oil, divided

½ tsp coarse sea salt, divided

1 bunch of Swiss chard (about 9oz [255g])

2 garlic cloves, sliced paper-thin

½ cup cooked **Red Lentils** (page 239)

FOR THE DRESSING

3 tbsp extra-virgin olive oil

2 tbsp balsamic vinegar

2 tbsp maple syrup

1 tbsp stone-ground mustard

¼ tsp coarse sea salt

¼ tsp ground black pepper

» QUICK TIPS

Save the dark green parts of the leeks to prepare zero-waste **Vegetable Broth** (page 232). Store the salad undressed in an airtight container in the fridge for up to 2 days. Separately store the dressing in a small lidded jar in the fridge. Add the dressing to the salad when ready to serve.

1 Preheat the oven to 425°F (220°C).

2 Cut the leeks into ⅜-inch-thick (1cm) rings (about 10 slices). Separate the rings and immerse them in water to wash well and remove any dirt. Dry thoroughly with paper towels.

3 On a baking tray, combine the leeks, 1 teaspoon of olive oil, and ¼ teaspoon of salt. Toss to coat and evenly space the leeks on the tray.

4 Place the tray on the top rack in the oven and cook until the leeks are seared and translucent, about 12 minutes. Remove the tray from the oven and allow the leeks to cool.

5 Wash the Swiss chard thoroughly. Separate the thick stalks from the leaves. Cut the stalks into ¼-inch-thick (0.5cm) sections. Stack the leaves on top of each other and roll tightly. Slice into ½-inch-thick (1.25cm) sections and separate into ribbons. Set the ribbons aside.

6 In a sauté pan on the stovetop, heat the remaining 2 teaspoons of olive oil over medium heat. Add the garlic and sauté for 1 minute, stirring often. Reduce the heat to medium-low. Add the stalks and cook for 4 minutes, stirring often. Add the remaining ¼ teaspoon of salt. Transfer everything to a medium bowl and set aside.

7 In a small bowl, make the dressing by whisking together all the ingredients until emulsified.

8 In a large bowl, combine the Swiss chard ribbons and stalks, lentils, and leeks. Toss well. Add ¼ cup of the dressing and toss again to coat.

9 Divide the salad into 2 to 4 bowls. Drizzle the remaining dressing over the top or serve separately. Serve immediately.

CURRIED CAULIFLOWER SALAD
WITH APPLES & CELERY

Ingredients in the curry seasoning used for this salad—turmeric, ginger, cinnamon, and others—contain immune-boosting properties that keep us healthy. They also infuse this dish with amazing flavors and aromas as well as a vibrant color. Eating plant-based doesn't have to be bland!

PREP TIME: **7 TO 10 MINUTES** // COOK TIME: **10 MINUTES** // YIELD: **2 TO 4 SERVINGS**

INGREDIENTS

2½ cups large-diced cauliflower, florets and stems

1 tbsp coconut oil

½ tbsp **Homemade Curry Powder** (page 240)

¼ tsp coarse sea salt, plus more

½ cup small-diced Fuji apples, unpeeled

½ cup small-diced celery

¼ cup minced red bell peppers

1 tbsp plus 1 tsp finely chopped fresh chives, divided

FOR THE DRESSING

2 tbsp **Aquafaba Mayonnaise** (page 235)

1½ tbsp freshly squeezed lime juice

½ tbsp maple syrup

pinch of coarse sea salt

1 Preheat the oven to 375°F (190°C). Line a large baking tray with parchment paper.

2 On the tray, combine the cauliflower, coconut oil, curry powder, and salt. Toss and rub with clean hands to make sure there's an even coating.

3 Place the tray on the top rack in the oven and bake until the cauliflower is golden brown, about 10 minutes, tossing halfway through.

4 In a small bowl, make the dressing by whisking together all the ingredients until creamy and consistent.

5 Remove the tray from the oven. In a large bowl, combine the cauliflower, apples, celery, bell peppers, and 1 tablespoon of chives. Drizzle the dressing over the top and gently toss to coat. Taste and adjust seasoning.

6 Transfer the salad to a serving bowl and top with the remaining 1 teaspoon of chives before serving. Serve warm, at room temperature, or cold.

» **QUICK TIP**
Store the salad in an airtight container in the fridge up to 1 week.

WILD RICE & TOMATO SALAD
WITH BALSAMIC & MAPLE DRESSING

Wild rice has more protein and minerals and twice as much fiber as white rice. Dietary fiber helps us maintain a healthy gut but also keeps us satiated for longer. Replace the heirloom tomatoes with other varieties, but avoid hothouse or air-freighted tomatoes—they have high foodprints.

PREP TIME: **5 TO 10 MINUTES** // COOK TIME: **NONE** // YIELD: **2 TO 4 SERVINGS**

INGREDIENTS

1 cup cooked **Wild Rice**
(page 242)

½ cup diced heirloom tomatoes,
cored and seeded

½ cup cucumbers, seeded
(peeled if desired)

3 tbsp roasted pistachios,
shelled

1 cup sliced romaine lettuce
(about ½-inch-thick [1.25cm]
and 2-inch-long [5cm] strips)

FOR THE DRESSING

2 tbsp extra-virgin olive oil

1½ tbsp balsamic vinegar

½ tbsp maple syrup

1 tsp stone-ground mustard

¼ tsp coarse sea salt, plus more

2 pinches of ground black pepper

1 In a small bowl, make the dressing by whisking together all the ingredients until emulsified. Taste and adjust seasoning.

2 In a large bowl, combine all the salad ingredients. Mix well. Drizzle the dressing over the top and toss until evenly coated. Serve immediately.

» QUICK TIPS

I like to buy unshelled roasted unsalted pistachios. They're usually more affordable than shelled pistachios. If you're preparing this salad ahead of time, hold the lettuce and add it to the dressed salad prior to serving. Store the salad in an airtight container in the fridge for up to 5 days.

CUCUMBER, PEA & DAIKON SALAD
WITH ALMOND & GINGER DRESSING

This salad has a great crunchy texture and is complemented by the creamy dressing. Adding snap peas to your diet helps increase the demand on a sustainable and soil-friendly ingredient, especially if you buy locally. Always remember: Legumes are important in a low-carbon diet!

PREP TIME: **10 MINUTES** // COOK TIME: **NONE** // YIELD: **2 TO 4 SERVINGS**

INGREDIENTS

1 medium garden cucumber

½ tsp coarse sea salt, divided

6oz (170g) daikon, peeled and cut into matchsticks

1 tbsp unseasoned rice vinegar

1 tsp maple syrup

1 tsp sesame oil

6oz (170g) sugar snap peas, sliced diagonally ¼ to ½ inch (0.5 to 1.25cm) thick

4 scallions, trimmed and sliced ¼ to ½ inch (0.5 to 1.25cm) thick

1½ to 2 tbsp thinly sliced fresh Fresno peppers (optional)

1 tsp **Furikake Seaweed Seasoning** (page 240)

FOR THE DRESSING

3 tbsp unseasoned rice vinegar

2½ tbsp raw almond butter

1 tbsp tamari

1 tbsp coconut sugar

½ to 1 tbsp crushed ginger

---

1 Trim 1 inch (2.5cm) from each end of the cucumber. Cut the cucumber in half lengthwise and use a small spoon to remove the seeds. Thinly slice the cucumber and place in a small bowl.

2 Add ¼ teaspoon of salt and toss to coat. Set aside until the slices have wilted and released some moisture, about 15 minutes. Drain and set aside.

3 In a small bowl, whisk together the rice vinegar, maple syrup, sesame oil, and the remaining ¼ teaspoon of salt. Add the daikon and toss to coat. Marinate for 5 to 10 minutes.

4 In a small bowl, make the almond and ginger dressing by whisking together all the ingredients. Set aside.

5 In a large bowl, combine the cucumber, daikon (with its marinade), snap peas, and scallions. Toss well.

6 Divide the salad into 2 to 4 bowls. Drizzle the dressing over the top. Garnish with the Fresno pepper (if using) and furikake seaweed seasoning before serving.

> » **QUICK TIPS**
> Any variety of cucumber will work for this recipe. Thinly sliced, they should add up to about 1¼ cups. I suggest keeping the skin on to minimize food waste and to benefit from their nutritional content. Store the salad undressed in an airtight container in the fridge for up to 2 days. Separately store and refrigerate the dressing in a small lidded jar and add to the salad when ready to serve.

CHAPTER 8
SIDES

114 Yuca with Leek Mojo Sauce

115 Domino Rice & Beans with Spicy Adobo Seasoning

116 Roasted Heirloom Carrots with Tahini Sauce

118 Acorn Squash with Wilted Kale

119 Roasted Okra with Maple Butternut Squash

120 Roasted Fingerling Potatoes with Caramelized Onions & Nuts

122 Crookneck Squash with King Oyster Mushrooms

123 Roasted Radishes with Garlic & Parsley

124 Edamame Pilaf with Ginger & Shaved Almonds

126 Plantain Dumplings

127 Sautéed Beet Greens

128 Corn Lollipops with Chipotle & Tofu Cream Sauce

YUCA
WITH LEEK MOJO SAUCE

Considered one of the most drought-tolerant crops, yuca is a tuber widely used in Venezuela and other Latin American countries. I grew up having boiled yuca as the starch served at barbecues. The leek mojo sauce is delectable and fragrant—it infuses the yuca with so much flavor.

PREP TIME: **5 MINUTES** // COOK TIME: **17 TO 20 MINUTES** // YIELD: **4 TO 6 SERVINGS**

INGREDIENTS

1 yuca (12 to 16oz [340 to 450g])

½ tsp coarse sea salt, divided

FOR THE SAUCE

2 tbsp pure olive oil

½ cup sliced leeks (¼ to ½ inch [0.5cm to 1.25cm] thick)

2 tbsp freshly squeezed lemon juice

1 tbsp finely chopped fresh curly parsley

½ tsp dried oregano

¼ tsp coarse sea salt

¼ tsp ground black pepper

1 In a small skillet on the stovetop, make the sauce by heating the olive oil over medium heat. Add the leeks and sauté for 2 minutes, stirring often. Remove the skillet from the heat and allow the leeks to cool completely.

2 In a small bowl, whisk together the lemon juice, parsley, oregano, salt, and pepper. Add the leeks and stir with a spoon until all the ingredients are well incorporated. Set aside.

3 Remove about ½ inch (1.25cm) from both ends of the yuca. Cut the yuca into 3-inch (7.5cm) segments. Score the skin lengthwise with a chef's knife. Pressing against the scored skin, use the edge of the knife to gently separate the skin from the flesh, working your way around until the yuca is completely peeled. Cut each segment into 4 pieces lengthwise and use a knife to remove the stem that runs through the center. Cut the pieces into 1½-inch (3.75cm) chunks.

4 In a medium saucepan on the stovetop over medium heat, place the yuca and cover with 1 inch (2.5cm) of water. Add the salt. Bring to a boil, then reduce the heat to medium-low. Cover and cook until the yuca is fork-tender, about 15 to 18 minutes. Use a colander to drain the water, then return the yuca to the saucepan and keep the saucepan covered.

5 Pour the leek mojo sauce over the yuca and mix until evenly coated by the sauce. Transfer to a serving bowl. Serve immediately.

» QUICK TIPS

You can make the leek mojo sauce a day or two ahead of time and refrigerate in a canning jar until ready to use. Immerse the lidded jar in hot water to warm the sauce prior to use. Store the yuca in an airtight container in the fridge for up to 10 days.

DOMINO RICE & BEANS
WITH SPICY ADOBO SEASONING

Inspired by the tiles used in one of my favorite games, this side dish is comforting and nourishing. Brown rice contains high amounts of fiber and vitamins, while black beans are high in protein, folate, manganese, magnesium, and iron. Serve with a side of vegetables and call this an entrée!

PREP TIME: **5 MINUTES** // COOK TIME: **6 TO 8 MINUTES** // YIELD: **2 TO 4 SERVINGS**

INGREDIENTS

2 tbsp coconut oil

¼ cup plus 2 tbsp small-diced brown onions

2 garlic cloves, minced

¼ cup small-diced red bell peppers

½ to 1 tsp **Spicy Adobo Seasoning** (page 240)

¼ tsp coarse sea salt, plus more

¼ tsp ground black pepper

1½ cups cooked **Brown Rice** (page 242), room temperature

1½ cups cooked **Black Beans** (page 238), room temperature

½ tsp freshly squeezed lime juice

1 In a large cast-iron skillet on the stovetop, heat the coconut oil over medium heat. Add the onions and sauté for 1½ to 2 minutes, stirring often.

2 Add the garlic and bell peppers. Sauté for 1 minute, stirring often. Add the spicy adobo seasoning, salt, and pepper. Mix well.

3 Add the brown rice and continue to stir until the onion mixture has evenly coated the rice. Stir in the black beans, reduce the heat to low, and cover. Cook for 3 to 5 minutes, stirring occasionally to prevent the food from sticking to the bottom of the skillet.

4 Remove the skillet from the heat and lightly drizzle the lime juice over the top. Mix well and serve immediately.

> **» QUICK TIP**
> For less heat, replace the **Spicy Adobo Seasoning** with ¼ teaspoon of ground coriander and ½ teaspoon of ground cumin.

ROASTED HEIRLOOM CARROTS
WITH TAHINI SAUCE

My dreams are as colorful as heirloom carrots! Their various hues are an ode to eating the rainbow. No matter their color, carrots are nutrient-dense—rich in vitamins, potassium, manganese, and powerful antioxidants. The tangy sauce complements the inherent sweetness of the carrots.

PREP TIME: **5 TO 7 MINUTES** // COOK TIME: **18 TO 20 MINUTES** // YIELD: **4 SERVINGS**

INGREDIENTS

1 bunch of heirloom carrots (about 1lb [450g]), unpeeled and thoroughly washed

1 tbsp coconut oil

½ tsp ground coriander

¼ tsp ground annatto

¼ tsp coarse sea salt, plus more

FOR THE SAUCE

1 tbsp tahini

1 tbsp finely minced carrot-top leaves

1 tbsp freshly squeezed lemon juice

½ tbsp water

¼ tsp finely grated garlic

2 pinches of coarse sea salt

2 pinches of ground black pepper

1 Preheat the oven to 425°F (220°C).

2 Cut the tops off the carrots and set aside about ¼ cup of leaves for the sauce and as garnish. Cut the carrots in half lengthwise, keeping the ends intact if possible.

3 Place the carrots on a baking tray. Add the coconut oil, coriander, annatto, and salt. Rub with clean hands until all the sides are evenly coated.

4 Place the tray on the bottom rack in the oven and roast until golden brown and tender, about 18 to 20 minutes, flipping halfway through.

5 In a small bowl, make the sauce by whisking together all the ingredients.

6 Remove the tray from the oven and transfer the carrots to a platter. Drizzle the sauce over the top. Garnish with several leaves before serving.

» QUICK TIPS

If you can't find heirloom or rainbow carrots, regular carrots will work just fine. Save carrot greens! Make **Carrot-Top Chimichurri** (page 218) or use them as you would any herb. Leave the carrots whole if they're thin or cut them into quarters lengthwise if they're thicker. Store in an airtight container in the fridge for up to 5 days.

ACORN SQUASH
WITH WILTED KALE

Beautifully contrasting colors make this dish extra special. I love the mildly sweet, nutty taste of acorn squash, which is enhanced by warming spices. The skin is edible and rich in fiber and antioxidants. Kale is one of the most nutrient-dense foods—loaded with vitamins A, C, and K.

PREP TIME: 5 TO 10 MINUTES // COOK TIME: 17 MINUTES // YIELD: 4 TO 6 SERVINGS

INGREDIENTS

1 medium acorn squash (about 1lb [450g])

1 tbsp avocado oil

¼ tsp ground cinnamon

pinch of ground cardamom

pinch of ground nutmeg

¼ tsp plus 2 to 3 pinches of coarse sea salt, divided, plus more

1 tbsp extra-virgin olive oil

½ tbsp maple syrup

1 tsp balsamic vinegar

½ tsp stone-ground mustard

2 cups kale, cut into 1-inch (2.5cm) pieces

1 Preheat the oven to 400°F (200°C).

2 Carefully trim the base and top of the acorn squash. Cut in half lengthwise and use a small spoon to remove the seeds and pulp. Place on a cutting board cut side down and slice about ½ inch (1.25cm) thick.

3 Place the squash on a baking tray. Drizzle the avocado oil over the top. Sprinkle the cinnamon, cardamom, nutmeg, and ¼ teaspoon of salt over the top. Rub with clean hands until the slices are evenly coated.

4 Place the tray on the bottom rack in the oven and roast until the edges are golden brown and the squash is cooked through, about 15 minutes, flipping halfway through.

5 In a small bowl, whisk together the olive oil, maple syrup, balsamic vinegar, mustard, and 1 pinch of salt. Set aside.

6 Place a steamer basket in a medium saucepan on the stovetop over medium heat. Fill the saucepan with enough water to get close to the bottom of the basket. Cover the saucepan. Bring to boil, then reduce the heat to low. Place the kale in the basket and steam covered for 1½ to 2 minutes. Remove the basket from the saucepan and transfer the kale to a platter. Season with the remaining 1 to 2 pinches of salt.

7 Use a spatula to transfer the squash to the serving platter and drizzle the sauce over the top. Serve immediately.

> **» QUICK TIPS**
>
> The skin easily detaches from the squash if the texture isn't desired. I used 1 cup of curly kale and 1 cup of lacinato kale. You can use whatever varieties are available to you, including white and purple flowering kale. Remove the thicker stems and save them for future use. If you have a steam pot set or insert, use that instead of the basket. Store leftovers in an airtight container in the fridge for up to 5 days.

ROASTED OKRA
WITH MAPLE BUTTERNUT SQUASH

Okra is a powerful but underappreciated vegetable (although botanically, it's a fruit). Five ounces provides nearly 3 grams of protein as well as minerals, vitamins, and antioxidants. It pairs well with butternut squash, which adds not only flavor and texture but also disease-fighting nutrients.

PREP TIME: **5 TO 7 MINUTES** // COOK TIME: **12 TO 14 MINUTES** // YIELD: **2 TO 4 SERVINGS**

INGREDIENTS

5oz (140g) okra (about 10 medium to large pods)

5oz (140g) butternut squash, peeled and seeded

1½ tbsp avocado oil, divided

½ tsp coarse sea salt, divided

¼ cup minced leeks

½ tbsp maple syrup

1 tsp balsamic vinegar

1 Preheat the oven to 425°F (220°C). Line a large baking tray with parchment paper.

2 Cut the okra in half lengthwise. Cut the butternut squash into rectangular sticks about ½ inch × ½ inch × 2 inches (1.25cm × 1.25cm × 5cm).

3 Place the okra cut side up on one half of the tray. Drizzle 1 tablespoon of avocado oil over the top and season with ¼ teaspoon of salt. Toss and rub with clean hands to evenly coat with oil and salt. Turn all the halves cut side down and evenly space them on their side of the tray.

4 In a medium bowl, combine the squash, leeks, maple syrup, balsamic vinegar, the remaining ½ tablespoon of avocado oil, and the remaining ¼ teaspoon of salt. Mix with a spatula until the squash is evenly coated. Transfer this mixture to the other half of the tray, spreading the squash evenly to leave some space in between the sticks.

5 Place the tray on the bottom rack in the oven and roast until the okra is golden and slightly crispy, about 12 to 14 minutes. After 6 minutes, toss the squash sticks with a spatula for even caramelization.

6 Remove the tray from the oven and use a spatula to transfer the vegetables to a platter. Serve immediately.

» QUICK TIPS

Okra is best enjoyed right out of the oven because it loses its crispy texture with time. Store leftovers in an airtight container in the fridge for up to 5 days. Reheat in the oven rather than in the microwave.

ROASTED FINGERLING POTATOES
WITH CARAMELIZED ONIONS & NUTS

Why settle for a common potato when there are so many varieties to choose from? Although all potatoes contain powerful antioxidants, colored varieties carry the most. Leaving the skin on helps us avoid food waste and enjoy a significant amount of nutrients, like fiber and minerals.

PREP TIME: **5 MINUTES** // COOK TIME: **58 TO 65 MINUTES** // YIELD: **6 SERVINGS**

INGREDIENTS

1½lb (680g) rainbow fingerling potatoes

1 to 2 sprigs of fresh rosemary

3 tbsp pure olive oil, divided

¾ tsp coarse sea salt, divided

1 red onion, thinly sliced

4 sprigs of fresh thyme

1 tbsp blackstrap molasses

1 tbsp balsamic vinegar

¼ cup chopped raw walnuts

1 Preheat the oven to 375°F (190°C).

2 Wash and scrub the potatoes thoroughly. Cut each in half and place them on a baking tray. Add the rosemary, 2 tablespoons of olive oil, and ½ teaspoon of salt. Toss to coat.

3 Fold a 15- × 30-inch (38 × 76cm) piece of parchment paper in half and place on a baking tray. Arrange the onion slices on one half of the paper. Add the thyme, blackstrap molasses, balsamic vinegar, the remaining 1 tablespoon of olive oil, and the remaining ¼ teaspoon of salt. Mix well. Fold the other half of the paper over the onions. To close the pouch, tightly fold the open edge of the paper, working from end to end.

4 Place the tray with the onions on the bottom rack in the oven. Cook for 25 minutes. Open the pouch and cut off the top layer of paper. Toss the onions and return the tray to the oven.

5 Add the tray with the potatoes to the top rack in the oven. Roast until golden and fork-tender, about 18 to 20 minutes, stirring occasionally. After 12 minutes, sprinkle the walnuts around the tray. Remove the tray from the oven and set on the stovetop to keep warm.

6 Continue to cook the onions until soft and caramelized, about 15 to 20 minutes. Remove the tray from the oven and set aside.

7 Transfer the onions, potatoes, and walnuts to a serving bowl. Mix to make sure the potatoes are evenly coated with the liquids. Serve immediately.

> **» QUICK TIPS**
> If some potatoes are much larger than others, cut them in quarters to make them evenly sized. Save the thyme and rosemary sprigs and freeze them in a reusable silicone bag. Repurpose them for **Vegetable Stock** (page 232). Store leftovers in an airtight container in the fridge for up to 3 days.

CROOKNECK SQUASH
WITH KING OYSTER MUSHROOMS

Can you say umami? This is packed with the fifth flavor—Japanese for "pleasant savory taste." Mushrooms are one the best sources of plant-based umami. Crookneck is such a beautiful summer squash and retains a crispy texture that balances the tenderness of the mushrooms.

PREP TIME: **5 MINUTES** // COOK TIME: **6 MINUTES** // YIELD: **2 TO 4 SERVINGS**

INGREDIENTS

1½ tbsp tamari

1 tsp grated garlic

½ tsp grated fresh ginger

½ tsp **Umami Mushroom Powder** (page 240)

4oz (110g) wild king oyster mushrooms (about 4 medium mushrooms)

1 tbsp toasted sesame oil

8oz (225g) crookneck squash (about 1 medium squash)

2 pinches of coarse sea salt, plus more

1 to 2 tbsp chopped scallion greens

1 to 2 tsp **Furikake Seaweed Seasoning** (page 240) (optional)

1 In a small bowl, combine the tamari, garlic, ginger, and mushroom powder. Set aside.

2 Thinly slice the mushrooms lengthwise at about ⅛ inch (3mm) thick.

3 In a large skillet on the stovetop, heat the sesame oil over medium-high heat. Add the mushrooms and sauté for 3 minutes, stirring often. Reduce the heat to medium and add the tamari mixture. Stir with a spatula until the sauce coats all mushrooms. Cook for 20 to 30 seconds more.

4 Add the squash and salt. Sauté for 1½ to 2 minutes, stirring often. (The squash will become mushy if overcooked.)

5 Transfer the mushrooms and squash to a platter. Taste and adjust seasoning. Sprinkle the scallion greens and furikake seaweed seasoning (if using) over the top. Serve immediately.

> **» QUICK TIPS**
> If you have any mushroom caps left from making **King Oyster Mushroom Arepas** (page 162), use them here (just slice them thinly crosswise). Wild mushrooms, like oyster and chanterelle, are a great substitute for king mushrooms. Thinly sliced portobello mushrooms will also work. Store the mushrooms and squash in an airtight container in the fridge for up to 5 days.

ROASTED RADISHES
WITH GARLIC & PARSLEY

This dish celebrates radishes in the tastiest way. The characteristic peppery taste is tamed by roasting while mild sweetness is heavenly developed. The Early Scarlet Globe is the most common radish in the United States, although you can use Watermelon, Easter Egg, or French Breakfast.

PREP TIME: **5 MINUTES** // COOK TIME: **15 MINUTES** // YIELD: **2 TO 4 SERVINGS**

INGREDIENTS

2 bunches of radishes

1 tbsp avocado oil

¼ coarse sea salt, plus more

2 pinches of ground black pepper

1 to 2 garlic cloves, grated

1 tbsp finely chopped fresh parsley stems (optional)

1 Preheat the oven to 400°F (200°C).

2 Gently cut off the greens from the radishes, then slice the radishes in half lengthwise. (If some of the radishes are very small, leave them whole.)

3 In a 9- × 15-inch (23 × 38cm) glass baking dish, combine the radishes, avocado oil, salt, and pepper. Rub with clean hands to make sure they're evenly coated and arrange them cut side down on the dish.

4 Place the dish on the bottom rack in the oven and roast until seared and golden, about 15 minutes. Because heat varies from oven to oven, start checking after 13 minutes to make sure the radishes don't burn.

5 Remove the dish from the oven. Add the garlic and parsley (if using). Stir with a spoonula for 45 seconds to 1 minute. The hot dish will cause the garlic to cook slightly and the stems to wilt. Taste and adjust seasoning. Serve immediately.

> **» QUICK TIPS**
>
> Save radish greens and refrigerate them for later use, like zero-waste **Salsa Verde** (page 215) or **Amaranth Tabbouleh with Cucumber & Pomegranate Seeds** (page 105). I love garlic even when it's raw or lightly cooked. If you're not a fan, substitute with **Roasted Garlic Paste** (page 237). Store the radishes in an airtight container in the fridge for up to 1 week.

EDAMAME PILAF
WITH GINGER & SHAVED ALMONDS

Edamame is sweet and has a nutty texture. It's highly sustainable and healthy, containing loads of protein as well as vitamins and minerals, like iron and calcium. Wild rice adds an earthy flavor and chewy texture that absorbs the fragrant spice of ginger and aromas from the leeks.

PREP TIME: **3 MINUTES** // COOK TIME: **6 MINUTES** // YIELD: **6 SERVINGS**

INGREDIENTS

1 quart (1 liter) water

1½ cups fresh shelled edamame

1 tbsp toasted sesame oil

⅓ cup minced leeks

2 to 3 tsp finely minced fresh ginger

1½ cups cooked **Wild Rice** (page 242)

1 tbsp tamari

2 tbsp shaved raw almonds

microgreens or chopped scallions

1 In a small saucepan on the stovetop over medium heat, bring the water to a boil. Add the edamame and cook for 2½ to 3 minutes. Strain. Set aside.

2 In a medium skillet on the stovetop, heat the sesame oil over medium heat. Add the leeks and ginger. Sauté for 2 minutes, stirring often. Stir in the wild rice and tamari. Cook until the rice has warmed through, about 1 minute. Add the edamame and mix well.

3 Transfer the pilaf to a serving bowl or portion directly into side dishes. Sprinkle the shaved almonds over the top and garnish with microgreens or scallions before serving.

> **» QUICK TIPS**
> To get 1½ cups of shelled edamame, you'll need about 3⅓ cups of pods. You can find them fresh at farmers markets as well as at Asian markets. Substitute with frozen shelled edamame, preferably organic.

PLANTAIN DUMPLINGS

Natural sweetness from the plantain contrasts beautifully with the savory flavors of the sofrito—the flavor base composed of sautéed vegetables and spices. These little pillows of goodness pair perfectly with **Salsa Verde** (page 215) or **Carrot-Top Chimichurri** (page 219).

PREP TIME: **10 MINUTES** // COOK TIME: **13 MINUTES** // YIELD: **4 TO 6 SERVINGS**

INGREDIENTS

1 large ripe unpeeled plantain, tips removed

4½ quarts (4½ liters) water, divided

2oz (30g) red bell pepper, roughly chopped

1 to 2 scallions, quartered

1 large garlic clove

½ cup gluten-free flour (or whole wheat flour)

½ cup rice crumbs (see Quick Tips)

2 tbsp plant-based milk

¼ tsp ground turmeric

¼ tsp ground cumin

½ tsp coarse sea salt

¼ tsp ground black pepper

1 Cut the plantain into 2-inch (5cm) segments.

2 In a medium saucepan on the stovetop over medium heat, bring 2 quarts of water to a boil. Add the plantain and poach until cooked through and you can easily insert a toothpick into the center, about 10 minutes. Remove the plantain from the saucepan. Allow to rest for 5 minutes before peeling.

3 In a food processor, combine the bell pepper, scallions, and garlic. Pulse until finely chopped. Use a rubber spatula to scrape down the sides of the bowl. Add the plantain and the remaining ingredients. Process on high until a consistent dough has formed. Use a spatula to transfer the dough to a working surface or wooden board.

4 With damp hands, break the dough into 4 equal portions. (Keeping your hands damp prevents the dough from sticking to anything.) Roll each portion into a ¾-inch-thick (2cm) rope. Use a knife to slice the ropes into ½-inch (1.25cm) pieces. (You might need to wipe the knife with a damp, clean towel to prevent the dough from sticking.)

5 In a clean medium saucepan on the stovetop over medium heat, bring the remaining 2½ quarts of water to a boil. Reduce the heat to medium-low. Use a slotted spoon to carefully immerse the dumplings in the boiling water. (They'll sink to the bottom of the pan.) Cook until they float to the surface, about 2½ minutes.

6 Use a slotted spoon to transfer the dumplings to a single layer on a platter. Serve immediately.

> **» QUICK TIPS**
> Choose plantains with peels that are dark yellow with many patches of black (at least 50%) and are soft to the touch. You can pan-sear the dumplings by heating 2 tablespoons of coconut oil or avocado oil in a large cast-iron skillet on the stovetop over medium heat. Add the dumplings to the pan and cook until golden brown on all sides, about 4 minutes, carefully stirring often with a spatula. You can substitute rice crumbs with panko or homemade breadcrumbs. (Save your stale bread. Toast and grind it to avoid food waste.)

SAUTÉED BEET GREENS

Did you know that beet greens are the most nutritious part of beets? That's why it saddens me to see people leave them behind at markets. They're similar in taste and texture to chard and mustard greens—slightly bitter but hearty. When cooked, they wilt as they absorb lots of flavor.

PREP TIME: **5 MINUTES** // COOK TIME: **3 TO 4 MINUTES** // YIELD: **2 TO 3 SERVINGS**

INGREDIENTS

5oz (140g) beet greens
(approximately 3 cups)

1 to 1½ tbsp pure olive oil

⅓ cup thinly sliced red onions

¼ tsp coarse sea salt, plus more

2 pinches of ground coriander

pinch of ground nutmeg

1 Stack the beet greens, starting with the bigger leaves at the bottom and the smallest leaves on top. Roll them up and slice to make 1-inch (1.25cm) strips. Loosen up the greens and cut longer strips in half.

2 In a large skillet on the stovetop, heat the olive oil over medium heat. Add the onions and sauté about 1½ to 2 minutes. Add the salt, coriander, and nutmeg. Stir with a spatula until the spices are well incorporated with the onions.

3 Add the beet greens and sauté for 1 to 1½ minutes, stirring often. (Don't overcook the greens.)

4 Transfer the beet greens to a serving bowl. Taste and adjust seasoning. Serve warm or at room temperature.

» QUICK TIPS

Don't throw away the red woody stalks of the beet greens. Shave the fibrous outer layer with a vegetable peeler, cut into 2- to 3-inch (5 to 7.5cm) batons, and pickle using the same recipe for **Pickled Carrots** (page 227). This recipe works very well with other hearty, zero-waste greens, like turnip greens and broccoli leaves. Store the cooled greens in an airtight container in the fridge for up to 5 days.

CORN LOLLIPOPS
WITH CHIPOTLE & TOFU CREAM SAUCE

Corn lollipops are great for barbecues or outdoor gatherings. The chipotle sauce is smoky and a little spicy—it goes well with the sweetness of the corn. And you don't have to tell anyone that what makes the sauce creamy also adds protein and minerals, like calcium and iron.

PREP TIME: **7 TO 10 MINUTES** // COOK TIME: **5 TO 6 MINUTES** // YIELD: **6 LOLLIPOPS**

INGREDIENTS

3 ears of corn

1 to 2 tbsp microgreens or finely chopped fresh chives (optional)

6 fresh lime wedges

FOR THE SAUCE

½ large dried chipotle pepper

½ cup boiling water

3oz (90g) organic sprouted tofu

1 tbsp **Aquafaba Mayonnaise** (page 235)

2 tbsp plant-based milk, plus more

1 tsp maple syrup

¼ tsp apple cider vinegar

1 tsp nutritional yeast

¼ tsp coarse sea salt

1   In a glass canning jar, begin to make the sauce by combining the chipotle pepper and water. Cover and allow to rest for at least 5 minutes.

2   In a high-powered blender, combine the pepper and the remaining sauce ingredients. Process on high until creamy and smooth, using the tamper to push down the ingredients. If the sauce is too thick, add ½ tablespoon of plant-based milk at a time to reach your desired consistency. Set aside.

3   Remove the husks and silk from the corn. Cut about ½ inch (1.25cm) from both ends of each ear and cut the ears in half.

4   Fill a large pot half full with water. Place the pot on the stovetop over medium heat. Bring the water to a boil, then reduce the heat to medium-low. Add the corn, cover, and cook for 5 to 6 minutes.

5   Transfer the corn to a cutting board and allow to cool slightly. Insert a wooden skewer at least 2 inches (5cm) deep into the center of each ear.

6   Transfer the lollipops to a platter or portion directly onto small plates. Drizzle the chipotle sauce over the top. Garnish with microgreens or chopped fresh chives. Serve each lollipop with 1 lime wedge.

> **» QUICK TIPS**
> Store the cooked corn in a reusable silicone bag in the fridge for up to 1 week. Poach in hot water to reheat. Separately store the sauce in an airtight container in the fridge for up to 5 days.

CHAPTER 9
SOUPS & STEWS

132 Mango & Ginger Gazpacho

134 Fava Bean & Avocado Soup

135 Split Pea Soup

136 Creamy Butternut Soup

138 Lentil Minestrone

139 Spiced Pumpkin Soup

140 Plant-Based Meatball Soup

142 Black-Eyed Pea & Vegetable Stew

143 Spicy Chayote & Tomato Casserole

144 Eggplant & Sweet Potato Curry

146 Broccoli Soup

147 Black Bean Chili

148 Chayote Tagine with Prunes & Apricots

150 Braised Nopal Cactus Pads

151 Garbanzo & Potato Stew

152 White Bean & Kale Stew

MANGO & GINGER GAZPACHO

Ginger has been used for medicinal purposes for many generations. Its natural oils, especially gingerol, have been proven to have health-promoting properties. That's a bonus because I just love its flavor and aroma. Mango is one of my favorite fruits—it makes for such a fun gazpacho.

PREP TIME: **5 TO 10 MINUTES** // COOK TIME: **NONE** // YIELD: **4 SERVINGS**

INGREDIENTS

2 large ripe mangoes, peeled, seeded, and cubed

½ cup small-diced seeded English cucumbers

¼ cup small-diced yellow bell peppers

2 tbsp puréed avocado pulp

1 tbsp minced ginger

1 tbsp minced shallots

1 garlic clove

3 to 4 cilantro stems, torn into pieces

¼ cup freshly squeezed orange juice

1 tbsp freshly squeezed lime juice

½ cup cold water, plus more

½ tsp coarse sea salt, plus more

whole cilantro leaves

FOR THE SALSA

1 tbsp minced yellow bell peppers

1 tbsp minced seeded English cucumbers

2 tsp minced Fresno peppers

2 tsp finely chopped fresh cilantro leaves

pinch of coarse sea salt

1 In a small bowl, make the salsa by combining the ingredients. Set aside.

2 In a high-powered blender, combine all the soup ingredients except the cilantro leaves. Process on high until smooth. Add water 1 tablespoon at a time to reach your desired consistency. Taste and adjust seasoning. Cover and refrigerate for at least 1 hour.

3 Divide the gazpacho into 4 bowls. Top with the salsa and garnish with the cilantro leaves before serving.

> **» QUICK TIPS**
>
> Persian cucumbers can also work well in this recipe. Because American cucumbers tend to have thicker, waxier skins, make sure to peel them if you're substituting the English cucumbers. Add the cucumber peels to your water bottle for a boost of flavor or save them for your compost pile! Gazpacho is best enjoyed immediately after chilling. Store any leftovers in an airtight container in the fridge for up 2 days.

FAVA BEAN & AVOCADO SOUP

Barely cooking fresh fava beans (plus giving them an ice-cold bath) helps them retain their vibrant green color while keeping their flavor bright. The avocado gives this dish such a creamy texture. The herbs and fragrant aromatics really enhance its flavor profile.

PREP TIME: **7 TO 10 MINUTES** // COOK TIME: **8 TO 10 MINUTES** // YIELD: **4 TO 6 SERVINGS**

INGREDIENTS

2 quarts (2 liters) water, divided

1 cup ice cubes

3oz (90g) fresh fava beans (from 7oz [200g] whole pods)

1 tbsp pure olive oil

¼ cup chopped shallots

2 garlic cloves, roughly chopped

½ tsp coarse sea salt, plus more

1 cup **Vegetable Broth** (page 232), room temperature

1 small Hass avocado (about 4oz [110g]), peeled and seeded

3 tbsp finely chopped fresh flat-leaf parsley

½ cup cold water, plus more

¼ cup plus 2 tbsp freshly squeezed lemon juice

---

1 In a medium bowl, combine 1 quart of water and the ice cubes.

2 In a small pot on the stovetop over medium-high heat, bring the remaining 1 quart of water to a boil. Add the fava beans and blanch until tender, about 2 minutes. Use a mesh strainer to transfer the fava beans to the iced water and shock for 1 minute. Strain with a colander.

3 Remove the skin (a light-colored membrane surrounding each bean) by scoring it and squeezing with your hands. Set the beans aside (and save the membranes for your compost pile).

4 In a small saucepan on the stovetop, heat the olive oil over medium heat. Add the shallots and sauté for 1 minute, stirring often.

5 Add the garlic, salt, and fava beans. Reduce the heat to low and add the vegetable broth. Bring to a soft boil. Cover and simmer until the fava beans are tender, about 5 to 7 minutes.

6 Remove the saucepan from the heat and allow the mixture to cool. Transfer to an airtight container and refrigerate for 1 hour or overnight.

7 In a high-powered blender, combine the fava bean mixture, avocado, parsley, cold water, and lemon juice. Process on high until smooth and velvety. Add cold water 1 tablespoon at a time if the soup needs to be thinner. Taste and adjust seasoning.

8 Divide the soup into 4 to 6 bowls and serve immediately.

> **» QUICK TIPS**
> This chilled soup is best enjoyed fresh. Save the fava bean pods for **Fava Bean Pod Bollitos** (page 83). You can sprinkle chopped fresh herbs, like cilantro or mint, and a little **Papaya Seed Powder** (page 231) over the top.

SPLIT PEA SOUP

Since I was a little girl, split-pea soup has made my heart smile. The USDA says we get 16.3 grams of protein per cup of cooked split peas. Adding vegetables and herbs makes this soup a full meal. Cooking the split peas ahead of time (page 239) makes the execution of this dish easy and quick.

PREP TIME: **5 MINUTES** // COOK TIME: **11 TO 13 MINUTES** // YIELD: **4 SERVINGS**

INGREDIENTS

2 tbsp unrefined coconut oil

½ cup finely chopped leeks

⅔ cup small-diced carrots

⅔ cup small-diced celery

½ cup small-diced green bell peppers

2 tsp **Spicy Adobo Seasoning** (page 240)

½ tsp coarse sea salt, plus more

2 cups **Vegetable Broth** (page 232)

2½ cups cooked yellow or green **Split Peas** (page 239)

½ to 1 tbsp freshly squeezed lime juice

2 tbsp finely chopped fresh herbs

1 In a saucepan or medium pot on the stovetop, heat the coconut oil over medium heat. Add the leeks, carrots, and celery. Sauté for 3 minutes, stirring often.

2 Add the bell peppers, adobo seasoning, and salt. Mix until the spices evenly coat the vegetables.

3 Add the vegetable broth and mix well. Bring to a boil, then reduce the heat to low.

4 Add the split peas. Cover and simmer until the vegetables are cooked through, about 8 to 10 minutes.

5 Add the lime juice and mix well. Taste and adjust seasoning.

6 Divide the soup into 4 bowls and sprinkle the fresh herbs over the top before serving.

> **» QUICK TIP**
> Store the soup in an airtight container in the fridge for up to 1 week or in the freezer for up to 6 months.

CREAMY BUTTERNUT SOUP

Roasting a mildly sweet winter squash as well as onion and herbs helps develop a depth of flavor and rich texture that make this dish just stunning. Butternut squash is rich in vitamins A and C. The cashew cream makes the soup velvety but also adds protein and heart-healthy fats.

PREP TIME: **5 TO 10 MINUTES** // COOK TIME: **45 MINUTES** // YIELD: **4 TO 6 SERVINGS**

INGREDIENTS

1 medium butternut squash, halved lengthwise and seeded

1 tbsp pure olive oil

1 tsp fresh thyme leaves

¾ tsp coarse sea salt, divided, plus more

¼ tsp ground black pepper, plus more

½ large Vidalia onion, skin on, halved

½ cup plus 2 tbsp **Cashew Cream** (page 230), divided

1½ tbsp plant-based milk

2 cups warm **Vegetable Broth** (page 232), plus more

2 tbsp **Roasted Garlic Paste** (page 237)

2 tsp freshly squeezed lemon juice

2 tsp maple syrup

fresh herbs

1 Preheat the oven to 425°F (220°C).

2 Place the butternut squash cut side up on a baking tray and drizzle the olive oil over the top. Sprinkle the thyme, ½ teaspoon of salt, and pepper evenly over the squash. Turn the squash cut side down. Place the onion cut side down on the baking tray.

3 Place the tray on the middle rack in the oven and roast until a fork easily perforates the skin of the squash, about 45 minutes. Remove the tray from the oven and allow the squash and onion to cool slightly.

4 Remove the outer layers from the onion and use a large spoon to scoop out the flesh from the squash. Set aside.

5 In a small bowl, whisk together 2 tablespoons of cashew cream, plant-based milk, and 1 pinch of salt. Set aside.

6 In a high-powered blender, combine the squash, onion, broth, garlic paste, lemon juice, maple syrup, the remaining ½ cup of cashew cream, and the remaining ¼ teaspoon of salt. Safely secure the lid and place a clean kitchen towel over the lid to prevent steam or liquid from escaping. Process on high until creamy and smooth. Add broth 1 tablespoon at a time to reach your desired consistency.

7 Divide the soup into 4 to 6 bowls. Top with the reserved cashew cream and garnish with fresh herbs and black pepper before serving.

> **» QUICK TIPS**
> If the roasted garlic paste hasn't already been made, cut ½ inch (1.25cm) from the top of a large head of garlic to expose the cloves. Wrap the garlic in aluminum foil and roast alongside the squash and onion. Once cooled, unwrap and squeeze the bottom of the bulb to get the needed amount of garlic paste. Store the soup in an airtight container in the fridge for up to 1 week.

LENTIL MINESTRONE

Many vegetables play an important role in this dish and each of them brings color, flavor, texture, and, most importantly, sustenance. Lentils are packed with plenty of nutrition despite being very affordable and having a long shelf life. Their carbon footprint is low and will help you lower yours.

PREP TIME: **10 MINUTES** // COOK TIME: **19 TO 20 MINUTES** // YIELD: **4 TO 6 SERVINGS**

INGREDIENTS

2 tbsp avocado oil

½ cup small-diced white onions

½ cup diced heirloom carrots, any color

½ cup diced potatoes

¼ cup diced celery

2 garlic cloves, minced

½ cup diced chayote squash

½ cup diced heirloom tomatoes, any color

½ tsp dried oregano

½ tsp dried basil

½ tsp smoked paprika

½ tsp ground cumin

½ tsp coarse sea salt, plus more

1 tbsp nutritional yeast

3 cups **Vegetable Broth** (page 232)

1½ cups cooked **Lentils** (any color) (page 239)

½ cup diced Italian squash

⅓ cup baby kale

¼ cup small-diced orange bell peppers

1 to 2 tsp freshly squeezed lemon juice

1 tbsp fresh basil chiffonade (see Quick Tips)

1 In a large saucepan on the stovetop, heat the avocado oil over medium heat. Add the onions and sauté for 1 to 2 minutes, stirring often. Add the carrots, potatoes, celery, and garlic. Sauté for 3 minutes, stirring often.

2 Add the chayote squash, tomatoes, oregano, basil, paprika, cumin, salt, and nutritional yeast. Mix well until the vegetables are evenly coated.

3 Stir in the vegetable broth. Bring to a boil, then reduce the heat to low. Cover and simmer for 10 minutes. Add the lentils, Italian squash, kale, and bell peppers. Mix well.

4 Cover and simmer until the lentils have warmed through and the squash is cooked but slightly firm, about 5 minutes more. Remove the saucepan from the heat and stir in the lemon juice. Taste and adjust seasoning.

5 Divide the soup into 4 to 6 shallow bowls. Sprinkle the basil chiffonade over the top before serving.

» QUICK TIPS

While most markets generally carry russet and Yukon potatoes, I suggest you try other varieties to promote biodiversity. Elba and red bliss potatoes are a couple of my favorites! You can use any variety of kale. If you're using grown/mature leaves, cut them into thin strips. To make basil chiffonade, roll 3 large basil leaves together and cut the leaves into ribbons. Store the soup in an airtight container in the fridge for up to 5 days.

SPICED PUMPKIN SOUP

Cumin, cardamom, and nutmeg provide delicious flavors to this soup. They also add healthful properties that improve the immune system, promote heart health, and help digestion. Kuri pumpkin is rich in vitamins A and C. Aromatics and fennel make this nothing short of magic.

PREP TIME: **5 TO 7 MINUTES** // COOK TIME: **28 TO 29 MINUTES** // YIELD: **4 SERVINGS**

INGREDIENTS

1 medium red kuri pumpkin/ squash (about 2½lb [1.2kg])

1 tbsp plus 2 tsp avocado oil, divided

½ tsp plus 4 pinches of coarse sea salt, divided, plus more

⅔ cup diced sweet onions

⅓ cup diced fennel

¼ cup diced red bell peppers

2 garlic cloves, roughly chopped

½ tsp ground cumin

¼ tsp ground black pepper

2 to 3 pinches of ground cardamom

2 pinches of ground nutmeg

3 cups **Vegetable Broth** (page 232)

½ tbsp maple syrup

1 to 2 tbsp fennel fronds

FOR THE SAUCE

2 to 3 tbsp **Cultured Cashew Yogurt** (page 235)

2 tsp cold water, plus more

2 pinches of coarse sea salt

> **» QUICK TIPS**
> Acorn, butternut, or kabocha squash can also work in this recipe. Store the soup in an airtight container in the fridge for up to 1 week or in the freezer for up to 6 months.

1 Preheat the oven to 425°F (220°C). Line a large baking tray with parchment paper.

2 Cut the pumpkin in half lengthwise and scoop out the seeds. Place the halves cut side up on the tray and sprinkle 1 teaspoon of avocado oil and 2 pinches of salt over the top of each half. Use clean hands to rub and season the cavities evenly. Flip the halves cut side down.

3 Place the tray on the middle rack in the oven and roast until you can easily perforate the skin with a fork, about 20 minutes.

4 Remove the tray from the oven and allow the pumpkin to cool. Use a spoon to scoop the flesh from the pumpkin and set aside.

5 In a small bowl, make the yogurt sauce by whisking together the ingredients until smooth enough to drizzle with a spoon. Set aside.

6 In a medium saucepan on the stovetop, heat the remaining 1 tablespoon of avocado oil over medium heat. Add the onions and sauté for 1 to 2 minutes, stirring often. Add the fennel, bell peppers, and garlic. Sauté for 2 minutes more, stirring often.

7 Stir in the cumin, black pepper, cardamom, nutmeg, and the remaining ½ teaspoon of salt. Mix well until the spices evenly coat the aromatics. Stir in the vegetable broth. Bring to a boil, then reduce the heat to low. Cover and simmer for 5 minutes.

8 In a high-powered blender, combine the pumpkin, maple syrup, and hot vegetable and broth mixture. Start blending on low speed and slowly increase to reach the highest speed. Process on high until very smooth.

9 Divide the soup into 4 bowls. Drizzle the yogurt sauce over the top and garnish with fennel fronds before serving.

PLANT-BASED MEATBALL SOUP

Because garbanzo beans and sprouted tofu are great sources of protein, the meatballs have nothing to envy. A classic mirepoix—onion, carrot, and celery—is enhanced by red peppers and corn. They combine to infuse the zero-waste vegetable broth with mouthwatering flavors.

PREP TIME: **10 MINUTES** // COOK TIME: **33 TO 34 MINUTES** // YIELD: **4 TO 6 SERVINGS**

INGREDIENTS

1 tbsp ground flaxseeds

3 tbsp warm water

5oz (150g) cooked **Garbanzo Beans** (page 238)

5oz (140g) crumbled organic sprouted tofu

⅓ cup minced leeks

2 garlic cloves, minced

1 tbsp finely chopped fresh flat-leaf parsley

⅓ cup all-purpose gluten-free flour (or whole wheat flour)

1 tbsp coarse sea salt, divided, plus more

½ tsp ground black pepper, plus more

½ tsp ancho chili powder (or chili powder)

½ tsp smoked paprika

2 tbsp avocado oil, divided

½ cup small-diced brown onions

1 cup small-diced carrots

1 cup small-diced celery

4 cups **Vegetable Broth** (page 232)

2 dried bay leaves

1 cup fresh corn kernels

¼ cup small-diced red bell peppers

finely sliced scallions or fresh herbs

1 Preheat the oven to 375°F (190°C). Line a medium baking tray with parchment paper.

2 In a small bowl, combine the flaxseeds and water, stirring to make sure no lumps remain. Allow to rest until viscous, about 3 minutes.

3 In a large bowl, mash the garbanzo beans with a fork or potato masher. Add the tofu, leeks, garlic, parsley, flour, ¾ teaspoon of salt, pepper, ancho chili powder, paprika, and the flaxseed mixture. Use clean hands to knead the mixture until all the ingredients are well incorporated. Allow the mixture to rest for 5 minutes.

4 Divide the mixture into 12 evenly sized balls. Place them 2 inches (5cm) apart on the tray. Brush the balls with 1 tablespoon of avocado oil.

5 Place the tray on the middle rack in the oven and bake until golden and firm to the touch, about 25 minutes.

6 In a medium pot on the stovetop, heat the remaining 1 tablespoon of avocado oil over medium heat. Add the onions and sauté for 2 minutes, stirring often. Add the carrots and celery. Sauté for 2 to 3 minutes more, stirring often.

7 Add the broth, bay leaves, and the remaining ¼ teaspoon of salt. Bring to a boil, then reduce the heat to low. Add the corn kernels and bell peppers. Cover and simmer for 4 minutes. Remove the pot from the heat. Taste and adjust seasoning.

8 Place 2 to 3 meatballs in each of 4 to 6 bowls. Use a ladle to pour the soup over the meatballs. Garnish with scallions or fresh herbs before serving.

» QUICK TIP

Separately store the meatballs and soup in airtight containers for up to 1 week.

BLACK-EYED PEA & VEGETABLE STEW

Although their name might imply otherwise, black-eyed peas aren't peas. They're pulses and part of the legume family, known for contributions to human health and the environment. Cooking with these cuties makes me think of my grandma, Mamaita, since she was probably their biggest fan.

PREP TIME: 5 TO 7 MINUTES // **COOK TIME: 21 TO 23 MINUTES** // **YIELD: 4 TO 6 SERVINGS**

INGREDIENTS

2 tbsp avocado oil

½ cup diced sweet onions

½ cup small-diced celery

½ cup small-diced heirloom carrots

1 cup diced skin-on red potatoes

½ cup small-diced parsnips

½ cup baby bella or cremini mushrooms

¼ cup small-diced green bell peppers

2 cups cooked **Black-Eyed Peas** (page 238)

2 tsp freshly squeezed lime juice

2 to 3 tbsp **Cashew Cream** (page 230)

1 tbsp finely chopped fresh flat-leaf parsley or fresh herbs

FOR THE SAUCE

2 large heirloom tomatoes

½ cup **Vegetable Broth** (page 232)

2 garlic cloves

1 tsp tapioca starch

½ tsp smoked paprika

½ tsp coarse sea salt, plus more

¼ tsp turmeric powder

¼ tsp ground black pepper

1 In a high-powered blender, make the sauce by processing on high all the ingredients until consistent. Taste and adjust seasoning. Set aside.

2 In a Dutch oven or enameled cast-iron pan on the stovetop, heat the avocado oil over medium heat. Add the onions, celery, and carrots. Sauté for 3 minutes, stirring often.

3 Add the potatoes, parsnips, mushrooms, and bell peppers. Cook until the potatoes and parsnips are just cooked through but still firm, about 5 minutes, stirring often.

4 Stir in the sauce. Bring to a boil, then reduce the heat to low. Cover and simmer until the vegetables are soft but not mushy and the sauce is thick and bubbly, about 5 minutes.

5 Add the black-eyed peas and lime juice. Mix well to incorporate all the ingredients. Cover and continue to simmer until all the vegetables are cooked through, about 8 to 10 minutes, stirring occasionally.

6 Divide the stew into 4 to 6 bowls and add an equal amount of cashew cream to each bowl. Sprinkle the parsley or fresh herbs over the top before serving.

> **» QUICK TIPS**
> If you're using a conventional blender or food processor, run the tomato sauce through a mesh sieve to strain any solids, pressing down with a spatula. Store the stew in an airtight container in the fridge for up to 10 days.

SPICY CHAYOTE & TOMATO CASSEROLE

Chayote is among my mother's favorite vegetables and it was always available at my home in Venezuela. It's a great vessel to carry the flavors of this casserole: umami from tomatoes, savory from aromatics, sweetness from bell pepper, and spicy from the serrano and seasoning blend.

PREP TIME: 10 MINUTES // COOK TIME: 28 TO 30 MINUTES // YIELD: 4 TO 6 SERVINGS

INGREDIENTS

3 to 4 quarts (3 to 4 liters) cold water

1 cup ice cubes

5 beefsteak tomatoes (about 3lb [1.4kg] total), divided

1 serrano pepper

2 garlic cloves, roughly chopped

½ cup chopped red onions

2 tbsp plus 2 tsp pure olive oil, divided

1 tbsp freshly squeezed lemon juice

½ tbsp coconut sugar

1 tsp **Spicy Adobo Seasoning** (page 240)

¾ tsp coarse sea salt, divided, plus more

½ tsp fresh lemon zest

2 to 3 large chayote squash (about 1½ to 2lb [680g to 1kg] total)

1 large yellow bell pepper

1 tbsp fresh dill or other fresh herbs

> » **QUICK TIPS**
> Serve over cooked **Quinoa** or **Brown Rice** (page 242). Store in an airtight container in the fridge for up to 5 days.

1 Preheat the oven to 400°F (200°C). Place a baking rack in the lower third.

2 In an extra-large bowl, combine the water and ice cubes. Set aside.

3 Score the bottom of each of tomato by using a paring knife to cut a small and shallow X. In a large pot on the stovetop over medium-high heat, place the tomatoes and add enough water to fully immerse them. Bring to a boil and blanch until the skin starts to loosen and to peel around the score, about 30 seconds.

4 Use a slotted spoon to transfer the tomatoes to the bowl of iced water to shock them. As soon as the tomatoes cool, use a paring knife to peel the skin, starting at the X. Place the tomatoes on a clean kitchen towel to absorb any extra water and set aside.

5 Roughly chop one peeled tomato. In a high-powered blender, combine the chopped tomato, serrano pepper, garlic, red onions, 2 tablespoons of olive oil, lemon juice, coconut sugar, adobo seasoning, ½ teaspoon of salt, and lemon zest. Process on high until consistent.

6 Core the remaining 4 tomatoes and cut into roughly 2-inch (5cm) chunks. Cut the chayote squash into 1- to 1½-inch (2.5 to 3.75cm) chunks and the bell pepper into 1½-inch (3.75cm) pieces. Brush the remaining 2 teaspoons of olive oil on the bottom and sides of a 9- × 12-inch (23 × 30.5cm) baking dish. Alternate the tomatoes, squash, and bell pepper around the dish. Sprinkle the remaining ¼ teaspoon of salt over the top. Pour the sauce over the vegetables, making sure to cover them evenly.

7 Place the dish in the oven and bake until the vegetables are cooked through and the sauce is bubbly, about 28 to 30 minutes.

8 Divide the casserole into 4 to 6 bowls. Sprinkle the dill or other fresh herbs over the top before serving.

EGGPLANT & SWEET POTATO CURRY

Perfectly spiced coconut creaminess makes this dish delicious and comforting. Eggplants are dense and meaty in texture—ideal as a meat substitute. The savory flavors beautifully complement the subtle sweetness of the sweet potatoes. This dish is a winner, amigos.

PREP TIME: 5 TO 10 MINUTES // COOK TIME: 41 TO 46 MINUTES // YIELD: 4 TO 6 SERVINGS

INGREDIENTS

1 medium eggplant, diced into large cubes

1 large sweet potato, diced into large cubes

2 tbsp avocado oil

¾ tsp coarse sea salt, divided, plus more

½ tsp ground black pepper

1 tbsp coconut oil

1 cup diced white onions

2 large garlic cloves, minced

2 tsp fresh crushed ginger

1 tbsp **Homemade Curry Powder** (page 240)

¼ tsp ground cayenne (optional)

1 medium globe tomato, diced

1 cup **Coconut Cream** (page 230)

¾ cup **Vegetable Broth** (page 232)

1 tbsp coconut sugar

fresh lemon balm or mint leaves

1 Preheat the oven to 400°F (200°C).

2 Place the eggplant and sweet potato on an extra-large baking tray. Drizzle the avocado oil over the top. Sprinkle ½ teaspoon of salt and the pepper over the top.

3 Place the tray on the middle rack in the oven and bake until golden, about 25 to 30 minutes. Use a metal spatula to flip halfway through to make sure they bake evenly. Remove the tray from the oven and allow the eggplant and sweet potato to cool. Set aside.

4 In a Dutch oven or an enameled cast-iron pot on the stovetop, heat the coconut oil over medium heat until smoking. Add the onions and sauté until soft and translucent, about 2 minutes, stirring often. Stir in the garlic and ginger. Cook for 1 minute.

5 Add the curry powder, cayenne (if using), and the remaining ¼ teaspoon of salt. Cook for 1 minute, stirring often. Add the tomatoes and mix well until evenly coated by the spices. Cook for 2 minutes.

6 Stir in the coconut cream, broth, and coconut sugar. Bring to a boil, then reduce the heat to low. Add the eggplant and sweet potato. Cover and simmer for 10 minutes. Taste and adjust seasoning. Remove the Dutch oven from the heat.

7 Divide the curry into 4 to 6 bowls. Garnish with fresh lemon balm or mint leaves before serving.

> **» QUICK TIPS**
> You can use two medium-sized trays and place one on the top rack and one on the bottom rack, switching their positions halfway through (after flipping the vegetables) to ensure even cooking. Serve the curry over cooked **Brown Rice** (page 242) or **Millets** (page 243).

BROCCOLI SOUP

This soup uses the whole crown of broccoli—florets, stems, and stalk—so nothing goes to waste. Broccoli might be a common vegetable, but nothing is common about this soup. Spinach bring extra color and nutrition to the mix, while cashew cream adds just the right amount of richness.

PREP TIME: **7 TO 10 MINUTES** // COOK TIME: **19 MINUTES** // YIELD: **4 TO 6 SERVINGS**

INGREDIENTS

1lb (450g) broccoli crown

2 tbsp pure olive oil

½ cup small-diced shallots

⅓ cup diced carrots

⅓ cup diced celery

½ tsp dried basil

½ tsp coarse sea salt, plus more

¼ tsp ground black pepper

2½ cups **Vegetable Broth** (page 232)

1 cup roughly chopped spinach

2 tbsp **Roasted Garlic Paste** (page 237)

½ cup **Cashew Cream** (page 230)

1 Cut the tops off the broccoli florets. Chop the broccoli stems and stalks into ½-inch (1.25cm) chunks. Set the florets aside separately from the stems and stalks.

2 In a saucepan on the stovetop, heat the olive oil over medium heat. Add the shallots, carrots, and celery. Sauté for 3 minutes, stirring often. Add the broccoli stems and stalks. Cook until slightly tender, about 3 minutes, stirring often.

3 Add the basil, salt, pepper, and broth. Mix well, making sure to scrape any brown bits from the bottom of the saucepan. Bring to a boil, then reduce the heat to low. Cover and simmer until the stems and stalks are soft and tender, about 8 minutes.

4 Add the florets and spinach. Cover and simmer until the florets are cooked through, about 5 minutes more.

5 In a high-powered blender, combine the broccoli mixture (including the liquids), garlic paste, and cashew cream. Start blending on low speed and slowly increase to reach the highest speed. Process on high until very smooth. Taste and adjust seasoning.

6 Divide the soup into 4 to 6 shallow bowls and serve immediately.

> **» QUICK TIPS**
> You can top the soup with a light drizzle of extra-virgin olive oil and freshly ground black pepper. Store the soup in an airtight container in the fridge for up to 1 week or in the freezer for up to 6 months.

BLACK BEAN CHILI

Without needing to simmer for an extended period of time, this chili still develops a mouthwatering and deep flavor thanks to the rich sauce and a variety of vegetables. Like other pulses, black beans are loaded with nutrients. However, they're particularly rich in fiber and magnesium.

PREP TIME: **10 MINUTES** // COOK TIME: **21 TO 23 MINUTES** // YIELD: **4 TO 6 SERVINGS**

INGREDIENTS

2 tbsp avocado oil

½ cup diced brown onions

⅓ cup small-diced carrots

½ cup small-diced celery

½ cup diced seeded vine-ripened tomatoes

1 cup fresh corn kernels (from 1 ear of corn)

1½ cup cooked **Black Beans** (page 238)

¼ cup small-diced green bell peppers

¼ tsp coarse sea salt, plus more

¼ cup loose cilantro leaves

2 tbsp thinly sliced serrano peppers

FOR THE SAUCE

2 vine-ripened tomatoes, cored and quartered

2 garlic cloves

¾ cup **Vegetable Broth** (page 232)

¼ cup **Barbecue Sauce** (page 214)

1½ tbsp finely chopped fresh cilantro stems

2 tsp tapioca starch

1½ tsp **Spicy Adobo Seasoning** (page 240)

½ tsp coarse sea salt, plus more

1 In a high-powered blender, make the sauce by combining all the ingredients, pressing down with the tamper if needed. Process on high until smooth. Set aside.

2 In a Dutch oven or enameled cast-iron pan on the stovetop, heat the avocado oil over medium heat. Add the onions, carrots, and celery. Sauté for 3 minutes.

3 Add the tomatoes, corn, black beans, bell peppers, and salt. Stir in the tomato sauce and mix well. Bring to a boil, then reduce the heat to low. Cover and simmer until the chili is thick and all the vegetables are cooked through, about 18 to 20 minutes, stirring occasionally to prevent the soup from sticking to the bottom. Taste and adjust seasoning.

4 Remove the Dutch oven from the heat and allow the chili to rest covered for 5 minutes. Taste and adjust seasoning.

5 Divide the chili into 4 to 6 bowls. Sprinkle the cilantro leaves and serrano peppers over the top before serving.

> **» QUICK TIPS**
> You can also top the chili with a dollop of **Cashew Cream** (page 230). Store the chili in an airtight container in the fridge for up to 10 days or in the freezer for up to 6 months.

CHAYOTE TAGINE
WITH PRUNES & APRICOTS

Chayote squash has folate, vitamin C, and manganese as well as powerful antioxidants that prevent damage at the cellular level and help reduce inflammation. Combined with root vegetables and tubers, dried fruits, and spices, chayote is the star of my plant-based interpretation of a tagine.

PREP TIME: **10 TO 15 MINUTES**   //   COOK TIME: **42 TO 46 MINUTES**   //   YIELD: **4 TO 6 SERVINGS**

INGREDIENTS

2 tbsp pure olive oil

1 cup thinly sliced brown onions

3 to 4 garlic cloves, minced

1½ tsp fresh crushed ginger

¼ tsp saffron threads

¼ tsp ground cardamom

¼ tsp ground cinnamon

¼ tsp ground cumin

2 large red potatoes, diced into large cubes

2 purple heirloom carrots, sliced ¾ inch (2cm) thick

1 tsp tapioca flour

¾ tsp coarse sea salt, plus more

2 cups **Vegetable Broth** (page 232)

¼ tsp fresh lemon zest

½ cup pitted prunes

½ cup dried apricots

2 large chayote squash, diced into large cubes

2 tsp maple syrup (optional)

fresh mint or chopped fresh herbs

1 In a Dutch oven or an enameled cast-iron pot on the stovetop, heat the olive oil over medium heat until smoking. Add the onions and sauté for 2 minutes, stirring often.

2 Stir in the garlic and ginger. Cook for 1 minute. Add the saffron, cardamom, cinnamon, and cumin. Cook for 1 minute more.

3 Add the potatoes, carrots, tapioca flour, and salt. Mix well with a spoonula to make sure the spices fully coat all the vegetables.

4 Add the broth, lemon zest, prunes, and apricots. Stir well. Bring to a boil, then reduce the heat to low. Cover and simmer for 28 to 30 minutes.

5 Stir in the squash and maple syrup (if using). Cover and cook for 10 to 12 minutes more. Taste and adjust seasoning.

6 Divide the tagine into 4 to 6 bowls. Garnish with fresh mint or chopped fresh herbs before serving.

> **» QUICK TIPS**
> Thinly slicing the onion widthwise (against the grain) allows for a greater release of flavor and for it to wilt and nearly blend into the sauce. You might want to wear gloves or oil your hands while working with the chayote. Serve the tagine with cooked **Quinoa** (page 242) or **Amaranth** (page 243) or topped with shaved almonds.

BRAISED NOPAL CACTUS PADS

Also known as nopales, prickly pear pads showcase the best qualities of low-carbon ingredients: climate-friendly, able to grow with little to no water, nourishing, and a good source of protein and other healthful nutrients. The red pepper sauce is infused with aromatics, dry herbs, and spices.

PREP TIME: 7 TO 10 MINUTES // COOK TIME: 28 TO 34 MINUTES // YIELD: 4 TO 6 SERVINGS

INGREDIENTS

1 large red bell pepper, halved lengthwise

1 tbsp plus 1 tsp pure olive oil, divided

1 tsp plus 2 pinches of coarse sea salt, divided, plus more

5 plum tomatoes (about 1lb [450g] total)

3 garlic cloves

1 tsp dried oregano

½ tsp ground coriander

½ tsp ground annatto

¼ tsp ground black pepper

4 large fresh nopal cactus pads (about 1¼lb [680g] total), thorns removed

2½ to 3 quarts (2½ to 3 liters) water

¾ cup julienned white onions

2 dried bay leaves

1 to 2 tbsp thinly sliced scallions or chopped fresh herbs

» QUICK TIPS

You can use nopalitos (jarred tender cactus) if you can't find fresh pads. Drain and discard the brine and rinse well before using. If using a conventional blender or food processor, run the pepper and tomato sauce through a mesh sieve, pressing down with a spatula to strain any solids.

1 Preheat the oven to 450°F (230°C).

2 Place the bell pepper cut side up on a baking tray. Drizzle ½ teaspoon of olive oil over each half and season each half with 1 pinch of salt. Flip the halves cut side down.

3 Place the tray on the top rack in the oven and roast until the pepper is soft and the skin has some golden brown marks, about 12 to 15 minutes.

4 Remove the tray from the oven and cover the pepper with a lid or aluminum foil. Allow to rest for 5 minutes. Once cooled, remove the stem and seeds. Gently peel the skin (and save it for your compost pile).

5 In a high-powered blender, combine the bell pepper, tomatoes, garlic, oregano, coriander, annatto, black pepper, and ½ teaspoon of salt. Process on high until smooth. Set aside.

6 Slice the cactus pads into ¼-inch (0.5cm) strips.

7 In a medium saucepan on the stovetop over medium heat, bring the water to a boil. Reduce the heat to low and add the remaining ½ teaspoon of salt. Add the cactus pads and cook covered for 5 minutes. Discard the water and rinse the cooked pads. Strain.

8 In a Dutch oven or enameled cast-iron pan on the stovetop, heat the remaining 1 tablespoon of olive oil over medium heat. Add the onions and sauté for 1 to 2 minutes. Add the cactus pads, bay leaves, and sauce. Stir well. Bring the sauce to a soft boil, then reduce the heat to low. Cover and simmer until the cactus pads have wilted and the sauce has thickened, about 10 to 12 minutes. Taste and adjust seasoning.

9 Divide into 4 to 6 shallow bowls and sprinkle the scallions or chopped fresh herbs over the top before serving.

GARBANZO & POTATO STEW

A plant-based interpretation of a dish I grew up eating in Venezuela, this stew is packed with flavorful memories. The fragrant and smooth coconut sauce is infused with a combination of green peppers, leafy greens, herbs, and gut-friendly ingredients, such as ginger and miso.

PREP TIME: **7 MINUTES** // COOK TIME: **13 TO 17 MINUTES** // YIELD: **4 TO 6 SERVINGS**

INGREDIENTS

1 tbsp unrefined coconut oil

½ cup diced brown onions

1½ cups large-diced heirloom potatoes

1 cup **Coconut Cream** (page 230)

¾ to 1 cup filtered water

2 cups cooked **Garbanzo Beans** (page 238)

¼ cup fresh English peas

2 to 3 tbsp thinly sliced jalapeños (optional)

4 lime wedges

FOR THE PASTE

3 large garlic cloves, roughly chopped

2 scallions, roughly chopped

½ cup baby arugula

¼ cup roughly chopped fresh curly parsley

¼ cup roughly chopped green bell peppers

2 tbsp freshly squeezed lime juice

1 to 2 tbsp minced jalapeños

1 tbsp coconut sugar

1 tbsp grated fresh ginger

½ tbsp chickpea miso paste

½ tsp coarse sea salt, plus more

¼ tsp ground coriander

¼ tsp ground cumin

¼ tsp ground black pepper

1 In a food processor, make the green paste by combining all the ingredients. Process on high until a thick paste has formed. Set aside.

2 In a Dutch oven or an enameled cast-iron pot on the stovetop, heat the coconut oil over medium heat. Once the oil starts to smoke, add the onions and sauté for 2 minutes, stirring often.

3 Add the potatoes and cook until just cooked through but still firm, about 3 minutes, stirring often. Add the green paste, coconut cream, and water. Mix with a wooden spoon until consistent.

4 Stir in the garbanzo beans, then reduce the heat to low. Cover and simmer until the potatoes are cooked through, about 7 to 10 minutes, stirring occasionally to make sure the stew doesn't stick to the bottom. Taste and adjust seasoning.

5 Stir in the peas and simmer for 1 to 2 minutes more. Remove the Dutch oven from the heat.

6 Divide the stew into 4 to 6 bowls. Garnish each with jalapeños (if using) and a lime wedge before serving.

> **» QUICK TIPS**
> Serve this dish with a side of cooked **Millets** (page 243) or **Farro** (page 243). With so many varieties of potatoes available, why not venture from those monopolizing our markets? Go for a delicious Early Rose, a Peach Blow, or a Green Mountain, although any potato or sweet potato will work well in this recipe. Store the stew in an airtight container in the fridge for up to 1 week. If the stew is too dense when reheating on the stovetop, add a little water.

WHITE BEAN & KALE STEW

This is my humble interpretation of a Tuscan dish called *Ribollita*. It's a hearty stew with deep, delectable flavors. White beans and cauliflower add a certain meatiness that complements the wilty texture of the kale. Because this dish reheats very well, add it to your meal-prep menu.

PREP TIME: **5 TO 10 MINUTES** // COOK TIME: **10 MINUTES** // YIELD: **4 SERVINGS**

INGREDIENTS

2 cups cooked **Black & White Beans** (Great Northern Beans) (page 238), divided

2 cups **Vegetable Broth** (page 232)

1 tbsp nutritional yeast, plus more

½ tsp coarse sea salt, plus more

½ tsp dried basil

¼ tsp red pepper flakes, plus more

2 tbsp pure olive oil

½ cup minced shallots

½ cup small-diced white heirloom carrots

¼ cup minced celery

¼ cup thinly sliced scallions

7oz (200g) small cauliflower florets

¼ cup minced green bell peppers

2 garlic cloves, minced

1 bunch of kale, stems removed, cut into 1- to 1½-inch (2.5 to 3.75cm) pieces

1½ tbsp freshly squeezed lemon juice

1 In a blender, combine ½ cup of beans, vegetable broth, nutritional yeast, salt, basil, and red pepper flakes. Process on high until smooth. Set aside.

2 In a medium pot on the stovetop, heat the olive oil over medium heat. Add the shallots and sauté for 1 minute, stirring often.

3 Stir in the carrots, celery, and scallions. Cook for 2 minutes, stirring often. Add the cauliflower, bell peppers, and garlic. Cook for 2 minutes more.

4 Add the broth mixture and the remaining 1½ cups of beans. Bring to a boil, then reduce the heat to low. Add the kale and mix well with a spoonula to coat the leaves with the stew liquids. Cover and simmer for 5 minutes. Stir in the lemon juice. Taste and adjust seasoning.

5 Divide the stew into 4 bowls. Sprinkle a little nutritional yeast and red pepper flakes over the top if desired. Serve immediately.

» QUICK TIPS

Save the cauliflower stems and leaves for **Cauliflower Leafstalk Kimchi** (page 226). This stew pairs perfectly with a side of **Roasted Radishes** (page 123). Store in an airtight container in the fridge for up to 5 days.

CHAPTER 10
MAIN DISHES

156 Cauliflower Ceviche with Coconut & Passion Fruit Marinade

158 Eggplant & Lentil Stacks

159 Mushroom Bánh Mì

160 Purple Sweet Potato Gnocchi with Carrot-Top Pesto

163 King Oyster Mushroom Arepas

164 Creamy Farro Casserole with Broccoli & Butternut Squash

165 Spaghetti Squash with Plant-Based Bolognese

166 Tostones Nachos with Crumbled Sprouted Tofu

168 Papaya Poke Stacks with Wasabi Slaw

170 Annatto Rice with Kidney Beans & Romanesco Florets

171 Crispy Sprouted Tofu with Stir-Fried Vegetables

172 Zucchini Noodles & Grilled Portobello Steaks

174 Quinoa-Stuffed Peppers

176 Cauliflower Steaks with Herbed Succotash

177 Jackfruit & Leafstalk Tacos with Avocado & Radish Greens Crema

178 Sweet Potato Tacos with Collard Greens Shells

CAULIFLOWER CEVICHE
WITH COCONUT & PASSION FRUIT MARINADE

Many versions of ceviche exist, but my favorite is Peruvian—traditionally served with sweet potatoes and corn, which add sweetness and texture. My interpretation showcases a *leche de tigre* (tiger's milk) prepared with coconut milk infused with flavors from lime and passion fruit.

PREP TIME: **10 TO 15 MINUTES** // COOK TIME: **17 TO 19 MINUTES** // YIELD: **2 SERVINGS**

INGREDIENTS

2½ quarts (2½ liters) water

1 tsp coarse sea salt

8oz (225g) cauliflower, cut into ½- to ¾-inch pieces (1.25 to 2cm)

1 ear of corn, shucked

1 unpeeled small sweet potato, thoroughly washed

⅓ cup small-diced celery

⅓ cup small-diced red bell peppers

¼ cup **Lime-Pickled Onions & Watermelon Rinds** (page 227)

2 to 3 tbsp whole cilantro leaves

4 small lime wedges

FOR THE MARINADE

⅓ cup **Coconut Cream** (page 230)

⅓ cup freshly squeezed lime juice

¼ cup roughly chopped fresh cilantro stems

¼ cup celery leaves

2 tbsp passion fruit pulp

1 to 2 garlic cloves

1 to 3 tbsp minced jalapeños

¼ tsp coarse sea salt, plus more

1 In a medium saucepan on the stovetop over medium-high heat, bring the water to a boil. Reduce the heat to medium and stir in the salt. Add the cauliflower and cook until slightly tender, about 2 minutes. Use a slotted spoon to transfer the cauliflower to a bowl with iced water.

2 To the still-simmering water, add the corn and cook for 5 minutes. Transfer the corn to a cutting board to cool slightly.

3 Add the sweet potato and cook covered until you can pierce it with a fork, about 10 to 12 minutes. Transfer the sweet potato to the cutting board to cool slightly.

4 Cut down each side of the corn cob to remove the kernels into a shallow bowl, making sure to remove any remaining silk. Use a paring knife to cut off the pointy ends of the sweet potato and to scrape the skin off. Cut into ½-inch (1.25cm) slices. Set aside.

5 In a high-powered blender, make the marinade by processing on high all the ingredients until smooth. Use a mesh sieve to strain into a bowl, pressing with a spoon to get most of the liquid. Taste and adjust seasoning.

6 Strain the cauliflower and transfer back to the chilled bowl. Add the celery and bell peppers. Mix well. Pour the marinade over the cauliflower mixture and toss to coat. Refrigerate for about 10 minutes.

7 Transfer the cauliflower and marinade to the center of 2 large shallow bowls. Add the sweet potato and corn. Top with the lime-pickled onions and watermelon rinds. Garnish with the cilantro leaves and lime wedges before serving.

> **» QUICK TIPS**
> Save the leftover corn cobs to make **Vegetable Broth** (page 232). For added nutrition, sprinkle a little **Papaya Seed Powder** (page 231) over the top.

EGGPLANT & LENTIL STACKS

Lentils are healthy, sustainable, and versatile pulses. They add meatiness to any dish, including a Bolognese sauce that helps layer stacks of balsamic-marinated eggplant slices and velvety cashew cream. This dish is inspired by eggplant lasagnas but is easier and quicker to make.

PREP TIME: 10 TO 12 MINUTES // **COOK TIME: 16 TO 18 MINUTES** // **YIELD: 4 TO 6 SERVINGS**

INGREDIENTS

1½ cups cooked **Lentils** (any color) (page 239)

½ medium brown onion, quartered

2 garlic cloves, minced

4 large plum tomatoes, cored and quartered

½ tbsp maple syrup

½ tsp dried basil

½ tsp smoked paprika

¼ cup plus 1 tbsp pure olive oil, divided, plus more

1 tsp coarse sea salt, divided, plus more

½ tsp ground black pepper, divided

1 tbsp balsamic vinegar

1 large eggplant, sliced into ½-inch (1.25cm) slices (about 12 total)

¾ to 1 cup **Cashew Cream** (page 230)

3 tbsp fresh basil chiffonade (see Quick Tip)

1½ to 2 tbsp nutritional yeast

1 tsp red pepper flakes (optional)

1 In a food processor, pulse the lentils 6 times. Transfer to a small bowl and set aside.

2 In the same food processor, combine the onions and garlic. Pulse until roughly chopped.

3 Add the tomatoes, maple syrup, basil, paprika, 2 tablespoons of olive oil, ½ teaspoon of salt, and ¼ teaspoon of pepper. Pulse until the sauce is chunky and consistent.

4 Transfer the sauce to a medium saucepan on the stovetop over medium-low heat. Bring to a soft boil, stirring often. Reduce the heat to low, add the lentils, and mix well. Cook covered until thick and bubbly, about 10 to 12 minutes, stirring often to prevent the sauce from sticking to the bottom of the saucepan. Taste and adjust seasoning. Remove the saucepan from the heat and keep covered until ready to serve.

5 In a small bowl, whisk together the balsamic vinegar, 1 tablespoon of olive oil, the remaining ½ teaspoon of salt, and the remaining ¼ teaspoon of pepper. Place the eggplant slices in a single layer on a baking tray and brush the balsamic mixture on both sides.

6 In a large cast-iron skillet on the stovetop, heat the remaining 2 tablespoons of olive oil over medium heat. Add the eggplant and cook until golden brown and slightly wilted, about 2 to 3 minutes per side. (You might need to do this in batches. If so, add more olive oil as needed.)

7 To assemble the stacks, place 6 eggplant slices on a platter. Top each slice with 1 to 1½ tablespoons of cashew cream and about ⅓ cup of the lentil Bolognese. Top each stack with 1 eggplant slice and 1 tablespoon of cashew cream. Garnish each stack with basil chiffonade. Sprinkle the nutritional yeast and red pepper flakes (if using) over the top before serving.

> **» QUICK TIP**
> To make basil chiffonade, roll 6 large basil leaves together and cut the leaves into ribbons.

MUSHROOM BÁNH MÌ

I became a big fan of bánh mì when I first tried it. A crispy and soft baguette serves as a vessel for cooked, raw, and pickled ingredients that are tender and crispy with savory, tangy, and sweet flavors. The mushrooms add an earthiness and umami taste that perfectly replace any meat.

PREP TIME: **10 MINUTES** // COOK TIME: **2 TO 3 MINUTES** // YIELD: **4 SERVINGS**

INGREDIENTS

⅔ cup finely julienned daikon

⅓ cup finely julienned carrots

½ cup unseasoned rice vinegar

2 tbsp coconut sugar

1 tsp coarse sea salt, divided, plus more

¼ cup boiling water

2 tbsp toasted sesame oil

½ tbsp maple syrup

2 tsp grated fresh ginger

2 tsp grated fresh garlic

2 tsp **Umami Mushroom Powder** (page 240)

½ tsp red pepper flakes (optional)

4 portobello mushrooms (about 1lb [450g] total), cut into ⅜-inch (1cm) slices

1 tbsp avocado oil

1 multi-grain baguette

12 thin slices of cucumber, plus more

16 thin slices of jalapeño, plus more (optional)

8 sprigs of fresh cilantro, plus more

FOR THE SPREAD

3 tbsp **Aquafaba Mayonnaise** (page 235)

1½ tbsp finely minced scallions

½ tsp freshly squeezed lime juice

¼ tsp coarse sea salt, plus more

1 In a glass container or canning jar, combine the daikon and carrots. Add the rice vinegar, coconut sugar, ½ teaspoon of salt, and water. Cover and close tightly. Carefully shake to mix all the ingredients and set aside for 5 minutes.

2 Shake the container again and place it in the back of the fridge. Refrigerate for at least 30 minutes. Strain the daikon and carrots before using.

3 In a large bowl, whisk together the sesame oil, maple syrup, ginger, garlic, mushroom powder, red pepper flakes (if using), and the remaining ½ teaspoon of salt. Add the mushrooms and use clean hands to evenly coat with the marinade. Marinate for 5 minutes.

4 In a small bowl, make the aquafaba spread by whisking together all the ingredients until consistent. Taste and adjust seasoning. Set aside.

5 In a large skillet on the stovetop, heat the avocado oil over medium-high heat. Add the mushrooms and sauté for 2 to 3 minutes, stirring often. Remove the skillet from the heat and keep the mushrooms in the skillet until ready to serve.

6 Cut the baguette into 4 even pieces, about 5 inches (12.5cm) long each. Slice each piece in half lengthwise. (You can toast the baguette slices on a cast-iron grill for a few minutes. This will give them grill marks and will make the bread warm and crispy.)

7 Place the baguette slices cut side up on a serving platter and add an equal amount of the spread to half or all the slices. On 1 slice of each pair, layer an equal amount of the daikon and carrots, 3 slices of cucumber, 4 slices of jalapeños (if using), and a couple sprigs of cilantro (or more!). On the other slice of each pair, add an equal amount of the mushrooms.

8 Place the two halves of each pair together to close the sandwiches and serve immediately.

PURPLE SWEET POTATO GNOCCHI
WITH CARROT-TOP PESTO

Did you know sweet potatoes come in orange, yellow, and even purple? Besides its bright color, the purple kind is also impressive for its health-promoting properties. This gnocchi is light but filling and perfectly balanced by the zero-waste pesto, which I might bottle and sell one day.

PREP TIME: **10 TO 15 MINUTES**   //   COOK TIME: **35 TO 41 MINUTES**   //   YIELD: **4 SERVINGS**

INGREDIENTS

1lb (450g) purple sweet potatoes

1 tsp plus 1½ tbsp pure olive oil, divided

½ cup whole wheat flour, plus more

½ tsp coarse sea salt

1 tsp nutritional yeast

¼ to ½ tsp red pepper flakes

FOR THE PESTO

2½ to 3 quarts (2½ to 3 liters) water

1¼ cups carrot tops, thick stems removed

¼ cup plus 1 tbsp crushed raw walnuts

2 garlic cloves, roughly chopped

¼ cup extra-virgin olive oil

2½ tbsp freshly squeezed lemon juice

1½ tbsp nutritional yeast

½ tsp coarse sea salt

½ tsp ground black pepper

> » **QUICK TIP**
> You can use the directions in Quick Tips on page 126 to pan-sear the gnocchi.

1 Preheat the oven to 375°F (190°C). Line a large baking tray with parchment paper.

To make the pesto, in a medium saucepan on the stovetop over medium-high heat, bring the water to a boil. Add the carrot tops and blanch for about 3 minutes. Use a mesh ladle to transfer to a bowl with iced water. Strain and set aside. (Retain the warm water in the saucepan. Turn off the heat but keep the saucepan covered.)

2 In a food processor, combine the carrot tops, walnuts, garlic, olive oil, lemon juice, nutritional yeast, salt, and pepper. Process on high until thick and consistent. Set aside.

3 Cut the purple sweet potatoes in half lengthwise. Rub with 1 teaspoon of olive oil. Place the potatoes cut side down on the tray. Place the tray on the top rack in the oven and bake until fork-tender, about 30 to 35 minutes. Remove the tray from the oven and allow the potatoes to cool completely.

4 Remove the skins from the potatoes and transfer the flesh to a food processor. Pulse until puréed (don't overprocess) and transfer to a large bowl. Add the flour, salt, and the remaining 1½ tablespoons of olive oil. Knead with clean hands. You might need to add flour a little at a time until the dough reaches the right consistency. Form the dough into a ball.

5 Transfer to a floured surface. Divide into 4 or more portions and roll each into a ¾-inch-thick (2cm) rope. Cut the ropes into ½-inch (1.25cm) pieces.

6 Uncover the saucepan and set the heat to medium. Bring the water to a rolling boil. Add the dough and cook uncovered until the pieces float to the surface, about 2 to 3 minutes. Use a slotted spoon to transfer the gnocchi to a platter in a single layer, making sure they don't stick together.

7 Spoon 2 to 3 tablespoons of pesto into a shallow bowl. Place the gnocchi on the pesto and sprinkle the nutritional yeast and red pepper flakes over the top. Garnish with small carrot-top leaves before serving.

KING OYSTER MUSHROOM AREPAS

"There's nothing more Venezuelan than an arepa" is a popular saying that highlights just how important these pockets of goodness are in our culture. And they are—arepas were the daily bread in my home growing up. The mushroom shreds will ensure you never miss meat.

PREP TIME: **10 MINUTES** // COOK TIME: **22 TO 23 MINUTES** // YIELD: **2 TO 3 AREPAS**

INGREDIENTS

½ cup plus 3 tbsp water, divided, plus more

¾ tsp coarse sea salt, divided, plus more

½ cup whole grain precooked white corn flour (Harina P.A.N. or arepa flour recommended)

1 tbsp plus 1 tsp avocado oil, divided

½ cup warm cooked **Black Beans** (page 238)

½ tbsp **Roasted Garlic Paste** (page 237)

2 extra-large king oyster mushrooms (about 10oz [285g] total)

3 tbsp finely julienned brown onions

3 tbsp finely julienned green bell peppers

1 tsp **Spicy Adobo Seasoning** (page 240)

1 Hass avocado, peeled, seeded, and thinly sliced

sunflower sprouts or chopped fresh herbs

> **» QUICK TIPS**
> Save the mushroom caps for **Crookneck Squash with King Oyster Mushrooms** (page 122). **Creamy Garlic Sauce** (page 214) and **Guasacaca** (page 215) are great condiments for arepas.

1 Preheat the oven to 375°F (190°C).

In a medium bowl, combine ½ cup plus 2 tablespoons of water and ¼ teaspoon of salt. Slowly add the corn flour, mixing with your hand or a spoon to make sure no lumps remain. Allow to hydrate for 5 minutes. Use clean, damp hands to divide the dough into 2 to 3 portions. Form each portion into a ball and then flatten into a ¾-inch (2cm) disc.

2 Brush the bottom of a cast-iron pan with ½ to 1 teaspoon of avocado oil. Place the pan on the stovetop over medium-low heat. Once hot, add the discs and sear until a crust with a few dark brown spots has formed, about 4 minutes per side. Place the arepas directly on the middle rack in the oven and bake until slightly puffed and the shell is crusty, about 8 minutes. Remove the arepas from the oven and wrap in a clean towel to keep warm.

3 In a tall blending cup or wide-mouthed glass jar, use an immersion blender to process the beans, garlic paste, 1 pinch of salt, and the remaining 1 tablespoon of water until a smooth paste forms. Set aside.

4 Cut the caps off the mushrooms. (Save them for later use.) Use two forks to thinly shred the stems: Work from the center lengthwise toward the end and then turn the mushroom the other way to repeat the process.

5 In a medium skillet on the stovetop, heat the remaining 1 tablespoon of avocado oil over medium heat. Add the onions and sauté for 1 to 2 minutes, stirring often. Add the bell peppers and sauté for 30 seconds.

6 Add the spicy adobo seasoning, mushrooms, and the remaining ½ teaspoon of salt. Mix until the shreds are evenly coated with spices. Reduce the heat to low and add a little water to deglaze the bottom of the skillet. Cook for about 4 minutes, stirring often. Taste and adjust seasoning.

7 Use a paring knife to slice the arepas in half to create pockets. Spread an equal amount of the bean paste inside each arepa. Use tongs to stuff them with the mushrooms and the avocado slices. Garnish with sunflower sprouts or chopped fresh herbs before serving.

CREAMY FARRO CASSEROLE
WITH BROCCOLI & BUTTERNUT SQUASH

The comfort level of this casserole is 100%. All the ingredients complement each other very well. Farro has a nutty flavor and chewy texture, and it's rich in protein and fiber. Thanks to make-ahead ingredients for this casserole, having dinner on the table in 20 minutes or less is quite possible.

PREP TIME: **7 TO 10 MINUTES** // COOK TIME: **15 TO 19 MINUTES** // YIELD: **4 TO 6 SERVINGS**

INGREDIENTS

2 tbsp pure olive oil, divided

¼ cup small-diced shallots

¾ cup small-diced fennel

2 cups medium-diced butternut squash

2 cups cooked **Farro** (page 243)

¼ cup small-diced red bell peppers

1½ tsp **Umami Mushroom Powder** (page 240)

1 tsp fresh thyme leaves

½ tsp coarse sea salt

½ tsp ground black pepper

½ cup plus 2 tbsp **Cashew Cream** (page 230)

½ cup plus 2 tbsp **Vegetable Broth** (page 232)

1 tbsp nutritional yeast

1 cup small broccoli florets

1 Preheat the oven to 450°F (235°C).

2 In a large cast-iron skillet on the stovetop, heat 1½ tablespoons of olive oil over medium heat. Add the shallots and fennel. Sauté for 2 minutes, stirring often. Add the butternut squash and cook until slightly firm but cooked through, about 5 to 6 minutes, stirring often.

3 Add the farro, bell peppers, mushroom powder, thyme leaves, salt, and black pepper. Mix until well incorporated. Stir in the cashew cream, broth, and nutritional yeast. Mix well. Cook until creamy and consistent, about 2 to 3 minutes, stirring occasionally.

4 Stir in the broccoli. Remove the skillet from the heat.

5 Brush an 11- × 7-inch (28 × 17.5cm) baking dish with the remaining ½ tablespoon of olive oil. Place the mixture in the dish and use a spatula or the back of a spoon to compact it slightly.

6 Place the dish on the top rack in the oven and bake until the top layer is golden and crusty, about 6 to 8 minutes.

7 Remove the dish from the oven and serve the casserole immediately.

» **QUICK TIPS**
Save the stalks to make **Broccoli Stalk Cakes** (page 79). Store leftovers in an airtight container in the fridge for up to 10 days.

SPAGHETTI SQUASH
WITH PLANT-BASED BOLOGNESE

Mama Earth's homemade spaghetti grows in a squash. It's naturally gluten-free and positively delicious. Cooking tomatoes in the Bolognese concentrates their flavor but also intensifies their healthful lycopene and lutein. Eggplant and walnuts give the Bolognese a heavenly meatiness.

PREP TIME: 10 MINUTES // **COOK TIME: 42 TO 44 MINUTES** // **YIELD: 4 TO 6 SERVINGS**

INGREDIENTS

1 medium spaghetti squash (about 2lb [1kg])

3 tbsp pure olive oil, divided

1½ tsp coarse sea salt, divided, plus more

1 small shallot

1 medium eggplant, peeled and roughly chopped

1 cup raw walnuts (halves and pieces)

1 tbsp nutritional yeast

½ tsp red pepper flakes (optional)

2 tbsp extra-small fresh basil leaves

FOR THE SAUCE

4 to 5 large ripe Roma tomatoes (about 1½lb [680g] total), quartered

2 to 3 garlic cloves

5 large fresh basil leaves

½ tbsp coconut sugar

1 tsp smoked paprika

½ tsp fennel seeds

½ tsp coarse sea salt, plus more

½ tsp ground black pepper

1 Preheat the oven to 400°F (200°C). Line a medium baking tray with parchment paper.

2 Cut the squash in half lengthwise and scoop out the seeds. Place both halves cut side up on the tray. Drizzle ½ tablespoon of olive oil and sprinkle ½ teaspoon of salt over the top of each half. Use clean hands to rub and evenly season the cavities. Flip the squash cut side down.

3 Place the tray on the middle rack in the oven and bake until you can easily perforate the squash skin with a fork, about 30 minutes. Remove the tray from the oven. Set aside.

4 In a high-powered blender, make the Bolognese by processing on high all the ingredients until smooth and consistent. Taste and adjust seasoning. Set aside.

5 In a food processor, combine the shallot, eggplant, and the remaining ½ teaspoon of salt. Pulse 6 times. Use a spatula to scrape down the sides of the bowl. Add the walnuts and pulse until all the ingredients are finely minced or ground.

6 In a medium saucepan on the stovetop, heat the remaining 2 tablespoons of olive oil over medium heat. Add the eggplant mixture and cook for 2 minutes, stirring often. Carefully pour the Bolognese over the mixture and bring to a simmer, stirring often. Reduce the heat to low and simmer until the Bolognese is cooked through and thick, about 10 to 12 minutes, stirring occasionally. Taste and adjust seasoning. Remove the saucepan from the heat and cover until time to serve.

7 Use a fork to scrape the inside of the squash and fluff the strands. Divide the noodles into 4 to 6 shallow bowls and pour the Bolognese sauce over the top. Sprinkle nutritional yeast and red pepper flakes (if using) over the top. Garnish with fresh basil leaves before serving.

TOSTONES NACHOS
WITH CRUMBLED SPROUTED TOFU

Tostones is the Venezuelan name for plantain chips. Baked to crispy perfection, they make an excellent bed for my plant-based version of nachos. The tofu absorbs flavors from the adobo seasoning and the tomatillo sauce is spicy in the best way possible.

PREP TIME: **25 TO 30 MINUTES** // COOK TIME: **10 TO 12 MINUTES** // YIELD: **2 SERVINGS**

INGREDIENTS

8oz (225g) organic sprouted tofu

½ tbsp coconut oil

¾ to 1 tsp **Spicy Adobo Seasoning** (page 240)

¼ tsp coarse sea salt, plus more

½ cup shaved purple cabbage

2½ to 3 cups round **Plantain Chips** (page 222)

2 tbsp raw or roasted pepitas

microgreens or fresh cilantro

FOR THE SAUCE

1 tsp avocado oil

2 medium tomatillos, husked, rinsed, and halved

2 small scallions, quartered

½ medium jalapeño, stem removed

1 lime, halved

¼ tsp coarse sea salt, plus more

FOR THE PICO DE GALLO

2 vine-ripened tomatoes, diced small

2 to 3 tbsp minced red onions

2 tbsp finely chopped fresh cilantro

1 tsp freshly squeezed lime juice

¼ tsp coarse sea salt

1 In a cast-iron grill pan on the stovetop over medium-high heat, make the tomatillo sauce by brushing the pan with the avocado oil. Once very hot, add the tomatillos, scallions, jalapeño, and lime. Grill until slightly soft and charred, about 7 to 8 minutes, flipping halfway through.

2 Use a lemon squeezer to juice the grilled lime into a food processor. Add the tomatillo mixture and salt. Pulse until consistent. Taste and adjust seasoning. Set aside.

3 In a small bowl, make the pico de gallo by combining the tomatoes, onions, cilantro, lime juice, and salt. Mix well and set aside.

4 Place the tofu between paper towels and press to remove excess moisture. Transfer the tofu to a cutting board and crumble finely with a fork or potato masher.

5 In a small skillet on the stovetop, heat the coconut oil over medium heat. Add the tofu and spicy adobo seasoning, stirring often to prevent the tofu from sticking to the bottom of the skillet. Cook until the tofu has browned a little, about 3 to 4 minutes. Turn the heat off and stir in the salt. Taste and adjust seasoning.

6 Place the cabbage on the perimeter of a shallow bowl and add the plantain chips as the nachos, leaving a 2- to 3-inch (5 to 6.5cm) space in the center for some tofu. Sprinkle the remaining tofu over the chips and add the pico de gallo and pepitas. Place a few mounds of the tomatillo sauce around the plate. Garnish with microgreens or cilantro before serving.

» QUICK TIPS
Creamy Garlic Sauce (page 214) really shines over the nachos. Because plantain chips are best/crispiest right out of the oven, I suggest you make only as much as you need: 1 medium green plantain usually yields 1¼ to 1½ cups. Store the pico de gallo in an airtight container in the fridge for up to 2 days. Store the tomatillo sauce in a canning jar in the fridge for up to 1 week.

PAPAYA POKE STACKS
WITH WASABI SLAW

Papaya works unexpectedly well as a replacement for the raw fish usually in this Hawaiian dish. It beautifully absorbs the umami marinade and complements the cucumbers, mango, and avocado. The wasabi slaw is pleasantly spicy and adds a depth of flavor that works well in this dish!

PREP TIME: **10 TO 15 MINUTES** // COOK TIME: **NONE** // YIELD: **2 STACKS**

INGREDIENTS

2 tbsp tamari

2 tsp toasted sesame oil

1½ tsp freshly squeezed lemon juice

2 cups large-diced ripe papaya

1½ tbsp **Aquafaba Mayonnaise** (page 235)

½ tbsp maple syrup

½ tbsp rice vinegar

½ tsp grated fresh ginger

¼ to ½ tsp ground fresh wasabi

pinch of coarse sea salt, plus more

¾ cup shredded Savoy cabbage

¼ cup shredded daikon

2 tbsp thinly sliced scallions, divided

½ cup diced ripe mangoes

½ cup diced avocados

1 tbsp minced jalapeños or serrano peppers (optional)

¼ cup thinly sliced seeded Persian cucumbers

2 to 3 tsp **Furikake Seaweed Seasoning** (page 240)

1 In a large bowl, whisk together the tamari, sesame oil, and lemon juice. Add the papaya and gently toss with a spoonula to thoroughly coat with the marinade. Allow to rest for 10 to 15 minutes.

2 In a medium bowl, whisk together the aquafaba mayonnaise, maple syrup, rice vinegar, ginger, wasabi, and 1 pinch of salt. Add the cabbage, daikon, and 1 tablespoon of scallions. Toss until the vegetables are fully coated. Refrigerate covered until time to serve.

3 In a small bowl, combine the mangoes, avocados, and jalapeños (if using).

4 Build the stacks on 2 large plates by using a large steel food ring or mold (about 3½ inches [9cm] wide). Layer half the mango mixture and use a spoon or spatula to press down. Layer the cucumbers and press down again. Add the papaya chunks and press down once more. Allow the layers to mound above the food ring.

5 Divide the slaw onto the plates around the food ring. Sprinkle the furikake seaweed seasoning over the top. Carefully remove the ring. Garnish with the remaining 1 tablespoon of scallions before serving.

» QUICK TIPS
You can substitute freshly ground horseradish for the wasabi. If you're unable to find fresh wasabi, you can use ½ teaspoon of wasabi powder.

ANNATTO RICE
WITH KIDNEY BEANS & ROMANESCO FLORETS

People often joke about annatto being a poor man's saffron, but I strongly disagree! This spice lends a vibrant color and a sweet and peppery taste to this dish. Brown rice absorbs flavor from the aromatics and spices, while the kidney beans and Romanesco add great texture and density.

PREP TIME: **5 TO 7 MINUTES** // COOK TIME: **8 TO 9 MINUTES** // YIELD: **4 TO 6 SERVINGS**

INGREDIENTS

2 tbsp avocado oil, divided

8oz (225g) small Romanesco broccoli florets

½ tsp plus 2 pinches of coarse sea salt, divided, plus more

⅓ cup small-diced sweet onions

1 tbsp minced fresh garlic

½ cup diced celery

⅓ cup diced carrots

½ cup cored, seeded, and diced vine-ripened tomatoes

⅓ cup small-diced yellow bell peppers

1½ tsp ground annatto

2 cups cooked **Brown Rice** (page 242)

1 cup **Kidney Beans** (page 238)

2 tbsp **Vegetable Broth** (page 232)

¼ tsp ground black pepper

1 to 1½ tbsp finely chopped fresh flat-leaf parsley

1 In a large cast-iron skillet on the stovetop, heat 1 tablespoon of avocado oil over medium heat. Add the broccoli and sauté for 2 to 3 minutes, stirring often.

2 Transfer the broccoli to a large bowl. Sprinkle 2 pinches of salt over the top and toss to coat evenly. Set aside.

3 In the same skillet, heat the remaining 1 tablespoon of avocado oil. Add the onions and sauté for 1 minute.

4 Add the garlic, celery, and carrots. Cook for 2 minutes, stirring often.

5 Add the tomatoes, bell peppers, and annatto. Mix well to incorporate with the aromatics. Cook for 1 minute, stirring occasionally.

6 Add the rice, beans, broth, black pepper, and the remaining ½ teaspoon of sea salt. Cook until the rice and beans are heated through, about 2 to 3 minutes, stirring often.

7 Return the broccoli to the skillet and mix well. Taste and adjust seasoning.

8 Remove the skillet from the heat and sprinkle the parsley over the top before serving.

» QUICK TIPS

Save the Romanesco broccoli stalks and use as you would those of broccoli or cauliflower to make various recipes from this book. A little side of **Carrot-Top Chimichurri** (page 218) would bring so much brightness and flavor to this rice dish! Store leftovers in an airtight container in the fridge for up to 1 week.

CRISPY SPROUTED TOFU
WITH STIR-FRIED VEGETABLES

Compared with regular tofu, sprouted tofu is believed to contain higher levels of protein and calcium. When cooked until perfectly crispy, it delivers wonderful umami flavors lent by the seasoning blend and complements the texture and flavors of the vegetables in the stir-fry.

PREP TIME: **10 MINUTES** // COOK TIME: **16 TO 18 MINUTES** // YIELD: **4 SERVINGS**

INGREDIENTS

1½ tbsp **Umami Mushroom Powder** (page 240)

½ tsp plus 2 pinches of coarse sea salt, divided, plus more

16oz (450g) extra-firm organic sprouted tofu, cubed and pressed

3 tbsp unrefined coconut oil, divided

½ cup julienned white onions

½ cup thinly sliced celery

½ cup julienned red bell peppers

½ cup julienned green bell peppers

3 garlic cloves, grated

⅔ cup sugar snap peas, cut in half lengthwise

4 cups zucchini noodles (2 large zucchini spiralized)

2 tbsp **Furikake Seaweed Seasoning** (page 240)

2 tbsp microgreens or thinly sliced scallion greens

FOR THE SAUCE

¼ cup tamari (or coconut aminos)

1½ tbsp maple syrup

1 tbsp freshly squeezed lime juice

1 On a large plate, combine the mushroom powder and ¼ teaspoon of salt. Add the tofu and carefully toss to coat. Marinate for at least 5 minutes.

2 In a small bowl, make the sauce by whisking together the tamari, maple syrup, and lime juice. Set aside.

3 In a large cast-iron skillet on the stovetop, heat 1 tablespoon of coconut oil over medium-high heat. Once the oil starts to smoke, add the tofu and sauté for 7 minutes, flipping to sear on all sides. Reduce the heat to low and cook for 3 minutes more, stirring often. (This allows the tofu to dry out a little more.) Transfer to a platter in a single layer and set aside.

4 In the same skillet, heat the remaining 2 tablespoons of coconut oil over medium heat. Add the onions and sauté for 1 to 2 minutes, stirring often. Add the celery, red and green bell peppers, garlic, and peas. Sauté for 3 to 4 minutes more, stirring often.

5 Add the zucchini noodles. Season with the remaining ¼ teaspoon and 2 pinches of salt. Use kitchen tongs or cooking chopsticks to carefully separate the noodles while they cook for 2 minutes. Add the sauce to the skillet and quickly toss until the vegetables are evenly coated. Remove the skillet from the heat.

6 Place equal amounts of the stir-fry on 4 large plates and top each with an equal amount of tofu. Use a spoon to scoop up any sauce left in the skillet and drizzle over the top of the tofu. Sprinkle the furikake seasoning over the top. Garnish with the microgreens or scallions before serving.

> **» QUICK TIP**
> To press the tofu, cut it into 1-inch (2.5cm) cubes and place them in a single layer on a flat surface lined with a clean towel. Cover with another clean towel, set a baking tray on top, and place something heavy, like a Dutch oven or a cast-iron pan, on the baking tray. Keep pressed for about 15 minutes.

ZUCCHINI NOODLES & GRILLED PORTOBELLO STEAKS

Inspired by a Peruvian dish called *Tallarines Verdes con Bistec* (green noodles with steak), this dish is just gorgeous. Portobello mushrooms are the perfect vessel for a flavor-rich marinade. The creamy green sauce slathers the zucchini noodles, infusing them with deep flavors.

PREP TIME: **10 MINUTES** // COOK TIME: **5 TO 6 MINUTES** // YIELD: **2 SERVINGS**

INGREDIENTS

1 tsp grated fresh garlic

1 tsp nutritional yeast

¾ tsp coarse sea salt, divided, plus more

¼ tsp ground black pepper

½ tsp dried basil

½ tsp dried oregano

2 tbsp avocado oil, plus more

2 tbsp freshly squeezed lemon juice, divided

2 large portobello mushroom caps (about 8oz [225g] total)

1 small radicchio

2½ quarts (2½ liters) water

2 medium zucchini (about 1lb [450g] total)

fresh basil

FOR THE SAUCE

1 cup packed spinach

¼ cup fresh flat-leaf parsley

¼ cup fresh basil

¼ cup roughly chopped leeks

2 tbsp tahini paste

2 tbsp extra-virgin olive oil

2 tbsp plant-based milk

1 tbsp freshly squeezed lemon juice

¼ tsp coarse sea salt, plus more

1 In a small bowl, whisk together the garlic, nutritional yeast, ½ teaspoon of salt, pepper, basil, oregano, avocado oil, and lemon juice until a soft paste forms.

2 Cut the stems from the mushrooms to create flat surfaces for the pan. Cut the radicchio into 2 wedges. Place the mushrooms and radicchio on a baking tray. Rub the marinade over the mushrooms and radicchio, coating all the surfaces. Marinate for at least 10 minutes.

3 Place a cast-iron grill pan on the stovetop over medium heat. Brush the pan with a little avocado oil to keep the vegetables from sticking. Once the pan is very hot, add the mushrooms and radicchio. Grill until tender and some grill marks appear, about 4 to 5 minutes, turning halfway through. Transfer the mushrooms and radicchio to a cutting board. Slice the mushrooms ¾ inch (2cm) thick. Set aside.

4 In a high-powered blender, make the green sauce by processing on high all the ingredients until creamy and smooth. Taste and adjust seasoning.

5 Use a spiralizer to turn the zucchini into noodles.

6 In a medium saucepan on the stovetop over medium-high heat, bring the water to a boil. Stir in the remaining ¼ teaspoon of salt. Add the zucchini and poach for 1 minute or less depending on noodle thickness. Drain with a mesh strainer and transfer back to the saucepan. Drizzle the green sauce over the noodles and stir gently with a spoonula to thoroughly coat.

7 Use a fork to roll the noodles into mounds and divide them evenly on 2 shallow plates. Use a spoon to add any remaining green sauce to the noodles. Use a spatula to transfer an equal amount of the mushrooms and radicchio to each plate. Garnish with fresh basil before serving.

QUINOA-STUFFED PEPPERS

I learned all about stuffed peppers from Mama Irene, my mother-in-law, whose recipe inspired this dish. I've used eggplant and lentils to add a comforting and satiating meatiness to the stuffing. I also added quinoa because it's a nutrition powerhouse that has great texture.

PREP TIME: **15 TO 20 MINUTES** // COOK TIME: **49 TO 52 MINUTES** // YIELD: **4 PEPPERS**

INGREDIENTS

4 large bell peppers (any colors)

3 quarts (3 liters) water

1½ tsp plus 2 pinches of coarse sea salt, divided

2 tbsp coconut oil

⅔ cup small-diced celery

⅔ cup thinly sliced scallions

2 large garlic cloves, minced

1 cup small-diced Japanese eggplant

½ cup small-diced tomato cores

¼ tsp ground annatto

¼ tsp ground coriander

¼ tsp ground black pepper

1¼ cups cooked **Quinoa** (page 242)

1 cup cooked **Green Lentils** (page 239)

2 tbsp **Vegetable Broth** (page 232)

2 cups red dandelion leaves

1 cup Swiss chard leaves

½ tbsp extra-virgin olive oil

½ tbsp balsamic vinegar

FOR THE JAM

1 lb (450g) ripe Roma tomatoes

¼ cup coconut sugar

1½ tbsp apple cider vinegar

1 tbsp blackstrap molasses

½ tbsp stone-ground mustard

¼ tsp coarse sea salt

¼ tsp ground cinnamon

1 To make the jam, core the tomatoes (and save for the quinoa mixture) and roughly chop the flesh. In a small saucepan on the stovetop over medium heat, add the tomatoes and the remaining jam ingredients. Bring to a boil, stirring often, then reduce the heat to low. Simmer until the liquids have evaporated and the jam is thick and sticky, about 25 minutes, stirring occasionally. Remove the saucepan from the heat and allow the jam to cool.

2 Preheat the oven to 375°F (190°C).

3 Cut off about ¾ inch (2cm) from the top of the peppers and remove all the seeds and white membranes. In a medium saucepan on the stovetop over medium-high heat, bring the water to a boil. Stir in 1 teaspoon of salt. Add the peppers and poach for 2 minutes. Use a mesh ladle to transfer the peppers to a baking tray lined with a clean kitchen towel. Keep the saucepan covered on the stovetop at a very low heat.

4 In a large sauté pan on the stovetop, heat the coconut oil over medium heat. Add the celery, scallions, and garlic. Sauté for 1 minute, stirring often. Stir in the Japanese eggplant and cook for 2 minutes.

5 Add the tomato cores, annatto, coriander, black pepper, and ½ teaspoon of salt. Cook for 2 minutes, stirring often. Add the quinoa, lentils, and broth. Cook for 2 minutes more, stirring occasionally.

6 Place the peppers in a glass baking dish. Stuff the peppers with the quinoa mixture and use a spoon or spatula to compact the filling as you go. Place the dish on the top rack in the oven and bake until the peppers are tender, about 15 to 18 minutes. Remove the dish from the oven and set aside.

7 Add the dandelion leaves and Swiss chard to the simmering saucepan. Poach for 1 minute, then strain. Transfer to a large bowl. Drizzle the olive oil and balsamic vinegar over the top. Season with the remaining 2 pinches of salt.

8 Place the peppers on 4 plates. Top each with a mound of leaves and chard as well as 1 to 1½ tablespoons of tomato jam. Serve immediately.

CAULIFLOWER STEAKS
WITH HERBED SUCCOTASH

Besides cauliflower's great aesthetic, this cruciferous vegetable has a desirable texture and the ability to carry flavors—all you want in a great "steak." Roasting it adds crispiness to a dish that contrasts the various consistencies of the succotash: crunchy, soft, and bitey.

PREP TIME: **7 TO 10 MINUTES** // COOK TIME: **26 TO 27 MINUTES** // YIELD: **2 TO 3 STEAKS**

INGREDIENTS

2½ tbsp avocado oil, divided

½ tsp smoked paprika

½ tsp ground coriander

1 tsp coarse sea salt, divided

½ tsp ground black pepper, divided

2 to 3 cauliflower steaks (about ¾ to 1 inch [2 to 2.5cm] thick)

¼ cup small-diced white onions

2 garlic cloves, minced

1 cup fresh corn kernels (from 1 ear of corn)

2½ tbsp small-diced green bell peppers

¼ cup fresh English peas

¼ cup diced ripe heirloom tomatoes

2 tbsp **Vegetable Broth** (page 232)

2 tbsp fresh basil chiffonade (see Quick Tips), divided

1 scallion, thinly sliced

1 Preheat the oven to 425°F (220°C).

2 In a small bowl or ramekin, whisk together 1½ tablespoons of avocado oil, paprika, coriander, ½ teaspoon of salt, and ¼ teaspoon of black pepper.

3 Place the cauliflower steaks on a baking tray and drizzle the avocado oil marinade over the top. Rub with clean hands or use a brush to coat the steaks thoroughly on both sides.

4 Place the tray on the top rack in the oven and roast until golden brown and crispy on the edges, about 20 minutes, gently flipping with a spatula halfway through. Remove the tray from the oven and keep the steaks on the tray until ready to serve.

5 In a large skillet on the stovetop, heat the remaining 1 tablespoon of avocado oil over medium heat. Add the onions and sauté for 1 to 2 minutes, stirring often. Add the garlic and corn. Sauté for 3 minutes, stirring occasionally.

6 Add the bell peppers, the remaining ½ teaspoon of salt, and the remaining ¼ teaspoon of black pepper. Add the peas, tomatoes, and broth. Cook for 2 minutes, stirring often and making sure to deglaze any bits from the bottom of the pan. Turn off the heat. Stir in 1 tablespoon of basil chiffonade and the scallions. Mix well.

7 Divide the succotash evenly onto 2 to 3 plates and garnish with the remaining 1 tablespoon of basil chiffonade. Add a cauliflower steak to each plate before serving.

> **» QUICK TIPS**
> Save the remaining florets for **Cauliflower Ceviche with Coconut & Passion Fruit Marinade** (page 156) and use the leaves and stalks to make **Cauliflower Leafstalk Kimchi** (page 226). To make basil chiffonade, roll 6 large basil leaves together and cut the leaves into ribbons. Store the succotash in an airtight container in the fridge for up to 5 days.

JACKFRUIT & LEAFSTALK TACOS
WITH AVOCADO & RADISH GREENS CREMA

Jícama forms the taco shells for this dish. I've upcycled cauliflower leafstalks to add a crunchy texture to the shredded jackfruit. These tacos are so good yet very easy (and quick!) to make. The avocado–radish crema pairs well with the piquant radishes and spicy jalapeños.

PREP TIME: **7 TO 10 MINUTES** // COOK TIME: **4 TO 5 MINUTES** // YIELD: **8 TO 12 TACOS**

INGREDIENTS

2 tbsp unrefined coconut oil

¼ cup shaved or finely julienned brown onions

1 cup finely sliced cauliflower leafstalks

¼ cup shaved or finely julienned green bell peppers

1 tbsp finely minced fresh garlic

1½ tsp **Spicy Adobo Seasoning** (page 240)

½ tsp coarse sea salt

1 cup cooked **Green Jackfruit** (page 234)

8 to 12 jícama tortillas (see Quick Tips)

2 radishes, thinly sliced

1 small jalapeño, thinly sliced (optional)

2 tbsp finely chopped fresh cilantro

Avocado Seed Powder (page 231)

FOR THE CREMA

1 Hass avocado, peeled, seeded, and quartered

⅓ cup radish greens

3 tbsp freshly squeezed lemon juice

¼ tsp coarse sea salt

1 In a large cast-iron skillet on the stovetop, heat the coconut oil over medium-high heat. Add the onions and sauté for 1 minute, stirring often. Add the cauliflower leafstalks, bell peppers, and garlic. Sauté for 1 minute, stirring often.

2 Reduce the heat to medium. Stir in the adobo seasoning and salt. Mix well until the aromatics are evenly coated.

3 Add the jackfruit and cook for 2 to 3 minutes, mixing well and breaking the shreds with the back of a wooden spoon. Remove the skillet from the heat and set aside.

4 In a tall blending cup or wide-mouthed glass jar, make the avocado and radish greens crema by using an immersion blender to process all the ingredients until smooth and creamy.

5 Place the jícama tortillas on a tray or platter. Add an equal amount of the jackfruit and leafstalk filling to each tortilla. Top each taco with hefty dollops of the crema as well as the radishes, jalapeños (if using), and cilantro. Sprinkle the avocado seed powder over the top before serving.

> **» QUICK TIPS**
> Use cauliflower leafstalks as well as leaves to prepare this recipe. If you're unable to source fresh jackfruit, use canned green jackfruit to make this dish. Just drain and rinse before adding to the pan. Use a mandoline on its lowest setting to finely slice the jícama (almost paper-thin) to create tortillas for the tacos. You can substitute these tortillas with corn or flour tortillas, preferably organic. These tacos pair perfectly with **Domino Rice & Beans** (page 115).

SWEET POTATO TACOS
WITH COLLARD GREENS SHELLS

To diversify your culinary palette, use new ingredients to make food fun. Collard greens have folate and vitamins C and K—and their bright green color makes a beautiful shell for tacos. Savory sweet potatoes are balanced by the tangy lime-marinated purple cabbage and spicy Fresno peppers.

PREP TIME: **5 TO 10 MINUTES** // COOK TIME: **9 MINUTES** // YIELD: **6 TACOS**

INGREDIENTS

6 small collard greens leaves

2½ quarts (2½ liters) water

1 tsp plus 1 to 2 pinches of coarse sea salt, divided

½ cup shredded purple cabbage

2 to 3 tbsp freshly squeezed lime juice

1½ tbsp coconut oil

½ cup diced brown onions

2 garlic cloves, minced

½ tsp ground coriander

½ tsp ancho chili powder

2 cups large-diced peeled sweet potatoes

¼ tsp ground black pepper

¼ cup **Cashew Cream** (page 230)

1 Easter egg radish, thinly sliced

2 to 3 tbsp thinly sliced Fresno peppers

microgreens or fresh herbs

2 to 4 small lime wedges

1 Cut the base off the leaves to remove the stems. In a medium saucepan on the stovetop over medium-high heat, bring the water to a boil. Stir in ½ teaspoon of salt. Add the leaves and poach until slightly wilted, about 20 to 30 seconds. Use a mesh skimmer to transfer the leaves to a baking tray lined with a clean kitchen towel to absorb as much water as possible.

2 In a small bowl, combine the purple cabbage, lime juice, and 1 to 2 pinches of salt. Toss to coat and set aside.

3 In a cast-iron skillet on the stovetop, heat the coconut oil over medium heat. Add the onions and sauté for 2 minutes, stirring often. Add the garlic and sauté for 30 seconds. Add the coriander and ancho chili powder. Stir until the aromatics evenly coat the vegetables.

4 Stir in the sweet potatoes, pepper, and the remaining ½ teaspoon of salt. Cook until golden and tender, about 6 minutes, stirring often. Taste and adjust seasoning.

5 To assemble the tacos, place the collard greens leaves on 2 to 3 plates. Divide the sweet potatoes evenly among the shells. Top with dollops of cashew cream and cabbage slaw. Top with the radish and Fresno peppers. Garnish with microgreens or fresh herbs. Serve immediately with the lime wedges.

» QUICK TIPS

Small collard greens leaves are generally rounder (and often found at farmers markets across the United States). You can use larger leaves and cut them into 2 even pieces to use as taco shells. Add collard greens stems to your vegetable scraps bag for later use. Use the pot of boiling water to blanch hearty greens or to cook any other vegetables and grains for the week. These tacos pair perfectly with a side of **Domino Rice & Beans** (page 115) or **Corn Lollipops with Chipotle & Tofu Cream Sauce** (page 128).

CHAPTER 11
BEVERAGES

182 Chunky Tropical Fruit Tizana

184 Tamarind Juice

185 Strawberry-Top Spritzer

186 Cinnamon-Spiced Brown Rice Smoothie

188 Loaded Breakfast Smoothie

189 Cocada Smoothie

190 Papaya Milkshakes

192 Spiced Hibiscus Tea

193 Watermelon Limeade

194 Maca & Cacao Latte

CHUNKY TROPICAL FRUIT TIZANA

I can't recall ever attending a kids party in Venezuela where tizana wasn't served. For this version, I used fresh pomegranate juice instead of grenadine to avoid processed ingredients and refined sugars. Adjust this recipe according to the seasonal fruits available to you.

PREP TIME: **7 TO 10 MINUTES** // COOK TIME: **NONE** // YIELD: **6 TO 8 SERVINGS**

INGREDIENTS

2 cups pomegranate seeds (from 1 medium-sized pomegranate)

¾ cup diced mangoes

¾ cup diced seedless watermelon

¾ cup diced Galia melon

¾ cup diced bananas

¾ cup halved green seedless grapes

4 cups freshly squeezed orange juice (from about 12 medium navel oranges)

¼ cup freshly squeezed lime juice

1 In a blender, process the pomegranate seeds until the arils have been crushed but the seeds remain mostly intact, about 10 to 15 seconds. Strain through a mesh sieve and press down with a spatula to get the most juice out of the pulp.

2 In a large punch bowl or pitcher, combine the mangoes, watermelon, Galia melon, bananas, and grapes. Stir in the pomegranate juice, orange juice, and lime juice. Allow to rest for at least 15 minutes.

3 Ladle the diced fruit and juice into 6 to 8 glasses. Serve immediately.

» QUICK TIPS

You can add ice cubes to the punch bowl to keep the tizana cool. You can also make this ahead and refrigerate overnight. Use other fruits according to season and availability (like apple, strawberries, pineapple, etc.).

TAMARIND JUICE

I grew up considering tamarind a fruit, but it's actually a legume (like lentils and string beans!). In Venezuela, it's often used to make juices and sweet treats as well as to flavor ice pops and shaved ice. In the United States, tamarind is featured in *aguas frescas* (fresh flavored waters).

PREP TIME: **7 TO 10 MINUTES** // COOK TIME: **NONE** // YIELD: **4 TO 6 SERVINGS**

INGREDIENTS

12 large tamarind pods

5 cups water

4 dates

1 quart (1 liter) filtered cold water

1 to 2 tsp chia seeds

1 Remove the outer shell from the pods and any strings surrounding the pulp of the fruit.

2 In a medium saucepan over medium-high heat, bring the water to a boil, then turn the heat off. In a glass jar, combine the dates and 1 cup of the hot water.

3 Add the tamarind pods to the saucepan and soak in the remaining 4 cups of hot water for 1½ to 2 hours.

4 With a mesh ladle, transfer the tamarind pods to a bowl or platter. Reserve the poaching water. Use clean hands to squeeze out the seeds and remove any remaining strings.

5 Once the dates have soaked for at least 10 minutes, strain and allow to cool slightly. Peel off the skins, remove the pits, and set aside.

6 In a high-powered blender, combine the tamarind pulp, dates, and reserved poaching water. Process for about 30 to 45 seconds. Use a fine mesh sieve to strain the liquid and transfer to a pitcher.

7 Add the cold water and chia seeds. Mix well with a wooden spoon. Cover the pitcher and refrigerate for at least 30 minutes. Serve cold.

» QUICK TIP

Save the tamarind shells, strings, and seeds for your compost pile.

STRAWBERRY-TOP SPRITZER

In the low-carbon kitchen, we don't let food go to waste, especially if we can upcycle ingredients like strawberry tops to make this spritzer. Strawberry leaves contain iron, calcium, and vitamin C. The top of the fruit also contains the same nutrients as the fruit itself, so why discard it?

PREP TIME: **5 MINUTES** // COOK TIME: **NONE** // YIELD: **1 TO 2 SERVINGS**

INGREDIENTS

1 cup strawberry tops, greens included

1½ tbsp maple syrup, plus more

1 tbsp freshly squeezed lime juice

2¼ to 2½ cups cold carbonated (sparkling) water

2 strips of lime peel

1 In a high-powered blender, process on high the strawberry tops, maple syrup, and lime juice until a smooth purée forms.

2 Pour or spoon the purée into 1 tall or 2 short glasses and top with the carbonated water. Stir well. Taste and adjust the sweetness.

3 Add a few ice cubes and garnish with the lime peel before serving.

» QUICK TIPS

High-powered blenders should yield a smooth purée that doesn't need straining. However, you can use a mesh sieve if needed. You might need to use the blender's tamper to push down the strawberry tops into the blades.

CINNAMON-SPICED BROWN RICE SMOOTHIE

A rice smoothie is known as *chicha* in Venezuela and it's somewhat similar to but thicker than *horchata* (a Mexican rice drink). This version is plant-based, free of refined sugar, and made with brown rice, which still contains the germ and bran (the most nutritious parts of the grain).

PREP TIME: **5 MINUTES** // COOK TIME: **NONE** // YIELD: **2 SERVINGS**

INGREDIENTS

1 cup cooked **Brown Rice** (page 242)

1 cup plant-based milk, plus more

2 tbsp coconut sugar

1 tbsp raw shelled hempseeds

½ tsp pure vanilla extract

½ cup small ice cubes

½ tsp ground cinnamon

1 In a high-powered blender, combine the brown rice, plant-based milk, coconut sugar, hempseeds, vanilla extract, and ice cubes. Process on high until smooth and creamy. Add milk 1 tablespoon at a time to reach your desired consistency.

2 Transfer the smoothies to 2 short glasses and sprinkle the cinnamon over the top. Stir and serve immediately.

> **» QUICK TIP**
> This smoothie is traditionally thick and has a grainy texture (think LOTS of fiber!). You can run the mixture through a mesh sieve and push with a spatula to get a finer, thinner texture if desired.

LOADED BREAKFAST SMOOTHIE

This is an easy and delicious way to get nutrients fast and conveniently. It's mildly sweet and has a creaminess from the cashew butter. It offers a great opportunity to use ripe or overly ripe fruits that might have been wasted. Hempseeds and flaxseeds add extra nutrition for a productive day!

PREP TIME: **3 MINUTES** // COOK TIME: **NONE** // YIELD: **1 TO 2 SERVINGS**

INGREDIENTS

2 small very ripe fresh or frozen bananas (about 3oz [90g] each)

2 cups baby spinach

1/2 cup fresh or frozen blackberries

1/2 cup fresh or frozen blueberries

1/2 cup plant-based milk

1 tbsp cashew butter

1 tbsp shelled hempseeds

1 tsp ground flaxseeds

2 to 3 ice cubes (optional)

1 In a high-powered blender, process all the ingredients until creamy and smooth. Add cold water 1 tablespoon at a time to thin out the mixture.

2 Pour into 1 or 2 glasses. Add the ice cubes (if using) before serving.

» **QUICK TIP**

When fresh bananas get very ripe (and I'm talking about their peels having lots of black spots), I like to peel and quarter them before freezing them in a reusable freezer bag for later use. This is an easy way to avoid food waste and to use them for something delicious!

COCADA SMOOTHIE

When we went to the beach in La Guaira near Caracas, my family stopped at a roadside food vendor who made *cocadas* (young coconut smoothies). He'd crack a coconut open with a machete, pour the water into a blender, scrape the young meat, and add some sugar to make this drink.

PREP TIME: **5 TO 10 MINUTES** // COOK TIME: **NONE** // YIELD: **1 TO 2 SERVINGS**

INGREDIENTS

1 fresh young coconut

1 tbsp maple syrup, plus more (optional)

1 Use the bottom corner of the blade of a meat cleaver to make the first cut on the top of the young coconut. You should hold the cleaver at about a 45-degree angle from the incision point. This cut should be approximately 2 inches (5cm) long and made 1 to 1½ inches (2.5 to 3.75cm) below the center tip on the top of the coconut.

2 Make the next three cuts perpendicular to the previous cut. All four cuts should create a square that will act as the "door" to open the coconut. Keep the coconut upright and use the base of the cleaver or a chef's knife to pull the "door" open. Pour the coconut water into a glass or a jar. (You should get about 1½ to 1¾ cups of coconut water.)

3 Turn the coconut on its side and use the meat cleaver's bottom corner to make a deep incision on the side of the coconut. Make enough incisions on the same side to crack it open. If the coconut gets stuck to the knife, hit the coconut against the working surface enough times to split it open.

4 Use a spoon, scraper, or grapefruit spoon to scrape the soft white flesh out of the shell. Inspect the flesh (and even rinse with water if needed) in case any pieces of hard shell remain attached while cracking the coconut open.

5 In a high-powered blender, combine the coconut water, coconut flesh, and maple syrup (if using). Cover tightly and process on high until creamy and consistent. (Depending on the kind of high-powered blender you use, you might not need to strain the smoothie. However, if any solid particles make it feel mealy, pass through a mesh strainer and use a spatula to push down and get the most liquids from the coconut meat.) Taste and adjust sweetness to your liking. Pour the smoothie into 1 or 2 glasses and serve immediately over ice.

> **» QUICK TIPS**
> Most US markets sell young coconuts with the green skin already removed. You'll likely find them in the refrigerated section of the produce department— covered in plastic wrap and with a flat enough base to stand on their own. If you find whole young coconuts (welcome to my world!), use a large knife or a meat cleaver to remove this outer skin and expose the soft fibrous layer that surrounds the hard coconut shell (where the water is!).

PAPAYA MILKSHAKES

My mama would make this often when I was a kid. I remember getting a papaya milkshake in the mornings when I was rushing off to university. The fruit grows really big in Venezuela—up to 2 feet long—and because it's quite affordable, we always had plenty in the house.

PREP TIME: **5 MINUTES** // COOK TIME: **NONE** // YIELD: **2 SERVINGS**

INGREDIENTS

1 to 2 large pitted dates

½ cup boiling water

2½ cups diced ripe papaya

½ cup plant-based milk

¾ cup small ice cubes

1 In a small bowl, combine the dates and water. Soak for 10 minutes. Strain and allow to cool. Peel off the skins.

2 In a blender, process on high the dates, papaya, plant-based milk, and ice cubes until smooth.

3 Transfer to 2 glasses and serve immediately.

> **» QUICK TIPS**
> Depending on how ripe and sweet the papaya, you'll need 1 or 2 dates (or none at all!). Save the papaya seeds! Minimize food waste and prepare **Papaya Seed Powder** (page 231). Store the milkshakes in an airtight container in the fridge for 2 to 3 days. Whisk before enjoying.

SPICED HIBISCUS TEA

This tea has a beautiful color and a delicious tart flavor from dried hibiscus petals. Warm spices lend comforting flavors and aromas, plus antioxidants and healthful compounds. In Latin America, people drink hibiscus tea for its medicinal properties, which include lowering blood pressure.

PREP TIME: **2 MINUTES** // COOK TIME: **NONE** // YIELD: **2 TO 4 SERVINGS**

INGREDIENTS

¾ cup loose whole hibiscus flowers

2 cinnamon sticks (about 3 inches [7.5cm] long)

2 whole star anise pods

10 whole allspice berries

1 quart (1 liter) or 4 cups water

1 to 2 tsp maple or date syrup (optional)

1 In the strainer basket of a teapot, combine the hibiscus flowers, cinnamon sticks, anise pods, and allspice berries.

2 In a medium saucepan on the stovetop over medium-high heat, bring the water to a boil. Add the water to the teapot. Cover and steep for 5 minutes.

3 Strain the tea solids and pour the tea into 2 to 4 cups. Taste and sweeten with maple syrup (if using) before serving.

» QUICK TIPS

If you're using cut or cut-and-sifted hibiscus flowers instead of whole, you might only need ⅓ cup. If you don't have a teapot, add the flowers and spices to a small pot with boiling water. Stir, cover, and turn the heat off. Steep for 5 minutes and strain the tea using a small mesh strainer. For cold-brew hibiscus tea, use room temperature water and steep the hibiscus flowers and spices for 12 hours in the refrigerator. Strain and enjoy cold. You can reuse the spices 2 to 3 times before they lose their flavor. Simply rinse them under hot water and allow to dry completely.

WATERMELON LIMEADE

This drink is yummy and refreshing, with sweet flavors from fresh watermelon and tartness from fresh lime juice. I love making two batches and keeping a large jar of this limeade in the fridge, where it doesn't last long. Only use maple syrup if the melon isn't sweet enough for your taste.

PREP TIME: **5 MINUTES** // COOK TIME: **NONE** // YIELD: **4 SERVINGS**

INGREDIENTS

2lb (1kg) peeled seedless watermelon, chopped (about 4 to 5 cups)

juice from 2 large limes

½ to 1 tbsp maple syrup (optional)

4 lime slices

1 In a blender, process the watermelon and lime juice on high until smooth. Pass the mixture through a mesh strainer to remove any solids. Taste and sweeten with maple syrup (if using).

2 Add ice cubes to 4 glasses and pour the limeade over the top. Garnish with a lime slice before serving.

» QUICK TIP
Avoid food waste and shrink your carbon footprint! Save the watermelon rinds to make **Lime-Pickled Onions & Watermelon Rinds** (page 227).

MACA & CACAO LATTE

Maca root and cacao powder add protein, fiber, vitamins, and minerals to this drink. Maca has an earthy taste and grainy texture that's balanced by the bitter cacao. Plant-based milk and comforting spices make this latte perfect to enjoy while reading a book on a cold morning.

PREP TIME: **2 MINUTES** // COOK TIME: **1 TO 2 MINUTES** // YIELD: **1 SERVING**

INGREDIENTS

1 cup plant-based milk

1 tbsp maca powder

1 tsp unsweetened cacao powder (preferably fair trade organic)

¼ tsp ground cinnamon

2 pinches of ground nutmeg

pinch of ground cardamom

1 tsp maple syrup (optional)

1 In a small saucepan on the stovetop, heat the plant-based milk over medium heat until it just starts to boil. Add the remaining ingredients and whisk until frothy.

2 Pour the latte into a coffee cup and serve immediately.

CHAPTER 12
DESSERTS

198 Quinoa Pudding

200 Cacao & Nut Truffles

201 Berry & Banana Sorbet

202 Mango & Coconut Sorbet

204 Pineapple Frozen Yogurt

205 Chocolate & Garbanzo Cookies

206 Buñuelos (Yuca Beignets) with Cacao Dipping Sauce

208 Yam & Maca Truffles

209 Leguminous Chocolate Pudding

210 Cantaloupe & Prickly Pear Ice Pops

QUINOA PUDDING

This nutritious and low-carbon take on a traditional rice pudding is made with quinoa, which is rich in protein (with all 9 essential amino acids) and contains healthy fats, minerals, and vitamins. This pudding is infused with fragrant spices and sweetened with molasses and maple syrup.

PREP TIME: **2 MINUTES** // COOK TIME: **26 MINUTES** // YIELD: **4 SERVINGS**

INGREDIENTS

1½ cups plant-based milk

2 whole star anise pods

4 whole allspice berries

2 cups cooked **Quinoa** (page 242)

1 tbsp blackstrap molasses

1 tbsp maple syrup

¼ cup **Cashew Cream** (page 230)

¼ cup raisins

½ tsp ground cinnamon

1 In a medium saucepan on the stovetop over medium heat, combine the plant-based milk, anise pods, and allspice berries. Cook until the milk starts to boil, about 4 minutes.

2 Add the quinoa, blackstrap molasses, and maple syrup. Stir well, then reduce the heat to low. Cook uncovered until the quinoa is soft and the mixture is dense, about 20 minutes, stirring occasionally.

3 Add the cashew cream and raisins. Mix until all the ingredients are well incorporated. Cook until creamy and thick, about 2 minutes more. Remove the saucepan from the heat. Remove the star anise and allspice berries from the mixture. (Don't discard them. See Quick Tip.)

4 Transfer the pudding to 4 bowls and sprinkle the cinnamon over the top. Serve immediately or at room temperature.

> **» QUICK TIP**
> You can reuse the spices two to three times before they lose their flavor. Simply rinse them under hot water and allow them to dry completely.

CACAO & NUT TRUFFLES

Dessert has never been this healthy and guilt-free! The sweetness of dates plays beautifully with the mild bitterness of cacao—the flavor combo makes me think of strong black chocolate, which is my favorite. These truffles are rich in antioxidants, healthy fats, fiber, and lots of YUM.

PREP TIME: *7 MINUTES* // COOK TIME: *NONE* // YIELD: *10 TO 12 TRUFFLES*

INGREDIENTS

5 to 6 large pitted dates

1 cup boiling water

4 tbsp unsweetened cacao powder (preferably fair trade organic), divided

½ cup raw cashews

¼ cup raw walnuts

2 tbsp rolled oats

1½ tbsp **Coconut Cream** (page 230)

1 In a medium bowl, combine the dates and water. Soak for 10 minutes. Strain and allow to cool slightly. Peel the skins.

2 In a food processor, combine the dates, 3 tablespoons of cacao powder, cashews, walnuts, oats, and coconut cream. Process on high until all the ingredients are well incorporated and a thick paste has formed. Separate the mixture into 10 to 12 equal portions and use clean hands to shape the dough into balls.

3 In a small bowl, place the remaining 1 tablespoon of cacao powder. Roll the balls in the powder to coat.

4 Refrigerate covered for at least 30 minutes before serving.

BERRY & BANANA SORBET

Seasonal berries make the healthiest and most colorful desserts! They're rich in healthful antioxidants that prevent cellular damage caused by free radicals. They can also help us combat inflammation—our body's way of battling infection or injuries. Talk about small but powerful!

PREP TIME: **2 MINUTES** // COOK TIME: **NONE** // YIELD: **2 SERVINGS**

INGREDIENTS

1 cup frozen blackberries

½ cup frozen raspberries

½ cup frozen blueberries

1 small frozen ripe banana

¼ cup plant-based milk

1 tbsp maple syrup, plus more

1 In a high-powered blender, process on high all the ingredients until smooth and consistent. Taste and adjust sweetness.

2 Divide the sorbet into 2 bowls and serve immediately.

» QUICK TIPS

Freeze overly ripe bananas and use them to give this sorbet the right amount of body and sweetness. Get your fresh berries at the farmers market! Rinse and allow them to air dry before using. Place them in reusable silicone storage bags and store in the freezer for up to 1 year. If the sorbet seems a little runny after processing, place the bowls in the freezer for 5 to 10 minutes.

MANGO & COCONUT SORBET

This creamy and tropical frozen treat brightens your day! The chia seeds offer heart-healthy fats, protein, and more. Did you know mangoes and cashews are related? Cousins, so to speak. They make an appearance in this dish (with one disguised in a make-ahead ingredient).

PREP TIME: **2 MINUTES** // COOK TIME: **NONE** // YIELD: **2 SERVINGS**

INGREDIENTS

2 cups cubed frozen mangoes (see Quick Tips)

½ cup **Coconut Cream** (page 230)

½ tbsp chia seeds

2 to 4 tbsp plant-based milk (optional)

fresh berries (like raspberries or blackberries) (optional)

1 In a high-powered blender, process on high the mangoes, coconut cream, chia seeds, and plant-based milk (if using) until smooth. If the blender gets stuck, add milk 1 tablespoon at a time until it runs smoothly.

2 Transfer the sorbet mixture to 2 bowls and top with fresh berries (if using) before serving.

> **» QUICK TIPS**
> Peel, seed, and cube the fresh ripe mangoes. Place them in a reusable silicone storage bag and freeze. If the mangoes aren't sweet enough, add a little maple syrup to the mixture. If the sorbet becomes a little runny after processing, place the bowls in the freezer for 5 to 10 minutes.

PINEAPPLE FROZEN YOGURT

Being able to make frozen treats in a jiffy is one of the perks of investing in a high-quality blender. Pineapple is rich in vitamin C and manganese, which gives me a great excuse to make this dish— the other being that it's DELICIOUS! The **Cultured Cashew Yogurt** features gut-healthy probiotics.

PREP TIME: **2 MINUTES** // COOK TIME: **NONE** // YIELD: **2 SERVINGS**

INGREDIENTS

½ cup (4 to 6 cubes) frozen **Cultured Cashew Yogurt** (page 235)

2½ cups frozen pineapple chunks (see Quick Tips)

1 to 2 tbsp coconut sugar

fresh berries (like goldenberries or blueberries) (optional)

1 Place the cashew yogurt in an ice cube tray and freeze for at least 2 hours before making the sorbet. (You can do this step ahead of time. Just pop the cubes out of the tray when frozen and store in a reusable freezer bag.)

2 In a high-powered blender, process on high the cashew yogurt cubes, pineapple, and coconut sugar until smooth and consistent. Use the tamper to press the ingredients toward the blades. Taste and adjust the sweetness.

3 Divide the sorbet mixture into 2 bowls and top with fresh berries (if using) before serving.

» QUICK TIPS

Use a whole ripe pineapple. Peel, core, and cube into ½-inch (1.25cm) pieces. Store the pineapple chunks in an airtight container in the freezer for up to 1 year. If the frozen yogurt looks slightly runny after processing, place the bowls in the freezer for 5 to 10 minutes.

CHOCOLATE & GARBANZO COOKIES

A dose of sustainable nourishment in my dessert? Yes please! Garbanzo bean flour carries the nutritional richness of the pulse itself, including protein and fiber. Cacao brings those as well as flavonoids, which can help lower blood pressure and reduce the risk of diabetes.

PREP TIME: **7 TO 10 MINUTES** // COOK TIME: **12 MINUTES** // YIELD: **12 COOKIES**

INGREDIENTS

1 tbsp plus 1 tsp ground flaxseeds

4 tbsp warm water

1½ cups garbanzo bean flour (see Quick Tips)

¼ cup unsweetened cacao powder

¾ tsp baking soda

¼ tsp coarse sea salt

½ cup melted unrefined coconut oil

1 tsp alcohol-free pure vanilla extract

½ cup coconut sugar

2 tbsp 100% unsweetened cacao chocolate chips, divided

1 Preheat the oven to 350°F (180°C). Line a large baking tray with parchment paper.

2 In a ramekin or small bowl, whisk together the flaxseeds and water until fully incorporated. Allow to rest until viscous, about 5 minutes. Set aside.

3 In a large bowl, whisk together the garbanzo bean flour, cacao powder, baking soda, and salt until evenly mixed. Set aside.

4 In a separate large bowl, whisk together the coconut oil, vanilla extract, coconut sugar, and flaxseed mixture until smooth, about 1 minute.

5 Add the dry ingredients to the wet ingredients. Mix until the batter is well combined. Fold in the cacao chips.

6 Use a spoon or cookie scoop to divide the dough into 12 even portions. Use your hands to roll the dough into balls. Place the dough on the tray, making sure to leave at least 3 inches (7.5cm) of space between the balls. With clean, slightly damp fingers, softly press down until each cookie is about ⅔ inch [1.7cm] thick.

7 Place the tray on the middle rack in the oven and bake until the edges are golden brown and the tops have cracked slightly, about 12 minutes.

8 Remove the tray from the oven. Allow the cookies to rest on the tray for 5 minutes before transferring them to a cooling rack.

> **» QUICK TIPS**
>
> For homemade garbanzo bean flour, process approximately 1¼ cup plus 1 tablespoon of dry garbanzo beans on the highest setting of a high-powered blender until pulverized as finely as possible, about 1 to 1½ minutes. Sift the flour through a mesh sieve before measuring. Allow the coconut oil to cool—it shouldn't be hot. Look for fair trade organic cacao powder and chips. Store the cookies in an airtight container in a dry place for up to 1 week.

BUÑUELOS (YUCA BEIGNETS)
WITH CACAO DIPPING SAUCE

This plant-based interpretation of a traditional Venezuelan dish features one of the most popular crops used in our cuisine: yuca. Starch from this humble root helps feed the good bacteria in our gut. I've added a dusting of coconut sugar and paired the beignets with a cacao sauce.

PREP TIME: 5 MINUTES // **COOK TIME: 18 TO 20 MINUTES** // **YIELD: 12 TO 14 BEIGNETS**

INGREDIENTS

9oz (255g) peeled fresh yuca, cut cross-sectionally into 1½-inch (3.75cm) pieces

1 tbsp ground flaxseeds

3 tbsp warm water

3 tbsp whole wheat flour

3 tbsp coconut sugar, divided

1 tbsp raw shelled hempseeds

pinch of coarse sea salt

1 cup avocado oil

FOR THE SAUCE

3 tbsp creamy almond butter

2 tbsp unsweetened cacao powder

1 to 2 tbsp maple syrup

2 tbsp hot water, plus more

> **» QUICK TIPS**
> Look for fair trade organic cacao powder. You can cook the yuca ahead and refrigerate overnight. Beignets are best enjoyed as soon as they're cooked. You can keep them warm in the oven at 200°F (95°C) for 1 to 2 hours.

1 In a small saucepan on the stovetop over medium-high heat, place the yuca and cover with 1 inch (2.5cm) of water. Bring to a boil, then reduce the heat to low. Simmer uncovered until the yuca is cooked through and you can easily insert a toothpick in the center, about 10 to 12 minutes. Strain and allow to cool completely. Remove the stiff core from the center of each segment. Set aside.

2 In a small bowl, make the dipping sauce by whisking together the almond butter, cacao powder, maple syrup, and hot water until smooth and consistent. If the sauce is too thick, add ½ tablespoon of hot water at a time to reach your desired consistency. Set aside.

3 In a small bowl, combine the flaxseeds and water, stirring to make sure no lumps remain. Allow to rest until viscous, about 3 minutes.

4 In a food processor, combine the whole wheat flour, 2 tablespoons of coconut sugar, hempseeds, salt, yuca, and flaxseed mixture. Process on high until a soft dough has formed, about 45 seconds to 1 minute.

5 Use damp hands to divide the dough into 12 to 14 equal portions. (Because the dough is very sticky, continue to dip your fingers in water while separating and rolling the dough.) Roll the dough into balls.

6 In a small saucepan on the stovetop, heat the avocado oil over medium-high heat until it reaches 365°F (185°C). Working in batches, place 3 to 4 balls in the saucepan and fry until crispy and golden brown on all sides, about 2 to 3 minutes.

7 Use a slotted spoon to transfer the beignets to a plate lined with absorbent paper to drain excess oil. Sprinkle the remaining 1 tablespoon of coconut sugar over the top. Toss to coat. Serve immediately with the dipping sauce.

YAM & MACA TRUFFLES

These will remind you of a comforting sweet potato pie! They're delicious as well as nourishing—packed with healthy fats, fiber, and healthful plant compounds. They're also great for dessert, as an afternoon sweet snack, and even with a warm cup of **Maca & Cacao Latte** [page 194].

PREP TIME: **7 TO 10 MINUTES** // COOK TIME: **20 MINUTES** // YIELD: **12 TRUFFLES**

INGREDIENTS

1 medium yam, peeled and cubed into ½-inch [1.25cm] pieces

½ tbsp melted coconut oil

3 dates

⅔ cup boiling water

2 tbsp maca powder

2 tbsp almond meal, plus more

2 tbsp roughly chopped walnuts

2 tbsp rolled oats

¼ tsp ground cinnamon

3 tbsp coarsely ground desiccated coconut, plus more

1 tbsp coconut sugar

1 Preheat the oven to 400°F (200°C). Line a large baking tray with parchment paper.

2 Place the yam on the tray and drizzle the coconut oil over the top. Toss to coat.

3 Place the tray on the middle rack in the oven and bake until fork-tender, about 20 minutes. Remove the tray from the oven and set aside.

4 In a medium bowl, combine the dates and water. Soak for 10 minutes, then strain well. Allow the dates to cool slightly before peeling the skins.

5 In a food processor, combine the yam, dates, maca powder, almond meal, walnuts, rolled oats, and cinnamon. Process on high until all the ingredients are well incorporated and the mixture is consistent. If the mixture is too thin, add ½ tablespoon of almond meal at a time to reach your desired consistency.

6 Divide the dough into 12 evenly sized portions. Shape the portions into balls with damp hands to prevent the dough from sticking to your hands.

7 In a shallow bowl, combine the desiccated coconut and coconut sugar. Roll the balls in the coconut mixture to coat. Refrigerate the truffles covered for at least 30 minutes before serving.

» QUICK TIP
Store the truffles in an airtight container in the fridge for up to 10 days.

LEGUMINOUS CHOCOLATE PUDDING

This pudding is velvety smooth and has a deep chocolate flavor—thanks, cacao! Use a ripe banana for texture and sweetness to help lower the need for added sugars. Using sprouted tofu as the base adds a significant nutritional value and thickness in the best way possible.

PREP TIME: **2 MINUTES** // COOK TIME: **NONE** // YIELD: **2 SERVINGS**

INGREDIENTS

8oz (225g) organic sprouted tofu

1 medium ripe banana

⅓ cup unsweetened cacao powder

¼ cup plus 2 tbsp plant-based milk, plus more

2 tbsp coconut sugar, plus more

pinch of coarse sea salt

4 to 6 fresh raspberries (optional)

½ tsp shelled hempseeds (optional)

1 In a high-powered blender, combine the tofu, banana, cacao powder, plant-based milk, coconut sugar, and salt. Process on high until smooth and velvety, about 1 minute. If it's too thick, add milk ½ tablespoon at a time and blend until the pudding reaches your desired consistency. Taste and adjust the sweetness.

2 Divide the pudding into 2 serving bowls. Cover and refrigerate for at least 20 minutes or until time to serve. Garnish with raspberries and hempseeds (if using) before serving.

» QUICK TIPS

Look for fair trade organic cacao powder. Store the pudding in an airtight container in the fridge for up to 5 days.

CANTALOUPE & PRICKLY PEAR ICE POPS

These are refreshing, delicious, and colorful. I grew up eating prickly pears because they're popular in Venezuela's Falcón State, my maternal "homeland." Adding cantaloupe—an underrated fruit rich in fiber, minerals, and vitamins—makes this sugar-free sweet treat poised to steal your heart.

PREP TIME: **7 TO 10 MINUTES** // COOK TIME: **NONE** // YIELD: **4 TO 8 ICE POPS (DEPENDING ON MOLD SIZE)**

INGREDIENTS

1 cup large-diced cantaloupe

2 tbsp freshly squeezed lime juice, divided

1 to 2 tbsp maple syrup, divided

5 tbsp cold water, divided

2 medium red prickly pears, peeled and roughly chopped

1 In a high-powered blender, combine the cantaloupe, 1 tablespoon of lime juice, ½ tablespoon of maple syrup, and 2 tablespoons of cold water. Process on high until smooth. Depending on the melon's ripeness or sweetness, you might need to add ½ tablespoon of maple syrup to the juice. Blend quickly. Fill the ice pop molds with the juice and freeze for at least 1 hour.

2 In the cleaned blender, combine the pears, the remaining 1 tablespoon of lime juice, the remaining 1 tablespoon of maple syrup, and the remaining 3 tablespoons of cold water. Process on high until smooth. Strain with a mesh strainer to remove seed fragments.

3 Fill the molds with the juice and freeze for at least 4 hours or overnight.

> » **QUICK TIPS**
> If you're using a regular blender and the juice still has many solids after processing, you can strain the juice with a mesh strainer. If properly covered, you can safely store the ice pops in the freezer for 6 months or more.

CHAPTER 13
SAUCES, DIPS, PICKLES & MORE

214 Barbecue Sauce / Creamy Garlic Sauce

215 Salsa Verde / Guasacaca (Spicy Avocado Sauce)

216 Roasted Red Pepper Dip

218 Black Bean Dip / Carrot-Top Chimichurri

219 Cucumber & Shallot Raita / Fava Bean Spread

220 Yellow Split Pea Hummus

222 Dippers: Plantain Chips

223 Dippers: Crispy Millet Crackers

224 Mango Salsa

226 Pickling & Fermenting: Cauliflower Leafstalk Kimchi

227 Pickling & Fermenting: Lime-Pickled Onions
& Watermelon Rinds / Pickled Carrots

BARBECUE SAUCE

Made from scratch using fresh tomatoes, coconut sugar, and spices,
this sweet and tangy sauce is wholesome and delicious.

PREP TIME: **2 MINUTES** // COOK TIME: **20 MINUTES** // YIELD: **ABOUT 1¼ CUPS**

INGREDIENTS

3 large vine-ripened tomatoes

⅓ cup coconut sugar

3 tbsp apple cider vinegar

½ tsp garlic powder

½ tsp onion powder

½ tsp smoked paprika

½ tsp coarse sea salt

½ tsp ground black pepper

¼ tsp ground cayenne

5 to 6 whole allspice berries

1 to 2 dried bay leaves

1 Wash the tomatoes thoroughly and remove all the stems. Cut the tomatoes in quarters. In a high-powered blender, combine the tomatoes, coconut sugar, apple cider vinegar, garlic powder, onion powder, paprika, salt, pepper, and cayenne. Process on high until smooth.

2 Transfer the mixture to a small saucepan on the stovetop over medium heat. Add the allspice berries and bay leaves. Bring to a soft boil, then reduce the heat to low. Cover and simmer for 10 minutes, stirring occasionally. Remove the lid and simmer until the sauce has thickened, about 10 minutes more, stirring occasionally.

3 Remove the saucepan from the heat and allow the sauce to cool slightly. Use a mesh ladle to remove the allspice berries and bay leaves.

4 Transfer the sauce to a glass canning jar. Cover and refrigerate for up to 10 days.

CREAMY GARLIC SAUCE

This sauce goes great on anything! Drizzle some over roasted
root vegetables or serve it with many of the recipes in Chapter 8.

PREP TIME: **5 MINUTES** // COOK TIME: **NONE** // YIELD: **1½ CUPS**

INGREDIENTS

1 cup **Cashew Cream** (page 230)

¼ cup **Roasted Garlic Paste** (page 237)

3 tbsp freshly squeezed lemon juice

½ tsp fresh lemon zest

⅛ coarse sea salt

1 In a medium bowl, whisk together the cashew cream, garlic paste, lemon juice, lemon zest, and salt until consistent.

2 Use immediately or store in an airtight container in the fridge for up to 1 week.

> **» QUICK TIP**
> For a little more pungent taste, add 2 to 3 tablespoons of finely chopped fennel fronds.

SALSA VERDE

Carrying a beautiful complexity of flavors, this zero-waste sauce is perfectly balanced and has a great consistency. Try it over cooked vegetables.

PREP TIME: **10 MINUTES** // COOK TIME: **NONE** // YIELD: **1¼ TO 1½ CUPS**

INGREDIENTS

1 to 1½ cups radish greens

1 cup fresh flat-leaf parsley

2 tbsp wild capers

2 to 3 garlic cloves, minced

½ tbsp stone-ground mustard

1 tsp chickpea miso

½ tsp ground black pepper

⅛ tsp coarse sea salt, plus more

¼ cup white wine vinegar

½ cup extra-virgin olive oil

1 In a food processor, combine all the ingredients. Pulse until the greens have been mostly chopped. Scrape the sides of the bowl and pulse until the salsa is chunky and consistent.

2 Use immediately or store in an airtight container in the fridge for up to 1 week.

» QUICK TIPS

You can use a blender for this recipe. Use the pulse button and don't overprocess. For a thinner consistency to the salsa, add 1 to 2 tablespoons of olive oil.

GUASACACA (SPICY AVOCADO SAUCE)

The most popular condiment in Venezuelan cuisine, guasacaca is made with all things green and that makes it a nutrition powerhouse.

PREP TIME: **10 MINUTES** // COOK TIME: **NONE** // YIELD: **1½ CUPS**

INGREDIENTS

2 ripe Hass avocados

½ cup chopped fresh cilantro

¼ cup chopped scallions

¼ cup chopped green bell peppers

2 tbsp minced serrano peppers

¼ cup plus 2 tbsp freshly squeezed lemon juice

¼ tsp coarse sea salt

¼ tsp ground black pepper

1 Cut the avocados in half and remove the seeds. Peel the avocados.

2 In a blender, combine all the ingredients and blend until smooth. Add 1 tablespoon of cold water at a time to thin out if needed.

3 Use immediately or store in an airtight container in the fridge for up to 2 days.

» QUICK TIPS

To avoid food waste, save the seeds and make **Avocado Seed Powder** (page 231). Use this as a dip, spread, or sauce.

ROASTED RED PEPPER DIP

This luscious dip is living proof there's no sacrifice in eating plant-based! It's the perfect combination of sweet, savory, and a little heat. The roasted bell peppers are flavorful and smoky, while the walnuts add great nutritional value, especially protein and heart-healthy fats.

PREP TIME: **5 TO 7 MINUTES** // COOK TIME: **33 TO 34 MINUTES** // YIELD: **ABOUT 1⅓ CUPS**

INGREDIENTS

2 large red bell peppers

2½ tbsp extra-virgin olive oil, divided, plus more

¾ cup roughly chopped raw walnuts

½ tbsp balsamic vinegar

½ tbsp blackstrap molasses

2 tsp **Roasted Garlic Paste** (page 237)

½ tsp ground cayenne, plus more

½ tsp coarse sea salt

¼ tsp ground black pepper

fresh parsley or other herbs

1 Preheat the oven to 400°F (200°C).

2 Cut the bell peppers in half lengthwise and place them cut side up in a baking dish. Drizzle ½ tablespoon of olive oil over the peppers and rub the oil throughout the cavities.

3 Place the dish on the bottom rack in the oven and roast for 30 minutes, flipping the peppers halfway through. Remove the dish from the oven, cover, and allow to rest for 10 minutes.

4 In a medium skillet on the stovetop over medium heat, toast the walnuts until golden brown, about 3 to 4 minutes. Remove the skillet from the heat and set aside to cool.

5 When the peppers are cool enough to handle, remove the stems and seeds, then peel the skins. Cut the peppers into large chunks.

6 In a food processor, combine the peppers, walnuts, balsamic vinegar, molasses, roasted garlic paste, cayenne, salt, pepper, and the remaining 2 tablespoons of olive oil. Process on high until smooth and consistent.

7 Transfer the dip to a serving bowl. Drizzle a little more olive oil over the top. Sprinkle 1 or 2 pinches of cayenne over the top if desired. Top with fresh parsley or other herbs. Enjoy at room temperature or chill covered for at least 30 minutes before serving.

> **» QUICK TIPS**
> Cover the baking dish to trap the steam. This will make it easier to peel the peppers. Serve with vegetable crudités (shown here) or **Crispy Millet Crackers** (page 223). Store in an airtight container in the fridge for up to 1 week.

BLACK BEAN DIP

Black beans are great for human health and that of the planet. Use this for paninis or wraps.

PREP TIME: **10 MINUTES** // COOK TIME: **2 MINUTES** // YIELD: **ABOUT 1½ CUPS**

INGREDIENTS

½ tbsp avocado oil

¼ cup chopped brown onions

¼ cup chopped green bell peppers

½ tsp ground cumin

¼ tsp ground coriander

¼ tsp ancho chili powder

2 tbsp freshly squeezed lime juice

1½ cups cooked **Black Beans** (page 238)

1 serrano pepper, quartered, plus more

2 tbsp extra-virgin olive oil, divided

½ tsp coarse sea salt

1 In a medium skillet on the stovetop, heat the avocado oil over medium heat. Add the onions and sauté for 2 minutes, stirring often. Add the bell peppers, cumin, coriander, and ancho chili powder. Stir until the spices evenly coat the onion mixture. Add the lime juice and deglaze the bottom of the skillet. Remove the skillet from the heat.

2 Transfer the mixture to a food processor and add the remaining ingredients. Process on high until smooth.

3 Transfer the dip to a serving bowl and garnish with slices of serrano pepper if desired. Serve warm or at room temperature.

> **» QUICK TIP**
> Store in an airtight container in the fridge for up to 10 days.

CARROT-TOP CHIMICHURRI

Popular in South American cuisine, this has a nutrient-dense ingredient often wasted: carrot tops.

PREP TIME: **10 MINUTES** // COOK TIME: **NONE** // YIELD: **1½ CUPS**

INGREDIENTS

½ cup extra-virgin olive oil

¼ cup red wine vinegar

2 tsp finely minced Fresno peppers

½ tsp dried oregano

2 garlic cloves, finely minced

½ tsp coarse sea salt

¼ tsp ground black pepper

1 cup finely chopped carrot tops, stems removed

1 In a medium bowl, whisk together the olive oil, red wine vinegar, Fresno peppers, oregano, garlic, salt, and pepper until emulsified. Add the carrot tops and mix well.

2 Allow the chimichurri to rest for at least 15 minutes before serving.

> **» QUICK TIPS**
> You can use any other type of fresh red pepper (like Calabrian or cherry pepper) or 1 teaspoon of red pepper flakes. Refrigerate/freeze carrot-top stems to make zero-waste **Vegetable Stock** (page 232). Store the chimichurri in an airtight container in the fridge for up to 1 week. Take the container out of the fridge at least 30 minutes before serving.

CUCUMBER & SHALLOT RAITA

Try this with **Potato & Eggplant Skewers** (page 85) or **Curried Cauliflower Salad** (page 108).

PREP TIME: **5 MINUTES** // COOK TIME: **NONE** // YIELD: **1¼ CUPS**

INGREDIENTS

¾ cup **Cultured Cashew Yogurt** (page 230)

¼ tsp ground cumin

½ tsp coarse sea salt

½ cup grated English cucumbers

1 tbsp finely minced shallots

1 tbsp fresh mint chiffonade (see Quick Tips)

2 tbsp plant-based milk (optional)

1 In a large bowl, whisk together the cashew yogurt, cumin, and salt. Allow to rest for 5 minutes, then whisk again. Add the cucumbers, shallots, and mint chiffonade. Mix well until consistent. If the mixture is too thick, add milk 1 tablespoon at a time to reach your desired consistency.

2 Serve immediately or store in an airtight container in the fridge for up to 3 days.

> **» QUICK TIPS**
> To make mint chiffonade, roll 4 to 6 mint leaves together and cut the leaves into ribbons. To avoid food waste, grate the whole cucumber, including the skin and seeds.

FAVA BEAN SPREAD

Fresh fava beans have a mild flavor and creamy texture—and they're healthy and planet-friendly!

PREP TIME: **20 MINUTES** // COOK TIME: **5 TO 6 MINUTES** // YIELD: **ABOUT 1⅓ CUPS**

INGREDIENTS

2 quarts (2 liters) water

1½ cups shelled fava beans (from about 4lb [1.8kg] of fresh fava bean pods)

3 tbsp **Cashew Cream** (page 230)

2 tbsp minced shallots

¼ cup loosely packed fresh lemon balm leaves

1½ tbsp freshly squeezed lemon juice

¼ tsp coarse sea salt

mint leaves or fresh herbs

1 In a medium saucepan on the stovetop over medium heat, bring the water to a boil. Add the fava beans and cook until tender, about 5 to 6 minutes. Drain with a mesh strainer and run the beans under cold water. Transfer the beans to a bowl and remove the skins (a light-colored membrane surrounding each bean) by squeezing the beans.

2 In a food processor, combine the beans, cashew cream, shallots, lemon balm leaves, lemon juice, and salt. Process on high until thick and creamy.

3 Transfer the spread to a serving bowl and garnish with mint leaves or fresh herbs. Chill covered for 30 to 45 minutes before serving.

> **» QUICK TIP**
> Store in an airtight container in the fridge for up to 5 days.

YELLOW SPLIT PEA HUMMUS

Part of the legume family, peas are planet-friendly crops. Not only do they help us shrink our carbon footprint, but they're also utterly yummy. I often tell people to diversify their culinary palette because it helps promote biodiversity—and split peas are great for this.

PREP TIME: **5 MINUTES** // COOK TIME: **NONE** // YIELD: **ABOUT 1⅔ CUPS**

INGREDIENTS

1½ cups cooked **Split Peas** (yellow) (page 239)

¼ cup plus 2 tbsp tahini

¼ cup freshly squeezed lemon juice

2 garlic cloves

1 to 2 tbsp extra-virgin olive oil, plus more

1 tsp ground flaxseeds

½ tsp smoked paprika, plus more

½ tsp coarse sea salt

¼ tsp ground black pepper

1 In a food processor, process on high all the ingredients until smooth.

2 Transfer the hummus to a serving bowl. Drizzle a little more olive oil over the top. Sprinkle 1 to 2 pinches of smoked paprika over the top if desired. Enjoy at room temperature or chill covered for 30 minutes before serving.

» QUICK TIP
Use this hummus immediately or store in an airtight container in the fridge for up to 10 days.

DIPPERS

These two dippers are great with some of the recipes in this chapter, including **Black Bean Dip** (page 218), **Yellow Split Pea Hummus** (page 220), and **Mango Salsa** (page 225). The plantain chips are a great substitute for the chips in **Tostones Nachos** (page 166).

PLANTAIN CHIPS

Green plantains are starchy and yield the crispiest chips. The molasses adds a touch of sweetness and is rich in iron and other minerals, like magnesium, calcium, and potassium. Although plantain chips are traditionally deep-fried, baked chips are healthier and just as delicious.

PREP TIME: **10 MINUTES** // COOK TIME: **15 TO 18 MINUTES** // YIELD: **4 TO 6 SERVINGS**

INGREDIENTS

2 large green plantains

2 to 3 tbsp melted coconut oil

1 tbsp blackstrap molasses

½ tsp coarse sea salt

1 Preheat the oven to 375°F (190°C). Line 2 large baking trays with parchment paper.

2 Cut the tips off both ends of each plantain. Use a paring knife to score the plantain skin lengthwise. Peel the plantains and cut the plantains in half cross-sectionally.

3 Set the mandoline to the lowest setting. (You want paper-thin slices because you get crispier chips.) Thinly slice the plantains cross-sectionally. Arrange the slices in a single layer on each tray.

4 In a small bowl, combine the coconut oil and blackstrap molasses. Blend with a spoon until consistent. Use a brush to coat all the slices evenly with the coconut oil mixture. (I prefer to brush both sides, but you can choose to brush one side only.)

5 Place the trays on the top and middle racks in the oven. Bake until crispy and golden brown, about 15 to 18 minutes, switching the trays once halfway through the baking process. (Check again after 12 minutes to make sure they don't burn.)

6 Remove the trays from the oven and sprinkle the salt evenly over the top. Because plantain chips are best/crispiest right out of the oven, enjoy them within a couple hours after baking.

> **» QUICK TIP**
> The peels from ripe plantains are edible, but that's not true for green plantains. Make sure to compost the peels.

CRISPY MILLET CRACKERS

Finger millets are on the "Future 50 Foods"—a list from the World Wildlife Fund that features sustainable foods with great nutritional value. Making food from scratch, like these crackers, helps us minimize the amount of processed foods we consume (and our foodprint!).

PREP TIME: **10 MINUTES** // COOK TIME: **20 TO 21 MINUTES** // YIELD: **40 CRACKERS**

INGREDIENTS

½ cup finger millet flour (ragi flour)

¼ cup rice flour

1 tsp raw sesame seeds

1 tsp chia seeds

½ tsp baking powder

½ tsp coarse sea salt

1 tbsp plus 2 tsp solid coconut oil

¼ cup plus 2 tbsp water

2 tsp melted coconut oil

1 Preheat the oven to 325°F (165°C).

2 In a large bowl, whisk together the millet flour, rice flour, sesame seeds, chia seeds, baking powder, and salt. Add the solid coconut oil. Use clean hands to blend until moist and crumbly. Add the water and knead until you can form the dough into a ball. If the dough is too dry, add water 1 teaspoon at a time. Break the dough into two even portions.

3 Place half the dough in the center of a piece of parchment paper and place another sheet of parchment paper on top. Flatten the dough a little with your hands, then use a rolling pin to roll out the dough until very thin. Repeat this process with the other half of dough.

4 Transfer the rolled dough (still attached to the 2 pieces of parchment paper) to 2 medium-sized baking trays. Place them in the freezer until the dough is stiff, about 8 minutes.

5 Remove the trays from the freezer and remove the top layer of parchment paper. Use a pizza cutter or a knife to cut the dough into equal squares, approximately 1 inch × 1 inch (2.5 × 2.5cm) each. Brush the squares with the melted coconut oil.

6 Place the trays on the top two racks in the oven. Bake for 15 minutes, rotating the trays halfway through to evenly bake the crackers. Remove the trays from the oven.

7 Raise the oven temperature to 425°F (220°C). Use a spatula to separate the crackers and turn them over. You can remove the parchment paper from the trays. Space out the crackers on the trays to evenly bake them.

8 Return the trays to the oven and bake until light golden brown and crispy, about 5 to 6 minutes more. Start checking after 4 minutes to make sure the crackers don't burn.

9 Remove the trays from the oven and allow the crackers to cool completely. Store the crackers in an airtight container in your pantry for up to 2 weeks.

MANGO SALSA

Besides being colorful and delicious, this is also nourishing. An unexpected addition—red lentils—adds protein, fiber, and tons of minerals. I just love the texture and flavor the mango—one of my favorite fruits—lends to this dish. Enjoy with **Plantain Chips** (page 222) or blue corn chips.

PREP TIME: **10 TO 15 MINUTES** // COOK TIME: **NONE** // YIELD: **2½ CUPS**

INGREDIENTS

1 large mango, peeled, pitted, and diced into small cubes (about 1½ cups)

½ cup cooked **Red Lentils** (page 239)

¼ cup chopped fresh cilantro

2 tbsp minced shallots

2 tbsp minced red bell peppers

1 tbsp minced jalapeños

3 tbsp freshly squeezed lime juice

¼ tsp coarse sea salt, plus more to taste

¼ tsp ground black pepper

1 In a medium bowl, combine the mango, red lentils, cilantro, shallots, red bell peppers, and jalapeños. Drizzle the lime juice over the top. Season with salt and pepper. Toss to coat.

2 Use immediately or cover the bowl and refrigerate for a couple hours.

> » *QUICK TIPS*
> Remove the jalapeño seeds if less heat is desired. Sprinkle the salsa with 1 teaspoon of **Papaya Seed Powder** (page 231) right before serving. Store in an airtight container in the fridge for up to 4 days.

PICKLING & FERMENTING

Pickling and fermenting allow us to preserve food and to produce mouthwatering sour flavors. These recipes give us the opportunity to upcycle ingredients that would normally end up in the trash bin. Pickled and fermented foods are beneficial for our digestive system and gut health.

CAULIFLOWER LEAFSTALK KIMCHI

PREP TIME: **15 TO 20 MINUTES** // COOK TIME: **NONE** // YIELD: **2 TO 3 CUPS**

INGREDIENTS

leaves and stalks from 2 heads of cauliflower

1 tbsp coarse sea salt

2 tbsp Korean chili powder or red pepper flakes

6 small garlic cloves

¼ cup chopped peeled fresh ginger

1 medium organic Gala apple, peeled, cored, and cubed

1 tbsp tamari

1 tbsp maple syrup

1 tbsp chickpea miso

¼ cup water

1 small bunch of scallions, cut into 1-inch (2.5cm) pieces

1 Separate the cauliflower leaves from the stalks. Cut the leaves into approximately 1-inch (2.5cm) pieces and thinly slice the stalks.

2 In a large bowl, combine the leaves, stalks, and salt. Massage and toss thoroughly until evenly seasoned. Add enough filtered water to the bowl to cover everything. Allow to rest for 1 hour, then strain. Set aside.

3 In a high-powered blender, combine the Korean chili powder, garlic, ginger, apple, tamari, maple syrup, chickpea miso, and water. Process until consistent.

4 Pour the mixture over the leaves and stalks. Use clean hands to mix well. Stir in the scallions and massage the mixture a few minutes more.

5 Transfer everything to a large canning jar, pressing down and packing tightly each new addition. Store the jar at room temperature, preferably on a tray in a kitchen cabinet, until the mixture ferments, about 3 days.

6 Transfer the jar to the fridge and store for up to 6 months. (Because the kimchi continues to ferment, it can last longer than this.)

> **» QUICK TIPS**
> Save leaves and stalks when making other recipes with cauliflower. Store in an airtight container in the fridge until you accumulate enough leaves for kimchi. During the fermentation process, you might see bubbles rising to the top of the jar or see some liquid spilling over. This is perfectly normal. Open the jar and stir the kimchi while making sure it remains submerged in the liquid. Close the jar and continue fermenting.

LIME-PICKLED ONIONS & WATERMELON RINDS

PREP TIME: **10 MINUTES** // COOK TIME: **NONE** // YIELD: **1½ CUPS**

INGREDIENTS

1lb (450g) watermelon rinds

1 cup finely julienned red onions

½ tsp coarse sea salt

½ cup freshly squeezed lime juice

1 Carefully peel/trim the dark green parts from the rinds. (It's okay if some pink parts remain.) Cut the rinds lengthwise into 2-inch (5cm) segments. Use a mandoline to finely julienne the rinds. (You can also use a chef's knife to thinly slice the rinds cross-sectionally.)

2 In a medium bowl, combine the rinds, onions, and salt. Toss to coat.

3 Transfer the rinds and onions to a canning jar. Add the lime juice. Seal the jar well and shake softly to coat.

4 Allow to marinate for at least 1 hour before serving.

> **» QUICK TIPS**
> For an extra punch of flavor, add 2 tablespoons of finely minced herb stalks (like parsley or cilantro). Store the jar in the fridge for up to 1 week.

PICKLED CARROTS

PREP TIME: **10 MINUTES** // COOK TIME: **7 MINUTES** // YIELD: **3 TO 4 CUPS**

INGREDIENTS

2 bunches of baby heirloom (rainbow) carrots, cut in half lengthwise (see Quick Tips)

2 scallions, cut in half

2 dried bay leaves

1¼ cup apple cider vinegar

¾ cup water

3 tbsp maple syrup

¼ tsp ground cinnamon

¼ tsp ground nutmeg

½ tsp coarse sea salt

1 Place half the carrots into each of two 16-ounce (450g) canning jars or glass containers. Add 1 scallion and 1 bay leaf to each jar. Set aside.

2 In a small saucepan on the stovetop over medium heat, combine the apple cider vinegar, water, maple syrup, cinnamon, nutmeg, and salt. Bring to a simmer and stir until the salt is fully dissolved. Reduce the heat to low and simmer covered for 7 minutes.

3 Carefully pour the brine over the carrots. If they're not fully submerged, add a little more vinegar or water. Seal the jars and allow them to cool before transferring them to the refrigerator. Allow the carrots to pickle for at least 24 hours before serving.

> **» QUICK TIPS**
> Baby heirloom carrots are usually 3 to 4 inches (7.5 to 10cm) long. If you're using larger carrots, cut them into smaller pieces. Also, leave the carrots unpeeled for extra nutrients. Store the carrots in the fridge for up to 3 weeks.

CHAPTER 14
MAKE-AHEAD

230 Creams: Cashew Cream / Coconut Cream

231 Seed Powders: Avocado Seed Powder / Papaya Seed Powder

232 Vegetable Broth

234 Green Jackfruit

235 Cultured Cashew Yogurt / Aquafaba Mayonnaise

236 Roasted Garlic Paste

238 Pulses: Black & White Beans / Black-Eyed Peas / Kidney Beans / Garbanzo Beans

239 Pulses: Split Peas / Green Lentils / Red Lentils

240 Seasoning Blends: Umami Mushroom Powder / Furikake Seaweed Seasoning / Spicy Adobe Seasoning / Homemade Curry Powder

242 Grains: Quinoa / Brown or Wild Rice

243 Grains: Amaranth / Millets / Farro

CREAMS

Cashew cream is as velvety and delicious as it is versatile. Use this cream to prepare other dishes or to top and finish dishes. Homemade coconut cream is used as a base for many savory and sweet dishes in this book. This version is easy to make without needing sophisticated equipment.

CASHEW CREAM

PREP TIME: **5 MINUTES** // COOK TIME: **NONE** // YIELD: **1 TO 1¼ CUPS**

INGREDIENTS

1½ cups raw cashews

2¼ cups filtered water, divided

1 tbsp freshly squeezed lemon juice

2 tsp nutritional yeast

½ tsp coarse sea salt, plus more

1 In a medium bowl, combine the cashews and 2 cups of water. Cover and refrigerate overnight (or for at least 10 hours). Drain the cashews with a mesh strainer.

2 In a high-powered blender, combine the cashews, lemon juice, nutritional yeast, salt, and the remaining ¼ cup of water. Process for 1 minute. Scrape the sides and process on high until smooth and velvety, about 10 seconds more. If the cream appears too thick, add water 1 tablespoon at a time to reach your desired consistency. Taste and adjust seasoning.

3 Use immediately if desired or refrigerate for up to 1 week.

COCONUT CREAM

PREP TIME: **2 MINUTES** // COOK TIME: **5 MINUTES** // YIELD: **2 CUPS**

INGREDIENTS

1½ cups plant-based milk

4oz (120g) unsweetened shredded coconut

¾ cup **Cashew Cream** (above)

> **» QUICK TIP**
> You can substitute fresh coconut for the shredded coconut.

1 In a small saucepan on the stovetop over medium-high heat, combine the plant-based milk and coconut. Bring to a simmer/soft boil, then reduce the heat to low. Simmer for 5 minutes. Remove the saucepan from the heat and set aside to cool.

2 In a high-powered blender, combine the coconut mixture and cashew cream. Process on high until creamy and smooth. Run the mixture through a mesh strainer and push with a silicone spatula to get the most amount of liquid.

3 Transfer the coconut cream to a lidded glass canning jar and store in the fridge for up 10 days.

SEED POWDERS

Want some easy ways to avoid food waste? Save your avocado and papaya seeds. In Venezuela, people have used ground avocado and papaya seeds for generations for medicinal purposes. Sprinkle these powders on myriad dishes in this book: breakfast, salads, casseroles, and more.

AVOCADO SEED POWDER

PREP TIME: **5 MINUTES** // COOK TIME: **NONE** // YIELD: **1 TO 3 TABLESPOONS**

INGREDIENTS
1 avocado seed

> » **QUICK TIP**
> If your location and/or weather doesn't allow for sun-drying, dehydrate the seed in the oven at 200°F (95°C) for 1 to 2 hours. To maximize the use of your oven, dehydrate other ingredients simultaneously.

1 Wash the avocado seed thoroughly and scrape any remainders of fruit from the surface. Rub dry with a clean towel.

2 Place the seed on a small plate in a sunny spot in your home. Allow the seed to sun-dry for 3 to 4 days.

3 Peel the outer skin off and use a chef's knife to carefully cut the seed into 2 to 4 pieces. Use a high-powered blender to process the seed on high until pulverized.

4 Transfer to a spice jar or a metal tin and store in a cool, dry place.

PAPAYA SEED POWDER

PREP TIME: **5 MINUTES** // COOK TIME: **NONE** // YIELD: **2 TO 4 TABLESPOONS**

INGREDIENTS
seeds from 1 papaya

1 Use a mesh strainer to wash the papaya seeds thoroughly. Pat dry with a clean towel.

2 Place the seeds on a layer of absorbent paper on a small tray. Separate the seeds to prevent them from sticking together.

3 Place the tray in a sunny spot in your home. Allow to sun-dry until the outer membranes have dried and are no longer sticky, about 2 to 3 days.

4 Use a high-powered blender or spice grinder to process the seeds on high until finely ground. Transfer to a spice jar or a metal tin and store in a cool, dry place.

> » **QUICK TIP**
> A medium papaya yields about ¼ to ⅓ cup of seeds.

VEGETABLE BROTH

This is one of the best ways to upcycle food and make something delicious. As you prepare more food from scratch, you'll accumulate lots of vegetable scraps. Use a reusable freezer bag to save them as you go—from peels and cores to ends, bits, and pieces as well as stems, stalks, and more.

PREP TIME: **5 MINUTES** // COOK TIME: **2 HOURS** // YIELD: **ABOUT 11 TO 13 CUPS**

INGREDIENTS

2lb (1kg) vegetable scraps

3½ quarts (3½ liters) water

2 dried bay leaves

8 to 10 whole peppercorns

3 to 4 tsp coarse sea salt

1 In a 7-quart (6½-liter) Dutch oven or enamel cast-iron pot on the stovetop over medium heat, combine all the ingredients. Bring to a boil, then reduce the heat to low. Cover and simmer for 2 hours.

2 Remove the pot from the heat and allow the broth to cool slightly. Strain the broth with a mesh strainer. Use immediately or save for later.

> **» QUICK TIPS**
> You can add whole vegetables to the pot rather than only scraps whenever you have too many available in your kitchen, including bell peppers, onions, garlic, celery, carrots, leeks, ginger, fennel, and corn cobs as well as cilantro, parsley, rosemary, and thyme stems. Store the broth in an airtight container in the fridge for up to 1 week or in the freezer for up to 6 months.

GREEN JACKFRUIT

Jackfruit is a large fruit common in Asian countries. When green, it's the ultimate meat substitute. Its texture and consistency when cooked highlight plant-based dishes. Because of its size, one jackfruit is sufficient to make many recipes. Freeze in smaller bags and use them as needed.

PREP TIME: **10 TO 15 MINUTES** // COOK TIME: **25 TO 30 MINUTES** // YIELD: **7½LB (3.4KG)**

INGREDIENTS
1 green jackfruit (about 11lb [5kg])

1 Wash the jackfruit thoroughly. Cover a cutting board with plastic wrap to avoid damage from the fruit's sap. Wear latex gloves.

2 Slice the fruit cross-sectionally in 2- to 2½-inch (5 to 6.25cm) slices. Cut each slice in half and remove most of the inner core.

3 In a large pot on the stovetop over medium-high heat, place the jackfruit sections (skin on) and cover with 1 to 2 inches (2.5 to 5cm) of water. Bring to a boil, then reduce the heat to medium-low. Simmer covered until the white strings around the pods are soft and tender, about 25 to 30 minutes.

4 Strain and allow to cool slightly. Peel off the skin and separate the edible parts: the fleshy strings, the pods nestled between them, and the seeds inside each pod.

5 Use the flesh and pods for cooking. Separate them into 1- to 2-pound (450g to 1kg) portions and freeze in reusable silicone bags. (Optional: Remove the thin white membrane surrounding the seeds and place the seeds on a baking tray. The seeds are edible once cooked and peeled. [See Quick Tips.])

» QUICK TIPS
You can use newspaper instead of plastic wrap. Make sure to rinse the fruit with water before cooking. If you're using a pressure cooker, cut the cooking time to 10 minutes. Some people consume the inner core, although I find its texture too harsh for my liking. You can compost it along with the skin of the fruit. For better flavor and texture, roast the seeds at 425°F (220°C) for 10 to 12 minutes. Sprinkle a little sea salt over the top right after removing the seeds from the oven. Eat the seeds as a snack or crush them and add to salads.

CULTURED CASHEW YOGURT

This homemade and wholesome yogurt is rich in probiotics—a type of healthy bacteria known to benefit our gut health. It's delicious, creamy, and somewhat tart—just as a yogurt should be. Use this to top fresh fruits; to make sauces, dips, and dressings; and even for desserts.

PREP TIME: 10 MINUTES // COOK TIME: 3 MINUTES // YIELD: 2 CUPS

INGREDIENTS

1 cup raw cashews

2½ cups filtered room temperature water, divided

3 capsules refrigerated probiotic

> **» QUICK TIPS**
> Check the probiotic label to make sure the product is plant-based and that no prebiotics have been added. If serving on its own, add a little maple syrup for sweetness or vanilla essence for flavoring. Store in the fridge for up to 1 week.

1 In a small pan on the stovetop over medium heat, combine the cashews and 1½ cups of water. Bring to a boil, then reduce the heat to low. Cover and simmer for about 3 minutes. Remove the pan from the heat and allow to rest covered for 10 to 12 minutes. Drain.

2 In a high-powered blender, combine the cashews and the remaining 1 cup of water. Process on high until creamy and smooth. Transfer to a clean wide-mouthed jar.

3 Empty the capsules one by one into the cashew mixture. Use a wooden spoon to stir until evenly incorporated. Cover the jar with cheesecloth or a clean thin towel and secure with kitchen twine. Place the jar in a warm place for 36 to 48 hours, then transfer to an airtight container. Refrigerate until the yogurt is cold and ready to serve, about 2 hours.

AQUAFABA MAYONNAISE

Aquafaba is the viscous liquid left after cooking garbanzo beans and other legumes. This liquid is also often discarded from a can of garbanzo beans. Instead, whisk together aquafaba and a good-quality oil to make a fluffy and delicious mayonnaise you can use for salads and sauces.

PREP TIME: 5 MINUTES // COOK TIME: NONE // YIELD: 2 CUPS

INGREDIENTS

½ cup aquafaba

2½ tsp yellow mustard

3 tsp apple cider vinegar

1½ to 2½ tsp molasses (optional)

½ tsp coarse sea salt

1½ cup avocado oil, plus more

1 In a tall blending cup or wide-mouthed glass jar, use an immersion blender to process the aquafaba, mustard, apple cider vinegar, molasses (if using), and salt for 30 seconds. With the blender running, add the avocado oil in a slow, steady stream over a 2-minute period. Move the blender up and down to aerate the mixture. If the mayonnaise hasn't thickened, slowly stream oil ½ tablespoon at a time to reach your desired consistency.

2 Transfer to an airtight container. Refrigerate the mayonnaise for at least 15 minutes before using. Store in the fridge for up to 2 weeks.

ROASTED GARLIC PASTE

Garlic loses its pungent flavor and becomes sweet and almost buttery when roasted. Use this paste to prepare other dishes in this book, like **Creamy Butternut Soup** [page 136] and **King Oyster Mushroom Arepas** [page 163]. But you can also spread this paste on crackers.

PREP TIME: **5 MINUTES** // COOK TIME: **45 MINUTES** // YIELD: **¾ TO 1¼ CUP (SEE QUICK TIP)**

INGREDIENTS

8 to 12 heads of garlic

4 to 6 tbsp pure olive oil

1 Preheat the oven to 400°F (200°C). Place a rack in the middle of the oven.

2 Peel off the loose, outer layers of each head of garlic, but leave all the cloves connected. Trim ¼ to ½ inch (0.5 to 1.25cm) off the top of each head to expose the cloves.

3 Place the heads in ramekins or in the cups of a muffin tray. Drizzle ½ tablespoon of olive oil over each head. Cover each ramekin or the entire muffin tray with aluminum foil.

4 Place the tray in the oven and roast until soft and slightly caramelized, about 45 minutes. Remove the tray from the oven and allow the garlic to cool enough to handle.

5 Press on the bottom of each clove to pull or squeeze the roasted garlic cloves from their skins. Place the garlic on a board and use a fork to mash until a smooth paste has formed.

6 Use immediately or separate into smaller portions (about ½ tablespoon) and freeze in ice cube trays.

> **» QUICK TIP**
> The yield depends on the size and type of garlic used. Usually, 1 head of roasted garlic equals 1½ tablespoons of garlic paste.

PULSES

I often proclaim my love for pulses! The most versatile plant-based protein comes in cute little beans you can eat on their own, sprinkle on salads, mash to creamy perfection, add to soups, stews, and entrees—and so much more. Pulses help fight the climate crises and provide healthful nutrients to humans. Talk about superpowers!

INGREDIENTS

1 cup beans:

- **black & white:** black beans, black turtle beans, Great Northern beans, navy beans
- **black-eyed peas:** black-eyed peas, creamer peas, crowder peas
- **kidney beans:** red kidney beans, speckled kidney beans, cannellini beans
- **garbanzo beans:** chickpeas

6 cups water, divided

BLACK & WHITE BEANS

PREP TIME: **5 MINS** // COOK TIME: **60 TO 70 MINS** // YIELD: **ABOUT 3 CUPS**

BLACK-EYED PEAS

PREP TIME: **5 MINS** // COOK TIME: **50 TO 60 MINS** // YIELD: **ABOUT 3 CUPS**

KIDNEY BEANS

PREP TIME: **5 MINS** // COOK TIME: **80 TO 90 MINS** // YIELD: **ABOUT 3 CUPS**

GARBANZO BEANS

PREP TIME: **5 MINS** // COOK TIME: **80 TO 90 MINS** // YIELD: **ABOUT 3 CUPS**

1 Spread out the beans and discard bad beans, small pebbles, and dirt. Wash and strain the good ones.

2 In a medium-sized container, place the beans and cover with 3 cups of water. Soak for at least 4 hours, then drain.

3 In a medium saucepan on the stovetop over medium heat, combine the beans and the remaining 3 cups of water. Bring to a boil, then reduce the heat to low. Cover and simmer until the beans are cooked through and tender or per the cook time instructions.

4 Remove the saucepan from the heat and allow the beans to cool. Strain with a colander over a large bowl.

5 Transfer the beans to an airtight container. Wait until the beans have cooled down completely before refrigerating for later use.

» QUICK TIPS

Bad beans are often shriveled and might have insect holes or dark spots. You can also soak the beans overnight. This will slightly reduce the cooking time. Save the cooking liquid (aquafaba) of the garbanzo and white beans (Great Northern, navy, or cannellini) to use in such zero-waste recipes as **Aquafaba Mayonnaise** (page 235). Store cooked beans in an airtight container in the fridge for up to 5 days or in the freezer for up to 6 months.

SPLIT PEAS

INGREDIENTS

1 cup split peas (green or yellow)

3 cups water

1 Spread out the peas and discard any bad ones. Wash and strain the good ones.

2 In a medium saucepan on the stovetop over medium heat, combine the peas and water. Bring to a boil, then reduce the heat to low. Cover and simmer until the peas are tender but still have a little bite, about 18 to 23 minutes.

3 Strain the peas and transfer to an airtight container. Allow the peas to cool completely before refrigerating for later use.

> **» QUICK TIPS**
> Split peas might become mushy when overcooked. Store in an airtight container in the fridge for up to 5 days or in the freezer for up to 6 months.

GREEN LENTILS

RED LENTILS

INGREDIENTS

1 cup lentils

3 cups water

1 Spread out the lentils and discard any bad ones. Wash and strain the good ones.

2 In a medium saucepan on the stovetop over medium heat, combine the lentils and water. Bring to boil, then reduce the heat to the lowest heat setting. Cover and simmer until the lentils are tender but still have a little bite or per the cook time instructions. Place a mesh strainer in the sink and drain the cooking water. Rinse the lentils under cold water to stop the cooking process.

3 Strain the lentils and transfer to an airtight container. Wait until the lentils have cooled down completely before refrigerating for later use.

> **» QUICK TIPS**
> Lentils might become mushy when overcooked. Store in an airtight container in the fridge for up to 5 days or in the freezer for up to 6 months.

SEASONING BLENDS

Spices aren't always hot. Cumin, smoked paprika, and turmeric are considered mild to me. They lend a lot of flavor, but they don't make food spicy. My seasoning blends will help you infuse lots flavor into your dishes! Hint: Customize the blends to your preference.

UMAMI MUSHROOM POWDER

PREP TIME: **2 MINS** // COOK TIME: **NONE** // YIELD: **ABOUT 1½ OZ (45G)**

INGREDIENTS

1 tbsp plus 2 tsp shiitake mushroom powder

2 tsp onion powder

2 tsp garlic powder

1½ tsp finely ground black pepper

½ tsp ground sage

½ tsp ground cayenne

FURIKAKE SEAWEED SEASONING

PREP TIME: **2 MINS** // COOK TIME: **NONE** // YIELD: **ABOUT 1½ (45G)**

INGREDIENTS

1 tbsp plus ½ tsp roasted nori seaweed

1 tbsp plus ½ tsp toasted sesame seeds

2 tsp black sesame seeds

1 tsp kelp powder

1 tsp red pepper flakes

SPICY ADOBO SEASONING

PREP TIME: **2 MINS** // COOK TIME: **NONE** // YIELD: **ABOUT 1½ OZ (45G)**

INGREDIENTS

3 tsp ancho chili powder

2¾ tsp smoked paprika

2 tsp ground cumin

1 tsp ground turmeric

1 tsp finely ground black pepper

¾ tsp garlic powder

½ tsp onion powder

HOMEMADE CURRY POWDER

PREP TIME: **2 MINS** // COOK TIME: **NONE** // YIELD: **ABOUT 1½ OZ (45G)**

INGREDIENTS

3¾ tsp ground turmeric

2¼ tsp ground ginger

2 tsp onion powder

1 tsp ground cumin

1 tsp finely ground black pepper

¾ tsp ground coriander

½ tsp ground cinnamon

1 In a small bowl, combine all the ingredients for each seasoning blend. Use a funnel to transfer the blend to a spice jar or an airtight container.

» QUICK TIPS

• *For the mushroom powder:* Break about 1 ounce (30 grams) of dried shiitake mushrooms into small chunks. In a spice grinder, process the mushroom until pulverized, about 1 minute. (You can also use a blender or food processor for this process.)

• *For the seaweed seasoning:* Use your hands to crumble 1 sheet of nori seaweed and thinly slice into very small pieces.

• Store the seasoning blends in airtight containers in a cool, dry place for up to 6 months.

GRAINS

Whole grains enrich our diets with fiber and heart-healthy carbohydrates. Some grains, like quinoa and amaranth, are very small but SO powerful, carrying lots of healthful nutrients needed for our well-being. Not all carbs are created equal—and these grains prove that.

QUINOA

PREP TIME: **2 MINUTES** // COOK TIME: **15 MINUTES** // YIELD: **3 CUPS**

INGREDIENTS

1 cup quinoa (white, red, black, or tricolor)

2 cups water

> **» QUICK TIPS**
> Not rinsing the quinoa results in a bitter taste. Quinoa might become mushy if overcooked. Store in an airtight container in the fridge for up to 5 days or in the freezer for up to 2 months.

1 Use a mesh strainer to thoroughly rinse the quinoa.

2 In a medium saucepan on the stovetop over medium heat, bring the water to a boil. Stir in the quinoa. Reduce the heat to low. Simmer uncovered until the quinoa is tender but still has a little bite, about 15 minutes. Use a mesh strainer to drain any water.

3 Transfer to an airtight container. Wait until the quinoa has cooled down completely before refrigerating for later use.

BROWN OR WILD RICE

PREP TIME: **2 MINUTES** // COOK TIME: **35 TO 40 MINUTES** // YIELD: **3 CUPS**

INGREDIENTS

1 cup brown or wild rice

2¼ cups water

> **» QUICK TIPS**
> The cooking time for short-grain brown rice might be slightly less than noted. Check the rice for tenderness after 28 to 30 minutes. Store in an airtight container in the fridge for up to 6 days or in the freezer for up to 6 months.

1 Use a mesh strainer to thoroughly rinse the rice.

2 In a medium saucepan on the stovetop over medium heat, combine the rice and water. Bring to a boil, then reduce the heat to low. Cover and simmer until the water has been fully absorbed and the rice is tender, about 35 to 40 minutes.

3 Remove the saucepan from the heat and allow to rest covered for 8 minutes. Transfer to an airtight container. Wait until the rice has cooled down completely before refrigerating for later use.

AMARANTH

PREP TIME: **5 MINUTES**   //   COOK TIME: **21 TO 23 MINUTES**   //   YIELD: **2½ CUPS**

INGREDIENTS

1 cup amaranth

1½ cups water

> » **QUICK TIP**
>
> Store in an airtight container in the fridge for up to 5 days or in the freezer for up to 6 months.

1 In a small saucepan on the stovetop over medium heat, place the amaranth and lightly toast for 3 minutes. Add the water. Bring to a boil, then reduce the heat to low. Cover and simmer until the water has been fully absorbed, about 18 to 20 minutes.

2 Remove the saucepan from the heat and allow to rest covered for about 3 minutes. Use a fork to fluff the amaranth and transfer to an airtight container. Wait until the seeds have cooled down completely before refrigerating for later use.

MILLETS

PREP TIME: **2 MINUTES**   //   COOK TIME: **22 TO 23 MINUTES**   //   YIELD: **3½ CUPS**

INGREDIENTS

1 cup millets

2 cups water

> » **QUICK TIP**
>
> Store in an airtight container in the fridge for up to 5 days or in the freezer for up to 3 months.

1 In a medium saucepan on the stovetop over medium heat, place the millets and lightly toast for 2 to 3 minutes. Add the water. Bring to a boil, then reduce the heat to low. Cover and simmer until the water has been fully absorbed and the millets are tender, about 20 minutes.

2 Remove the saucepan from the heat and allow to rest covered for about 5 minutes. Use a fork to fluff the millets and transfer to an airtight container. Wait until the millets have cooled down completely before refrigerating for later use.

FARRO

PREP TIME: **1 MINUTE**   //   COOK TIME: **35 TO 40 MINUTES**   //   YIELD: **3 CUPS**

INGREDIENTS

1 cup whole farro

2½ cups water

> » **QUICK TIPS**
>
> If you're using pearled farro, cut the cooking time to 15 to 20 minutes. Store in an airtight container in the fridge for up to 6 days or in the freezer for up to 6 months.

1 In a medium saucepan on the stovetop over medium heat, combine the farro and water. Bring to a boil, then reduce the heat to low. Cover and simmer until the water has been fully absorbed and the farro is tender, about 35 to 40 minutes.

2 Remove the saucepan from the heat and allow to rest covered for 5 minutes. Fluff the farro with a fork and transfer to an airtight container. Wait until the farro has cooled down completely before refrigerating for later use.

ENDNOTES

CHAPTER 1

1 Crutzen, P.J. "Geology of Mankind." *Nature* 415. 2002.

2 Ripple, W., C. Wolf, T. Newsome, P. Barnard, and W. Moomaw. "World Scientists' Warning of a Climate Emergency." *BioScience* 70. 2020.

3 Crippa, M., G. Oreggioni, D. Guizzardi, M. Muntean, E. Schaaf et al. "Fossil CO_2 and GHG Emissions of All World Countries." Publications Office of the European Union. 2019.

4 Natural Resources Defense Council. "Global Warming 101." 2016.

5 Rogelj, J., D. Shindell, K. Jiang, S. Fifita, P. Forster et al. "Mitigation Pathways Compatible with 1.5°C in the Context of Sustainable Development." Intergovernmental Panel on Climate Change Special Report. 2018.

6 Lindsey, R., and L. Dahlman "Climate Change: Global Temperature." NOAA. Climate.gov. 2020.

7 National Oceanic and Atmospheric Administration. "Global Climate Report." 2019.

8 Arrhenius, S. "On the Influence of Carbonic Acid in the Air Upon the Temperature of the Ground." *Philosophical Magazine and Journal of Science* 5, 41. 1896.

9 Lindsey, R. "Climate Change: Atmospheric Carbon Dioxide." NOAA. Climate.gov. 2020.

10 Settele, J., R. Scholes, R. Betts, S. Bunn, P. Leadley et al. "Terrestrial and Inland Water System." Climate Change 2014: Impacts, Adaptation, and Vulnerability. Intergovernmental Panel on Climate Change Report. 2014.

11 Environmental Protection Agency. "Overview of Greenhouse Gases." 2019.

12 Food and Agriculture Administration of the United Nations. "Tackling Climate Change Through Livestock—A Global Assessment of Emissions and Mitigation Opportunities." 2013.

13 Yadvinder, M., J. Franklin, N. Seddon, M. Solan, M. Turner et al. "Climate Change and Ecosystems: Threats, Opportunities and Solutions." *The Royal Society* 375, 1974. 2020.

14 Convention on Biological Diversity. "Article 2: Use of Terms." 2006.

15 Sintayehu, D. "Impact of Climate Change on Biodiversity and Associated Key Ecosystem Services in Africa: A Systematic Review." *Ecosystem Health and Sustainability* 4, 9. 2018.

16 Travis, J. M. J. "Climate Change and Habitat Destruction: A Deadly Anthropogenic Cocktail." *The Royal Society* 270, 1514. 2003.

17 Dullinger, S., A. Gattringer, W. Thuiller, D. Moser, N. Zimmermann et al. "Extinction Debt of High-Mountain Plants Under Twenty-First-Century Climate Change." *Nature Climate Change* 2. 2012.

18 United Nations Foundation. "Ecosystems and Climate Change." 2018.

19 Lovejoy, T., and L. Hannah. "Avoiding the Climate Failsafe Point." *Science Advances* 22. 2018.

20 Scheelbeek, P., F. Bird, H. Tuomisto, R. Green, F. Harris et al. "Effect of Environmental Changes on Vegetable and Legume Yields and Nutritional Quality." Proceedings of the National Academy of Sciences. 2018.

21 Environmental Protection Agency. "Climate Change Impacts: Climate Impacts on Agriculture and Food Supply." 2017.

22 Development Initiatives. "Global Nutrition Report 2017: Nourishing the SDGs." 2017.

23 United Nations Educational, Scientific, and Cultural Organization. "World Water Assessment Programme: Facts and Figures." 2014.

24 Gornall, J., R. Betts, E. Burke, R. Clark, R. Camp et al. "Implications of Climate Change for Agricultural Productivity in the Early Twenty-First Century." *The Royal Society* 365, 1554. 2010.

25 Bierkens, M., and Y. Wada. "Non-Renewable Groundwater Use and Groundwater Depletion: A Review." *Environmental Research Letters* 14, 6. 2019.

26 Dalin, C., Y. Wada, T. Kastner, and M. Puma. "Groundwater Depletion Embedded in International Food Trade." *Nature* 543. 2017.

27 Scaven, V., and N. Rafferty. "Physiological Effects of Climate Warming on Flowering Plants and Insect Pollinators and Potential Consequences for Their Interactions." *Current Zoology* 59. 2013.

28 Ihsan, M., F. El-Nakhlawy, S. Ismail et al. "Wheat Phenological Development and Growth Studies as Affected by Drought and Late Season High Temperature Stress Under Arid Environment." *Frontiers in Plant Science* 7. 2016.

29 Oxfam. "Extreme Carbon Inequality: Why the Paris Climate Deal Must Put the Poorest, Lowest Emitting and Most Vulnerable People First." 2015.

30 United States Global Change Research Program. "Fourth National Climate Assessment: Volume II: Impacts, Risks, and Adaptation in the United States." 2018.

31 Gasparrini, A., Y. Guo, F. Sera, A.M. Vicedo-Cabrera, and V. Huber. "Projections of Temperature-Related Excess Mortality Under Climate Change Scenarios." *The Lancet Planetary Health* 1. 2017.

32 United States Global Change Research Program. "The Impacts of Climate Change on Human Health in the United States: A Scientific Assessment." 2016.

33 The Rockefeller Foundation–Lancet Commission on Planetary Health. "Safeguarding Human Health in the Anthropocene Epoch: Report of The Rockefeller Foundation–Lancet Commission on Planetary Health." 2015.

34 World Health Organization. "Coronavirus Disease 2019 (COVID-19) Situation Report." 2020.

35 United Nations Framework Convention on Climate Change. "Paris Agreement." 2015.

36 United Nations. "Sustainable Development Goals Knowledge Platform: Climate Change." 2015.

37 "United States First Nationally Determined Contribution to the Paris Agreement." 2015.

38 United Nations Development Programme. "Sustainable Development Goals: Background on the Goals." 2012.

39 United Nations. "Sustainable Development Goals: 17 Goals to Transform Our World." 2015.

40 United Nations. "Sustainable Development Goals Knowledge Platform: Climate Change." 2015.

41 Poore, J., and T. Nemecek. "Reducing Food's Environmental Impacts Through Producers and Consumers." *Science* 1. 2018.

42 Ritchie, H., and M. Roser. "Environmental Impacts of Food Production." *Our World in Data*. 2020.

43 Azevedo, L., R. van Zelma, A. Hendriks, R. Bobbink, and M. Huijbregts. "Global Assessment of the Effects of Terrestrial Acidification on Plant Species Richness." *Environmental Pollution* 174. 2013.

44 Chislock, M., E. Doster, R. Zitomer, and A. Wilson. "Eutrophication: Causes, Consequences, and Controls in Aquatic Ecosystems." *Nature Education Knowledge*. 2013.

45 Willet, W., J. Rockström, B. Loken, M. Springmann, T. Lang et al. "Food in the Anthropocene: The EAT–Lancet Commission on Healthy Diets from Sustainable Food Systems." *The Lancet*. 2019.

46 Ritchie, H. "Food Production Is Responsible for One-Quarter of the World's Greenhouse Gas Emissions." *Our World in Data*. 2019.

47 Food and Agriculture Administration of the United Nations. "Tackling Climate Change Through Livestock—A Global Assessment of Emissions and Mitigation Opportunities." 2013.

48 Climate and Clean Air Coalition. "Enteric Fermentation." 2014.

49 Keith Paustian, K., N.H. Ravindranath, A. van Amstel, M. Gytarsky, and V. Kurz. "Volume 4: Agriculture, Forestry and Other Land Use: IPCC Guidelines for National Greenhouse Gas Inventories." 2006.

50 Intergovernmental Panel on Climate Change. "Refinement to the 2006 IPCC Guidelines on National Greenhouse Gas Inventories." 2019.

51 UN Food and Agriculture Organization. "Global Livestock Environmental Assessment Model (GLEAM)." 2010.

52 World Wildlife Fund. "Appetite for Destruction." 2017.

53 Dunkley, C. "Global Warming: How Does It Relate to Poultry?" University of Georgia Extension: Bulletin 1382. 2014.

54 UN Food and Agriculture Organization. P. Gerber, C. Opio, and H. Steinfeld. "Poultry Production and the Environment—A Review." 2007.

55 Gerber, P., P. Chilonda, G. Franceschini, and H. Menzi. "Geographical Determinants and Environmental Implications of Livestock Production Intensification in Asia." *Bioresource Technology* 96. 2005.

56 Ritchie, H., and M. Roser. "Seafood Production." *Our World in Data*. 2019.

57 Parker, R. J. Blanchard, C. Gardner, B. Green, K. Hartmann et al. "Fuel Use and Greenhouse Gas Emissions of World Fisheries." *Nature Climate Change* 8. 2018.

58 MacLeod, M., M. Hasan, D. Robb, M. Mamun-Ur-Rashid et al. "Quantifying Greenhouse Gas Emissions from Global Aquaculture." *Nature Scientific Reports*. 2017.

59 United States Department of Agriculture: Economic Research Service. "The Estimated Amount, Value, and Calories of Postharvest Food Losses at the Retail and Consumer Levels in the United States." *Economic Information Bulletin* 121. 2014.

60 Climate Watch. "Historical GHG Emissions." 2020.

61 UN Food and Agriculture Organization. "Food Wastage Footprint: Impacts on Natural Resources." 2013.

62 United Nations: Sustainable Development Goals. "Goal 12." 2015.

63 Bajželj, B., K. Richards, J. Allwood, P. Smith, J. Dennis et al. "Importance of Food-Demand Management for Climate Mitigation." *Nature Climate Change* 4. 2014.

64 Hawken, P., and A. Ravenhill. "The Drawdown Project: Table of Solutions." 2017.

65 National Agricultural Library. "Agricultural Thesaurus and Glossary."

66 United States Department of Agriculture. "National Agricultural Statistics Service."

67 National Sustainable Agriculture Coalition. "Agriculture and Climate Change: Policy Imperatives and Opportunities to Help Producers Meet the Challenge." 2019.

68 Potera, C. "Agriculture: Pesticides Disrupt Nitrogen Fixation." *Environmental Health Perspectives* 115:12. 2007.

69 Rodale Institute. "Regenerative Organic Agriculture and Climate Change: A Down-to-Earth Solution to Global Warming." 2013.

70 Carbon Cycle Institute. "Carbon Farming." 2020.

71 UN Food and Agriculture Organization. "Soil Carbon Sequestration."

72 Zomer, R., D. Bossio, R. Sommer, and L. Verchot. "Global Sequestration Potential of Increased Organic Carbon in Cropland Soils." *Scientific Reports* 7. 2017.

73 The Carbon Underground and Regenerative Agriculture Initiative. "What Is Regenerative Agriculture?" 2017.

CHAPTER 2

1 Amend, T., B. Barbeau, B. Beyers, S. Burns, S. Eißing et al. "A Big Foot on a Small Planet? Accounting with the Ecological Footprint. Succeeding in a World with Growing Resource Constraints." *Sustainability Has Many Faces* 10. 2010.

2 Rees, W., and M. Wackernagel. *Our Ecological Footprint: Reducing Human Impact on the Earth*. New Society Publishers. 1996.

3 Global Footprint Network. "Ecological Footprint."

4 National Foodprint Accounts. "2019 National Footprint and Biocapacity Accounts Data Set (1961–2016)."

5 Global Footprint Network. "Earth Overshoot Day."

6 Wackernagel, M., and B. Beyers. *Ecological Footprint: Managing Our Biocapacity Budget*. New Society Publishers. 2019.

7 Lin, D., L. Hanscom, A. Murthy et al. "Ecological Footprint Accounting for Countries: Updates and Results of the National Footprint Accounts, 2012–2018." *Resources*. 2018.

8 Global Footprint Network. "Climate Change: Carbon Footprint."

9 Ritchie, H. "Who Emits the Most CO_2 Today?" *Our World in Data*. 2019

10 Ritchie, H. "Where in the World Do People Emit the Most CO₂?" *Our World in Data*. 2019.

11 World Health Organization. "Reducing Your Carbon Footprint Can Be Good for Your Health." 2008.

12 Goldstein, B., M. Birkved, J. Fernández, and M. Hauschild. "Surveying the Environmental Footprint of Urban Food Consumption." *Journal of Industrial Ecology* 21. 2016.

13 FoodPrint. "What Is a FoodPrint?"

14 Weber, C., and H. Matthews. "Food-Miles and the Relative Climate Impacts of Food Choices in the United States." *Environmental Science and Technology* 42. 2008.

15 Kim, B., R. Neff, R. Santo, and J. Vigorito. "The Importance of Reducing Animal Product Consumption and Wasted Food in Mitigating Catastrophic Climate Change." Johns Hopkins Center for a Livable Future. 2015.

16 Burlingame, B., and S. Dernini. "Sustainable Diets and Biodiversity: Directions and Solutions for Policy, Research and Action." International Scientific Symposium, Biodiversity and Sustainable Diets United Against Hunger. Rome, Italy: Food and Agriculture Organization (FAO). 2010.

17 Ritchie, H., and M. Roser. "Environmental Impacts of Food Production." *Our World in Data*. 2020.

18 Ritchie, H. "Less Meat Is Nearly Always Better Than Sustainable Meat, to Reduce Your Carbon Footprint." *Our World in Data*. 2020.

19 Neufeld, D. "The Carbon Footprint of the Food Supply Chain." *Visual Capitalist*. 2020.

20 Poore, J., and T. Nemecek. "Reducing Food's Environmental Impacts Through Producers and Consumers." *Science* 360. 2018.

21 Intergovernmental Panel on Climate Change. "Special Report on Climate Change and Land." 2019.

22 Shrink That Footprint. "The Carbon Foodprint of 5 Diets Compared." 2015.

23 Schaeffer, J. "The Low-Carbon Diet: A Protection Plan for the Planet." *Today's Dietitian* 10. 2008.

24 Poore, J., and T. Nemecek. "Reducing Food's Environmental Impacts Through Producers and Consumers. *Science* 360. 2018.

25 Ritchie, H. "Very Little of Global Food Is Transported by Air; This Greatly Reduces the Climate Benefits of Eating Local." *Our World in Data*. 2020.

26 Sims, R., R. Schaeffer, F. Creutzig, X. Cruz-Núñez, M. D'Agosto et al. "Climate Change 2014: Mitigation of Climate Change." Contribution of Working Group III to the Fifth Assessment Report of the Intergovernmental Panel on Climate Change. 2014.

27 Alfoeldi, T., A. Fliessbach, U. Geier, L. Kilcher, U. Niggli et al. "Organic Agriculture and the Environment." Organic Agriculture, Environment and Food Security Report by the Food and Agriculture Organization (FAO). 2002.

28 The Carbon Underground and Regenerative Agriculture Initiative. "What Is Regenerative Agriculture?" 2017.

29 Rodale Institute. "Regenerative Organic Agriculture."

30 US Department of Agriculture. Agricultural Marketing Service. "National Organic Program."

31 UN Food and Agriculture Organization. "Once Neglected, These Traditional Crops Are Our New Rising Stars." 2018.

32 UN Food and Agriculture Organization. "What Is Happening to Agrobiodiversity?" 2018.

33 FoodPrint. "Raising Crops Sustainably."

CHAPTER 3

1 Eshel, G., P. Stainier, A. Shepon, and A. Swaminathan. "Environmentally Optimal, Nutritionally Sound, Protein and Energy Conserving Plant Based Alternatives to U.S. Meat." *Scientific Reports* 9. 2019.

2 US Department of Agriculture. "What Foods Are in the Grains Group?" 2019.

3 Feeney, M.J., A. Miller, and P. Roupas. "Mushrooms—Biologically Distinct and Nutritionally Unique: Exploring a Third Food Kingdom." *Nutrition Today* 49. 2014.

4 Knorr, WWF, and Washington University. "Future 50 Foods: 50 Foods for Healthier People and a Healthier Planet." 2019.

5 Willett, W., J. Rockström, B. Loken, M. Springmann, T. Lang et al. "Food in the Anthropocene: The EAT–Lancet Commission on Healthy Diets from Sustainable Food Systems." *The Lancet*. 2019.

6 Physicians Committee for Responsible Medicine. "Plant-Based Diets: The Power of a Plant-Based Diet for Good Health."

7 US Department of Agriculture. National Agricultural Library. "Dietary Reference Intakes."

8 Campbell, T.C. "The Mystique of Protein and Its Implications." *Nutrition Studies*. 2019.

9 Global Citizen. "7 Foods You Can Eat to Help the Environment." 2016.

10 Goldhamer, A. "Where Do You Get Your Protein?" *Nutrition Studies*. 2018.

11 US Department of Agriculture. Natural Resources Conservation Service. "Cover Crops and Soil Health."

12 Library of Congress. "Food Preservation: Selected Titles." Science Reference Guides.

13 Sacks, K. "How Sustainable Are Sugar Substitutes?" Published at Foodprint.org. 2020.

14 Marie, A. "TOFU: Ingredient Guide for Health, Environment, Animals, Laborers." Published at HEALabel.com. 2020.

15 Loken, B., and F. DeClerck. "Diets for a Better Future: Rebooting and Reimagining Healthy and Sustainable Food Systems in the G20." EAT Foundation. 2020.

16 World Health Organization. "Noncommunicable Diseases." 2018.

17 Alexander, H. "5 Benefits of a Plant-Based Diet." *Focused on Health*. 2019.

18 Clark, M., M. Springmann, J. Hill, and D. Tilman. "Multiple Health and Environmental Impacts of Foods." *Proceedings of the National Academy of Sciences* 116. 2019.

REGIONAL & SEASONAL SWAPS

BREAKFAST

AMARANTH PANCAKES (p. 60)

Gala apple: any variety of apple

OVERNIGHT BEET OATS (p. 62)

Beet: carrot

Fuji apple: any variety of apple, pear, peach

Dried apricots: dried mango/goldenberries/cranberries

Raw cashews: raw walnuts/pecans/sliced almonds

TOFU PERICO SCRAMBLE (p. 63)

White onion: brown/sweet onion, scallion whites, leek

Baby bella mushroom: shiitake/cremini/portobello mushrooms, eggplant

Roma tomato: vine-ripened/beefsteak/heirloom tomato, red bell pepper

Orange bell pepper: yellow/green bell pepper, sweet pepper

WATERMELON PIZZA (p. 64)

Blackberries, blueberries: strawberries, raspberries, goldenberries, cherries

Fresh mint: fresh basil

AVOCADO SMOOTHIE BOWL (p. 67)

Kiwi: mango, nectarine

Baby spinach: baby kale

Pitaya: prickly pear fruit, guava

Raspberries, goldenberries: strawberries, blackberries, blueberries, cherries

OAT WAFFLES (p. 72)

Mango: pineapple, nectarine

SMALL BITES

JACKFRUIT EMPANADITAS (p. 76)

Shallots: red/white/brown onions, scallion whites

Shredded green jackfruit: shredded king oyster mushrooms

STUFFED SQUASH BLOSSOMS (p. 78)

Butternut squash: sweet potato, yam, acorn squash

Parsley stems: cilantro stems

Squash blossoms: pumpkin flowers

BROCCOLI STALK CAKES (p. 79)

Broccoli stalk/stem: cauliflower, Romanesco stalk/stem

Scallion: leek, chives, shallots

PLANTAIN CUPS (p. 80)

Vine-ripened tomato: Roma/beefsteak/heirloom tomato

Brown onion: white/red onion, shallot, leek

Red bell pepper: orange/yellow/green bell pepper, sweet pepper

STUFFED SHIITAKE MUSHROOMS (p. 82)

Shiitake: baby bella, cremini, button mushroom

Carrot: golden beet, sweet potato, yam

Spinach: arugula, dandelion, radicchio

FAVA BEAN POD BOLLITOS (p. 83)

Shallot: red/white/brown onion, scallion whites, leek

Poblano pepper: Anaheim/jalapeño/green bell pepper

POTATO & EGGPLANT SKEWERS (p. 84)

Eggplant: portobello mushroom, red bell pepper

Baby potato: celeriac, rutabaga, parsnip

Red onion: white/brown onion

BARBECUE CAULIFLOWER (p. 86)

Cauliflower: broccoli, Romanesco

SAVORY QUINOA BEIGNETS (p. 87)

Cauliflower: broccoli, Romanesco

Brown onion: white/red onion, leek

FALAFEL BITES (p. 88)

White onion: brown/red onion, leek

Parsley: basil, scallion greens

Vine-ripened tomato: Roma/beefsteak/heirloom tomato

SALADS

NOPAL CACTUS PAD & QUINOA SALAD (p. 92)

Tomatillos: underripe/green tomato

Red nopal fruit: pink dragon fruit, guava

Red bell pepper: orange/yellow bell pepper, sweet pepper

FAVA BEAN & ZUCCHINI SALAD (p. 94)

Fresh fava beans: fresh lima beans, soybeans

Zucchini: crookneck, white squash, chayote

Arugula: watercress, dandelion greens

Yellow bell pepper: orange/red bell pepper, sweet pepper

JÍCAMA & CORN SALAD (p. 95)

Jícama: Asian pear, sunchoke, white radish

Cilantro: parsley, chives, scallion greens

Fresno pepper: jalapeño/serrano pepper, sweet/red pepper

SWEET POTATO & GREAT NORTHERN BEAN SALAD (p. 96)

Sweet potato: purple/white/Japanese sweet potato, yam/ube

Great Northern beans: garbanzo beans, broad/fava beans

Arugula: dandelion/radish greens, watercress, spinach

Purple cabbage: green/savoy/napa cabbage, radicchio

Pomegranate seeds: dried cranberries/cherries

MUSHROOM & STRING BEAN SALAD (p. 98)

Wild brown beech mushroom: white beech/shimeji, enoki mushroom

String bean: white/dragon tongue bean, snap/snow pea

Heirloom carrot: golden/purple beet, parsnip

Fresh ginger: fresh turmeric

ASPARAGUS SALAD (p. 99)

Asparagus: white asparagus, white/string beans

Grape tomato: cherry/yellow currant/tiny Tim tomato

Cilantro: parsley, chives, scallion greens

Red onion: shallot, brown/white/sweet onion

MILLET & OKRA SALAD (p. 100)

Okra: nopales/prickly pear pad, string bean

Purple cauliflower: white cauliflower, Romanesco, broccoli

Millet: quinoa, amaranth, fonio

Red pepper: orange/yellow bell pepper, sweet pepper

Mint: lemon balm, basil, flat-leaf/curly parsley

SHAVED FENNEL, CELERY & PINK GRAPEFRUIT SALAD (p. 102)

Fennel bulb: bok choy, raw celeriac

Shallot: red onion, scallion whites

Pink grapefruit: red/white grapefruit, blood orange, pomelo

Red globe radish: Easter egg/daikon radish

CHAYOTE & MANGO SLAW (p. 104)

English peas: garden peas, fresh fava beans, edamame

Purple cabbage: green/savoy/napa cabbage, radicchio

Chayote squash: green papaya, cucuzza/ summer squash

Green mango: unripe peach/nectarine

Scallions: chives

AMARANTH TABBOULEH (p. 105)

Persian cucumber: English/garden cucumber, zucchini

Amaranth: millet, quinoa, bulgur, couscous

Radish greens: dandelion, watercress, arugula

Pomegranate seeds: dried cranberries/ cherries

Mint: basil, flat-leaf/curly parsley

Shallot: red onion, scallion whites

SWISS CHARD & LENTIL SALAD (p. 106)

Leeks: scallions, spring/white/brown onions

Swiss chard: rainbow chard, mustard greens, spinach, kale

Red lentil: green/black lentil

CURRIED CAULIFLOWER SALAD (p. 108)

Cauliflower: purple/yellow cauliflower, Romanesco, broccoli

Fuji apple: any variety of apple, pear

Celery: fennel bulb

Red pepper: orange/yellow bell pepper, sweet pepper

Chives: scallion greens, parsley, ramson/ wild garlic

WILD RICE & TOMATO SALAD (p. 109)

Wild rice: brown rice, farro, wheatberry

Heirloom tomato: vine-ripened/Roma/ beefsteak tomato

Cucumber: English/Persian cucumber, zucchini/summer squash

Romaine lettuce: butter lettuce, kale, chard

CUCUMBER, PEA & DAIKON SALAD (p. 110)

Garden cucumber: English/Persian cucumber

Sugar snap pea: snow pea, string/white bean

Scallion: chives, spring onion green

Fresno pepper: jalapeño/serrano pepper, sweet/red pepper

SIDES

YUCA (p. 114)

Leek: spring onion, scallion, ramson/wild garlic

Curly parsley: flat-leaf parsley, cilantro, chive

DOMINO RICE & BEANS (p. 115)

Brown onion: white/sweet/red onion

Red bell pepper: orange/yellow/green bell pepper, sweet pepper

Brown rice: farro, white quinoa, barley

Black beans: adzuki/kidney beans

ROASTED HEIRLOOM CARROTS (p. 116)

Heirloom carrot: Danvers/Nantes/ Chantenay carrot, parsnip

Carrot-top leaves: radish greens, curly/flat-leaf parsley

ACORN SQUASH (p. 118)

Acorn squash: butternut/Hubbard/delicata squash

Kale: chard, collard/mustard greens, turnip/kohlrabi tops

ROASTED OKRA (p. 119)

Okra: fiddlehead green, string/green beans

Butternut squash: acorn/Hubbard squash, sweet potato, yam

Leeks: scallions, spring onions

ROASTED FINGERLING POTATOES (p. 120)

Red onion: shallot, brown/sweet onion

Fresh thyme: fresh oregano/marjoram

Rainbow fingerling potatoes: peewee/red thumb/baby Yukon potato

Fresh rosemary: fresh sage

Raw walnuts: raw pecans/pistachio

CROOKNECK SQUASH (p. 122)

Fresh ginger: fresh turmeric

Wild king oyster mushrooms: shiitake/ portobello mushroom

Crookneck squash: zucchini/white/Zephyr squash

Scallion greens: chives, ramson/wild garlic

ROASTED RADISHES (p. 123)

Red globe radish: Easter egg/white beauty/fresh breakfast radish

Parsley stems: cilantro stems, chives

EDAMAME PILAF (p. 124)

Fresh edamame: fresh fava/lima beans, fresh garden/English peas

Fresh ginger: fresh turmeric

Wild rice: brown rice, quinoa, wheatberry

Raw almonds: raw macadamia/pine nuts

PLANTAIN DUMPLINGS (p. 126)

Red bell pepper: orange/yellow bell pepper, sweet pepper

Scallions: chives, spring onions

SAUTÉED BEET GREENS (p. 127)

Beet greens: turnip/kohlrabi tops, Swiss/rainbow chard

Red onions: shallots, leeks

CORN LOLLIPOPS (p. 128)

Dried chipotle pepper: dried ancho chili

SOUPS & STEWS

MANGO AND GINGER GAZPACHO (p. 132)

English cucumber: Persian/garden cucumber

Yellow bell pepper: orange bell pepper, sweet pepper

Shallot: scallion whites, spring onion bulb

Cilantro leaves and stems: parsley leaves and stems

Fresno pepper: jalapeño/serrano pepper, red bell pepper

FAVA BEAN & AVOCADO SOUP (p. 134)

Fresh fava beans: fresh lima beans, edamame, English/garden peas

Shallot: scallion whites, spring onion bulb

Flat-leaf parsley: curly parsley, scallion greens

SPLIT PEA SOUP (p. 135)

Leek: scallion, white/brown onion

Carrot: parsnip, golden beet

Celery: fennel

Green bell pepper: yellow/orange bell pepper, Anaheim pepper (mildly spicy)

CREAMY BUTTERNUT SOUP (p. 136)

Butternut squash: acorn/Hubbard squash, red kuri pumpkin

Vidalia onion: sweet/Maui/brown onion

LENTIL MINESTRONE (p. 138)

White onion: brown/sweet onion, leek

Heirloom carrot: Danvers/Nantes/Chantenay carrot, parsnip

Celery: fennel bulb

Chayote squash: cucuzza squash

Heirloom tomato: Roma/vine-ripened/beefsteak tomato

Italian squash: crookneck/Zephyr/white squash

Baby kale: baby spinach, chopped collard greens/chard

Orange bell pepper: yellow/red bell pepper, sweet pepper

SPICED PUMPKIN SOUP (p. 139)

Red kuri pumpkin: butternut/acorn squash

Sweet onion: Vidalia/brown onion

Fennel: celery

Red bell pepper: orange/yellow/green bell pepper

Fennel fronds: dill

PLANT-BASED MEATBALL SOUP (p. 140)

Leek: shallot, scallion whites

Flat-leaf parsley: curly parsley, cilantro, scallion greens

Carrot: heirloom carrot, parsnip

Celery: fennel

Brown onion: white/sweet onion

Red bell pepper: orange/yellow/green bell pepper

BROCCOLI SOUP (p. 142)

Broccoli: Romanesco

Shallot: scallion whites, spring onion bulb

Carrot: parsnip, golden beet

Celery: fennel

Spinach: arugula, kale

BLACK BEAN CHILI (p. 143)

Brown onion: Vidalia/sweet onion

Carrot: heirloom carrot, golden beet

Celery: fennel

Vine-ripened tomato: Roma, beefsteak tomato

Green bell pepper: yellow/orange/green bell pepper

Cilantro leaves and stems: parsley leaves and stems

Serrano pepper: jalapeño/Fresno pepper

EGGPLANT & SWEET POTATO CURRY (p. 144)

Eggplant: Japanese eggplant, portobello mushrooms

Sweet potato: yams, ube

White onion: brown/sweet/Maui onion

Fresh ginger: fresh turmeric

Globe tomato: ripe heirloom/beefsteak tomato, red bell pepper

BLACK-EYED PEA & VEGETABLE STEW (p. 146)

Sweet onion: Vidalia/Maui onion

Celery: fennel

Heirloom carrot: Danvers/Nantes/Chantenay carrot, parsnip

Red potato: Yukon potato, rutabaga

Heirloom tomato: vine-ripened/Roma/beefsteak tomato

SPICY CHAYOTE & TOMATO CASSEROLE (p. 147)

Beefsteak tomato: globe/heirloom tomato

Serrano pepper: jalapeño/Fresno/habanero pepper

Red onion: shallot

Chayote squash: cucuzza squash

Yellow bell pepper: orange/red bell pepper, sweet pepper

CHAYOTE TAGINE (p. 148)

Brown onion: sweet/Maui onion

Fresh ginger: fresh turmeric

Red potato: Yukon potato, rutabaga

Heirloom carrot: Danvers/Nantes/Chantenay carrot, parsnip

Chayote squash: cucuzza squash

BRAISED NOPAL CACTUS PADS (p. 150)

Red bell pepper: orange/yellow bell pepper

Plum tomato: Roma/globe/beefsteak tomato

White onion: spring onion bulb, brown onion

Scallion: chives, spring onion

GARBANZO & POTATO STEW (p. 151)

Brown onion: Maui/sweet onion, shallot

Heirloom potato: Yukon/red/fingerling potato, celeriac

English peas: garden peas, fresh fava/lima beans

Jalapeño: serrano, green bell pepper

Baby arugula: watercress, dandelion, spinach

Curly parsley: flat-leaf parsley, cilantro, chive

Green bell pepper: yellow/orange bell pepper

WHITE BEAN & KALE STEW (p. 152)

Great Northern bean: cannellini, white kidney beans

White heirloom carrot: Danvers/Nantes/Chantenay carrot, parsnip

Celery: fennel, leek

Cauliflower florets: broccoli/Romanesco florets, Brussels sprouts (quartered)

Green bell pepper: yellow/orange bell pepper

Kale: collard/mustard greens, Swiss/rainbow chard

MAIN DISHES

CAULIFLOWER CEVICHE (p. 156)

Sweet potato: purple/Japanese sweet potato, yam, ube

Red bell pepper: orange/yellow bell pepper, sweet pepper

Jalapeño: serrano/habanero pepper

EGGPLANT & LENTIL STACKS (p. 158)

Plum tomato: Roma/globe/beefsteak tomato

Fresh basil: fresh flat-leaf parsley

Brown onion: white/red/sweet onion, shallot, leek"

MUSHROOM BÁNH MÌ (p. 159)

Daikon: white radish, jícama

Portobello mushroom: shiitake/king oyster/baby bella mushroom

Garden cucumber: English/Persian cucumber

Jalapeño: serrano/Fresno pepper

Scallion: spring onion, chives

PURPLE SWEET POTATO GNOCCHI (p. 160)

Purple sweet potato: orange/Japanese sweet potato, yam, ube

Carrot tops: radish tops, parsley

Raw walnuts: raw pecans, pine nuts

Garlic: ramson/wild garlic, shallot

KING OYSTER MUSHROOM AREPAS (p. 163)

Black beans: adzuki/pinto/kidney beans

Brown onion: Vidalia/sweet/white onion

Green bell pepper: red/orange/yellow bell pepper

CREAMY FARRO CASSEROLE (p. 164)

Shallot: scallion whites, spring onion bulb

Fennel: celery

Butternut squash: acorn/Hubbard squash

Farro: wheatberry, barley

Red bell pepper: orange/yellow bell pepper, sweet pepper

Fresh thyme: fresh oregano/marjoram

Broccoli florets: Romanesco/cauliflower florets, Brussels sprouts (sliced)

SPAGHETTI SQUASH BOLOGNESE (p. 165)

Shallot: white/red/brown onion, spring onion bulb

Eggplant: portobello mushrooms

Raw walnuts: raw pecans

Roma tomatoes: beefsteak/globe/vine-ripened tomatoes

TOSTONES NACHOS (p. 166)

Purple cabbage: green/savoy/Napa cabbage

Pepitas: sunflower seeds

Tomatillos: green/unripe tomato

Scallion: spring onion

Jalapeño: serrano, Fresno

Vine-ripened tomatoes: Roma/heirloom/cherry tomato

Cilantro: parsley, scallion greens

PAPAYA POKE STACKS (p. 168)

Savoy cabbage: green/Napa/purple cabbage

Daikon: white radish, jícama

Ripe mango: pineapple, nectarine

Persian cucumber: English/garden cucumber

ANNATTO RICE (p. 170)

Romanesco: broccoli, cauliflower, quartered Brussels sprouts

Sweet onions: Maui/brown onions, leeks

Celery: fennel

Carrots: golden beets, yams, butternut squash

Vine-ripened tomatoes: Roma/heirloom/cherry tomato

Yellow bell pepper: orange/red bell pepper, sweet pepper

Flat-lea parsley: curly parsley, basil, chives

CRISPY SPROUTED TOFU (p. 171)

White onions: brown/red/sweet onion

Celery: daikon, fennel

Red bell pepper: orange/yellow/green bell pepper, sweet pepper

Sugar snap peas: snow peas, string/green beans

Zucchini: crookneck/Zephyr/white squash

ZUCCHINI NOODLES (p. 172)

Portobello mushroom: shiitake/cremini/maitake mushroom

Radicchio: purple/green cabbage, Belgian endive

Zucchini: crookneck/Zephyr/white squash

Fresh basil: fresh parsley

Spinach: arugula, kale, chard

Leek: scallion, spring onions

QUINOA-STUFFED PEPPERS (p. 174)

Celery: fennel, leek

Japanese eggplant: globe/Rosa Bianca/American eggplant

Dandelion leaves: mature watercress, arugula

Roma tomatoes: heirloom/vine-ripened tomatoes

CAULIFLOWER STEAKS (p. 176)
Cauliflower: Romanesco

White onion: brown/red onion

Green bell pepper: red/orange/yellow bell pepper

Fresh English peas: fresh garden peas, edamame, lima beans

Heirloom tomato: Roma/vine-ripened/beefsteak tomato

Fresh basil: fresh parsley

Scallion: spring onion, chives

JACKFRUIT & LEAFSTALK TACOS (p. 177)
Brown onion: sweet/white/red onion

Cauliflower leafstalk: broccoli/Romanesco leafstalk, chard stalks

Green bell pepper: red/orange/yellow bell pepper

Radish: turnip, parsnip

Jalapeño: serrano/Fresno pepper

SWEET POTATO TACOS (p. 178)
Collard greens: Swiss/rainbow chard, mustard greens, kale

Purple cabbage: green/Napa/savoy cabbage

Brown onions: sweet/Maui onions

Garlic: ramson/wild garlic

Sweet potato: yam, ube

Easter egg radish: red globe/French breakfast/white radish

Fresno pepper: jalapeño/serrano pepper, red pepper

BEVERAGES
CHUNKY TROPICAL FRUIT TIZANA (p. 182)

Pomegranate seeds: fresh passion fruit seeds

Mango: pineapple, nectarine

Galia melon: cantaloupe/honeydew melon

Green seedless grapes: red seedless/globe grapes

Fresh orange juice: fresh grapefruit juice

LOADED BREAKFAST SMOOTHIE (p. 188)
Baby spinach: baby kale

Blackberries: raspberries

Blueberries: pitted cherries, goldenberries

Cashew butter: peanut/almond/macadamia butter

DESSERTS
QUINOA PUDDING (p. 198)

Raisins: currants, dried cranberries

BUÑUELOS (p. 206)

Almond butter: cashew/peanut/pecan butter

YAM & MACA TRUFFLES (p. 208)

Yam: orange/white/purple/Japanese sweet potatoes

LEGUMINOUS CHOCOLATE PUDDING (p. 209)

Raspberries: blackberries/blueberries/strawberries/goldenberries

SAUCES, DIPS, PICKLES & MORE
BARBECUE SAUCE (p. 214)

Vine-ripened tomatoes: Roma/globe/beefsteak tomatoes

SALSA VERDE (p. 215)

Radish greens: carrot tops, dandelion, watercress

Parsley: cilantro, basil

Garlic: ramson, shallot

GUASACACA (p. 215)

Cilantro: parsley

Scallion: chive

Green bell pepper: Anaheim/hatch pepper

Serrano: jalapeño

ROASTED RED PEPPER DIP (p. 216)

Red bell pepper: orange/yellow bell pepper, sweet pepper

Raw walnuts: raw pecans, pine nuts

BLACK BEAN DIP (p. 218)
Brown onion: sweet/white/red onion

Green bell pepper: red/orange/yellow bell pepper

Serrano pepper: jalapeño/Fresno/habanero pepper

CUCUMBER & SHALLOT RAITA (p. 219)
English cucumber: garden/Persian cucumber

Fresh mint: fresh basil, lemon balm, parsley

FAVA BEAN SPREAD (p. 219)
Shallots: scallion whites, spring onion bulbs

Fresh lemon balm: fresh mint, basil

MANGO SALSA (p. 224)
Red lentils: green/black lentils

Cilantro: parsley, chive

Shallots: scallion whites, spring onion bulbs

Red bell pepper: orange/yellow/green bell pepper

Jalapeño: serrano/Fresno pepper

INDEX

A

Acorn Squash with Wilted Kale, 118
action plan, 51–57
amaranth
  Amaranth, 243
  Amaranth Pancakes with Apple Compote, 61
  Amaranth Tabbouleh with Cucumber & Pomegranate Seeds, 105
  Coconut & Chia Bowl with Warm Ancient Grains, 69
Annatto Rice with Kidney Beans & Romanesco Florets, 170
apples
  Amaranth Pancakes with Apple Compote, 61
  Cauliflower Leafstalk Kimchi, 226
  Curried Cauliflower Salad with Apples & Celery, 108
  Overnight Beet Oats, 62
Aquafaba Mayonnaise, 235
Asparagus Salad with Avocado & Grape Tomatoes, 99
avocados
  Asparagus Salad with Avocado & Grape Tomatoes, 99
  Avocado Seed Powder, 231
  Avocado Smoothie Bowl with Fresh Fruits, 67
  Avocado Toast, 70
  Fava Bean & Avocado Soup, 134
  Guasacaca (spicy avocado sauce), 215
  Jackfruit & Leafstalk Tacos with Avocado & Radish Greens Crema, 177
  King Oyster Mushroom Arepas, 163
  Papaya Poke Stacks with Wasabi Slaw, 169

B

baby potatoes, Potato & Eggplant Skewers, 85
baby spinach, Avocado Smoothie Bowl with Fresh Fruits, 67
bananas
  Avocado Smoothie Bowl with Fresh Fruits, 67
  Berry & Banana Sorbet, 201
  Chunky Tropical Fruit Tizana, 183
  Leguminous Chocolate Pudding, 209
  Loaded Breakfast Smoothie, 188
  Quinoa Porridge with Stewed Bananas & Prunes, 66
  Watermelon Pizza, 64

Barbecue Cauliflower, 86
Barbecue Sauce, 214
beans. See also string beans
  black
    Black Bean Chili, 147
    Black Bean Dip, 218
    Black & White Beans, 238
    Domino Rice & Beans with Spicy Adobo Seasoning, 115
    King Oyster Mushroom Arepas, 163
  fava
    Fava Bean & Avocado Soup, 134
    Fava Bean Pod Bollitos, 83
    Fava Bean Spread, 219
    Fava Bean & Zucchini Salad with Apple Cider Dressing, 94
  garbanzo
    Falafel Bites on Endive Boats, 88
    Garbanzo Beans, 238
    Garbanzo & Potato Stew, 151
    Plant-Based Meatball Soup, 141
  Great Northern
    Black & White Beans, 238
    Sweet Potato & Great Northern Bean Salad with Tahini Dressing, 96
    White Bean & Kale Stew, 152
  kidney
    Annatto Rice with Kidney Beans & Romanesco Florets, 170
    Kidney Beans, 238
beets, Overnight Beet Oats, 62
bell peppers
  Annatto Rice with Kidney Beans & Romanesco Florets, 170
  Black Bean Dip, 218
  Braised Nopal Cactus Pads, 150
  Cauliflower Ceviche with Coconut & Passion Fruit Marinade, 157
  Cauliflower Steaks with Herbed Succotash, 176
  Creamy Farro Casserole with Broccoli & Butternut Squash, 164
  Crispy Sprouted Tofu with Stir-Fried Vegetables, 171
  Domino Rice & Beans with Spicy Adobo Seasoning, 115
  Fava Bean & Zucchini Salad with Apple Cider Dressing, 94
  Guasacaca (Spicy Avocado Sauce), 215
  Jackfruit & Leafstalk Tacos with Avocado & Radish Greens Crema, 177
  Nopal Cactus Pad & Quinoa Salad, 93

Plantain Dumplings, 126
Quinoa-Stuffed Peppers, 175
Roasted Red Pepper Dip, 217
Spicy Chayote & Tomato Casserole, 143
Split Pea Soup, 135
Berry & Banana Sorbet, 201
beverages, 181–195
  Chunky Tropical Fruit Tizana, 183
  Cinnamon-Spiced Brown Rice Smoothie, 186
  Cocada Smoothie, 189
  Loaded Breakfast Smoothie, 188
  Maca & Cacao Latte, 194
  Papaya Milkshakes, 191
  Spiced Hibiscus Tea, 192
  Strawberry-Top Spritzer, 185
  Tamarind Juice, 184
  Watermelon Limeade, 193
black beans
  Black Bean Chili, 147
  Black Bean Dip, 218
  Black & White Beans, 238
  Domino Rice & Beans with Spicy Adobo Seasoning, 115
  King Oyster Mushroom Arepas, 163
blackberries
  Berry & Banana Sorbet, 201
  Loaded Breakfast Smoothie, 188
  Watermelon Pizza, 64
black-eyed peas
  Black-Eyed Peas, 238
  Black-Eyed Pea & Vegetable Stew, 142
blueberries
  Berry & Banana Sorbet, 201
  Loaded Breakfast Smoothie, 188
  Watermelon Pizza, 64
Braised Nopal Cactus Pads, 150
breakfasts, 59–73
  Amaranth Pancakes with Apple Compote, 61
  Avocado Smoothie Bowl with Fresh Fruits, 67
  Coconut & Chia Bowl with Warm Ancient Grains, 69
  Loaded Breakfast Smoothie, 188
  Oat Waffles with Mango Sauce, 72
  Overnight Beet Oats, 62
  Quinoa Porridge with Stewed Bananas & Prunes, 66
  toasts, 70–71
    Avocado Toast, 70
    Hummus Toast, 70

    Pea Purée Toast, 71
    Vegetable Toast, 71
  Tofu Perico Scramble, 63
  Watermelon Pizza, 64
broccoli
  Annatto Rice with Kidney Beans & Romanesco Florets, 170
  Broccoli Soup, 146
  Broccoli Stalk Cakes, 79
  Creamy Farro Casserole with Broccoli & Butternut Squash, 164
brown rice
  Annatto Rice with Kidney Beans & Romanesco Florets, 170
  Brown or Wild Rice, 242
  Cinnamon-Spiced Brown Rice Smoothie, 186
  Domino Rice & Beans with Spicy Adobo Seasoning, 115
Buñuelos (Yuca Beignets) with Cacao Dipping Sauce, 207
butternut squash
  Creamy Butternut Soup, 136
  Creamy Farro Casserole with Broccoli & Butternut Squash, 164
  Roasted Okra with Maple Butternut Squash, 119
  Stuffed Squash Blossoms, 78

C

cabbage (purple)
  Chayote & Mango Slaw with English Peas, 104
  Sweet Potato & Great Northern Bean Salad with Tahini Dressing, 96
  Sweet Potato Tacos with Collard Greens Shells, 178
  Tostones Nachos with Crumbled Sprouted Tofu, 166
cabbage (Savoy), Papaya Poke Stacks with Wasabi Slaw, 169
Cacao & Nut Truffles, 200
cactus
  Braised Nopal Cactus Pads, 150
  Cantaloupe & Prickly Pear Ice Pops, 210
  Nopal Cactus Pad & Quinoa Salad, 93
cantaloupe, Cantaloupe & Prickly Pear Ice Pops, 210
carbon footprint, 27–39
carrots
  Carrot-Top Chimichurri, 218
  Chayote Tagine with Prunes & Apricots, 149
  Lentil Minestrone, 138

Mushroom Bánh Mì, 159

Mushroom & String Bean Salad with Roasted Heirloom Carrots, 98

Pickled Carrots, 227

Purple Sweet Potato Gnocchi with Carrot-Top Pesto, 160

Roasted Heirloom Carrots with Tahini Sauce, 117

Split Pea Soup, 135

Cashew Cream, 230

cauliflower

Barbecue Cauliflower, 86

Cauliflower Ceviche with Coconut & Passion Fruit Marinade, 157

Cauliflower Leafstalk Kimchi, 226

Cauliflower Steaks with Herbed Succotash, 176

Curried Cauliflower Salad with Apples & Celery, 108

Jackfruit & Leafstalk Tacos with Avocado & Radish Greens Crema, 177

White Bean & Kale Stew, 152

cauliflower (purple)

Millet & Okra Salad, 101

Savory Quinoa Beignets, 87

celery

Curried Cauliflower Salad with Apples & Celery, 108

Lentil Minestrone, 138

Shaved Fennel, Celery & Pink Grapefruit Salad with Dill & Yogurt Dressing, 102

Split Pea Soup, 135

chayote squash

Chayote & Mango Slaw with English Peas, 104

Chayote Tagine with Prunes & Apricots, 149

Lentil Minestrone, 138

Spicy Chayote & Tomato Casserole, 143

chia seeds

Coconut & Chia Bowl with Warm Ancient Grains, 69

Crispy Millet Crackers, 223

Oat Waffles with Mango Sauce, 72

Tamarind Juice, 184

Watermelon Pizza, 64

chipotle pepper, Corn Lollipops with Chipotle & Tofu Cream Sauce, 128

Chocolate & Garbanzo Cookies, 205

Chunky Tropical Fruit Tizana, 183

Cinnamon-Spiced Brown Rice Smoothie, 186

climate and food crises, 11–25

coconut

Cocada Smoothie, 189

Coconut & Chia Bowl with Warm Ancient Grains, 69

Coconut Cream, 230

collard greens, Sweet Potato Tacos with Collard Greens Shells, 178

corn

Black Bean Chili, 147

Cauliflower Ceviche with Coconut & Passion Fruit Marinade, 157

Cauliflower Steaks with Herbed Succotash, 176

Corn Lollipops with Chipotle & Tofu Cream Sauce, 128

Fava Bean Pod Bollitos, 83

Jícama & Corn Salad with Aquafaba Mayonnaise Vinaigrette, 95

Plant-Based Meatball Soup, 141

creams, 230

Cashew Cream, 230

Coconut Cream, 230

Creamy Butternut Soup, 136

Creamy Farro Casserole with Broccoli & Butternut Squash, 164

Creamy Garlic Sauce, 214

Crispy Millet Crackers, 223

Crispy Sprouted Tofu with Stir-Fried Vegetables, 171

crookneck squash, Crookneck Squash with King Oyster Mushrooms, 122

cucumbers

Cucumber, Pea & Daikon Salad with Almond & Ginger Dressing, 110

English, Cucumber & Shallot Raita, 219

Mushroom Bánh Mì, 159

Wild Rice & Tomato Salad with Balsamic & Maple Dressing, 109

cucumbers (English), Mango & Ginger Gazpacho, 133

cucumbers (Persian), Amaranth Tabbouleh with Cucumber & Pomegranate Seeds, 105

Cultured Cashew Yogurt, 235

Curried Cauliflower Salad with Apples & Celery, 108

D

daikon

Cucumber, Pea & Daikon Salad with Almond & Ginger Dressing, 110

Mushroom Bánh Mì, 159

Papaya Poke Stacks with Wasabi Slaw, 169

dandelion leaves, Quinoa-Stuffed Peppers, 175

dates

Cacao & Nut Truffles, 200

Papaya Milkshakes, 191

Yam & Maca Truffles, 208

desserts, 197–211

Berry & Banana Sorbet, 201

Buñuelos (Yuca Beignets) with Cacao Dipping Sauce, 207

Cacao & Nut Truffles, 200

Cantaloupe & Prickly Pear Ice Pops, 210

Chocolate & Garbanzo Cookies, 205

Leguminous Chocolate Pudding, 209

Mango & Coconut Sorbet, 202

Pineapple Frozen Yogurt, 204

Quinoa Pudding, 199

Yam & Maca Truffles, 208

dips. See sauces, dips, pickles & more

Domino Rice & Beans with Spicy Adobo Seasoning, 115

E

Edamame Pilaf with Ginger & Shaved Almonds, 125

eggplant

Eggplant & Lentil Stacks, 158

Eggplant & Sweet Potato Curry, 144

Japanese, Quinoa-Stuffed Peppers, 175

Potato & Eggplant Skewers, 85

Spaghetti Squash with Plant-Based Bolognese, 165

English cucumber

Cucumber & Shallot Raita, 219

Mango & Ginger Gazpacho, 133

English peas

Chayote & Mango Slaw with English Peas, 104

Pea Purée Toast, 71

F

Falafel Bites on Endive Boats, 88

farro

Creamy Farro Casserole with Broccoli & Butternut Squash, 164

Farro, 243

fava beans

Fava Bean & Avocado Soup, 134

Fava Bean Pod Bollitos, 83

Fava Bean Spread, 219

Fava Bean & Zucchini Salad with Apple Cider Dressing, 94

fennel, Shaved Fennel, Celery & Pink Grapefruit Salad with Dill & Yogurt Dressing, 102

flaxseeds

Amaranth Pancakes with Apple Compote, 61

Broccoli Stalk Cakes, 79

Buñuelos (Yuca Beignets) with Cacao Dipping Sauce, 207

Chocolate & Garbanzo Cookies, 205

Loaded Breakfast Smoothie, 188

Plant-Based Meatball Soup, 141

Yellow Split Pea Hummus, 220

Fresno peppers

Carrot-Top Chimichurri, 218

Jícama & Corn Salad with Aquafaba Mayonnaise Vinaigrette, 95

Fuji apples

Curried Cauliflower Salad with Apples & Celery, 108

Overnight Beet Oats, 62

Furikake Seaweed Seasoning, 240

G

Gala apples

Amaranth Pancakes with Apple Compote, 61

Cauliflower Leafstalk Kimchi, 226

galia melon, Chunky Tropical Fruit Tizana, 183

garbanzo beans

Falafel Bites on Endive Boats, 88

Garbanzo Beans, 238

Garbanzo & Potato Stew, 151

Plant-Based Meatball Soup, 141

garlic, Roasted Garlic Paste, 237

goldenberries (cape gooseberries), Avocado Smoothie Bowl with Fresh Fruits, 67

grains, 242–243

Amaranth, 243

Brown or Wild Rice, 242

Farro, 243

Millets, 243

Quinoa, 242

grapefruit (pink), Shaved Fennel, Celery & Pink Grapefruit Salad with Dill & Yogurt Dressing, 102

grapes (seedless), Chunky Tropical Fruit Tizana, 183

Great Northern beans

Sweet Potato & Great Northern Bean Salad with Tahini Dressing, 96

White Bean & Kale Stew, 152

Green Jackfruit, 234

green lentils

Green Lentils, 239

Quinoa-Stuffed Peppers, 175

Guasacaca (Spicy Avocado Sauce), 215

H

hempseeds

Buñuelos (Yuca Beignets) with Cacao Dipping Sauce, 207

Cinnamon-Spiced Brown Rice Smoothie, 186

Coconut & Chia Bowl with Warm Ancient Grains, 69

Loaded Breakfast Smoothie, 188

hibiscus flowers, Spiced Hibiscus Tea, 192

Homemade Curry Powder, 240

hummus, Hummus Toast, 70

J

jackfruit
Green Jackfruit, 234
Jackfruit Empanaditas, *77*
Jackfruit & Leafstalk Tacos with
Avocado & Radish Greens Crema,
177
Japanese eggplant, Quinoa-Stuffed
Peppers, 175
jícama
Jackfruit & Leafstalk Tacos with
Avocado & Radish Greens Crema,
177
Jícama & Corn Salad with Aquafaba
Mayonnaise Vinaigrette, 95

K

kale
Acorn Squash with Wilted Kale, 118
White Bean & Kale Stew, 152
kidney beans
Annatto Rice with Kidney Beans &
Romanesco Florets, 170
Kidney Beans, 238
King Oyster Mushroom Arepas, 163
kiwi, Avocado Smoothie Bowl with
Fresh Fruits, 67

L

latte, Maca & Cacao Latte, 194
leeks
Split Pea Soup, 135
Swiss Chard & Lentil Salad with
Balsamic Dressing, 107
Yuca with Leek Mojo Sauce, 114
Leguminous Chocolate Pudding, 209
lentils
Eggplant & Lentil Stacks, 158
Lentil Minestrone, 138
lentils (green)
Green Lentils, 239
Quinoa-Stuffed Peppers, 175
lentils (red)
Mango Salsa, 225
Red Lentils, 239
Swiss Chard & Lentil Salad with
Balsamic Dressing, 107
lettuce (romaine), Wild Rice & Tomato
Salad with Balsamic & Maple
Dressing, 109
lime
Lime-Pickled Onions & Watermelon
Rinds, 227
Watermelon Limeade, 193
Loaded Breakfast Smoothie, 188
low-carbon diet, 41–49

M

Maca & Cacao Latte, 194
main dishes, 155–179

Annatto Rice with Kidney Beans &
Romanesco Florets, 170
Cauliflower Ceviche with Coconut &
Passion Fruit Marinade, 157
Cauliflower Steaks with Herbed
Succotash, 176
Creamy Farro Casserole with Broccoli
& Butternut Squash, 164
Crispy Sprouted Tofu with Stir-Fried
Vegetables, 171
Eggplant & Lentil Stacks, 158
Jackfruit & Leafstalk Tacos with
Avocado & Radish Greens Crema,
177
King Oyster Mushroom Arepas, 163
Mushroom Bánh Mì, 159
Papaya Poke Stacks with Wasabi
Slaw, 169
Purple Sweet Potato Gnocchi with
Carrot-Top Pesto, 160
Quinoa-Stuffed Peppers, 175
Spaghetti Squash with Plant-Based
Bolognese, 165
Sweet Potato Tacos with Collard
Greens Shells, 178
Tostones Nachos with Crumbled
Sprouted Tofu, 166
Zucchini Noodles & Grilled Portobello
Steaks, 172
make-ahead recipes, 229–243
Aquafaba Mayonnaise, 235
creams, 230
Cashew Cream, 230
Coconut Cream, 230
Cultured Cashew Yogurt, 235
grains, 242–243
Amaranth, 243
Brown or Wild Rice, 242
Farro, 243
Millets, 243
Quinoa, 242
Green Jackfruit, 234
pulses, 238–239
Black-Eyed Peas, 238
Black & White Beans, 238
Garbanzo Beans, 238
Green Lentils, 239
Kidney Beans, 238
Red Lentils, 239
Split Peas, 239
Roasted Garlic Paste, 237
seasoning blends, 240
Furikake Seaweed Seasoning, 240
Homemade Curry Powder, 240
Spicy Adobo Seasoning, 240
Umami Mushroom Powder, 240
seed powders, 231
Avocado Seed Powder, 231
Papaya Seed Powder, 231
Vegetable Broth, 232

mangoes
Chayote & Mango Slaw with English
Peas, 104
Chunky Tropical Fruit Tizana, 183
Mango & Coconut Sorbet, 202
Mango & Ginger Gazpacho, 133
Mango Salsa, 225
milk (plant-based)
Amaranth Pancakes with Apple
Compote, 61
Barbecue Cauliflower, 86
Berry & Banana Sorbet, 201
Coconut Cream, 230
Maca & Cacao Latte, 194
Oat Waffles with Mango Sauce, *72*
Overnight Beet Oats, 62
Papaya Milkshakes, 191
Quinoa Pudding, 199
millets
Crispy Millet Crackers, 223
Millet & Okra Salad, 101
Millets, 243
Stuffed Shiitake Mushrooms, 82
mushrooms
Black-Eyed Pea & Vegetable Stew,
142
Crookneck Squash with King Oyster
Mushrooms, 122
King Oyster Mushroom Arepas, 163
Mushroom Bánh Mì, 159
Mushroom & String Bean Salad with
Roasted Heirloom Carrots, 98
Stuffed Shiitake Mushrooms, 82
Tofu Perico Scramble, 63
Zucchini Noodles & Grilled Portobello
Steaks, 172

N

nopal cactus pads
Braised Nopal Cactus Pads, 150
Nopal Cactus Pad & Quinoa Salad, 93
nuts
Cacao & Nut Truffles, 200
Cultured Cashew Yogurt, 235
Edamame Pilaf with Ginger & Shaved
Almonds, 125
Roasted Fingerling Potatoes with
Caramelized Onions & Nuts, 120
Roasted Red Pepper Dip, 217
Spaghetti Squash with Plant-Based
Bolognese, 165
Yam & Maca Truffles, 208

O

oat flour, Oat Waffles with Mango
Sauce, *72*
oats, Overnight Beet Oats, 62
okra
Millet & Okra Salad, 101
Roasted Okra with Maple Butternut

Squash, 119
onions
Black Bean Dip, 218
Cauliflower Ceviche with Coconut &
Passion Fruit Marinade, 157
Chayote Tagine with Prunes &
Apricots, 149
Creamy Butternut Soup, 136
Crispy Sprouted Tofu with Stir-Fried
Vegetables, 171
Lentil Minestrone, 138
Lime-Pickled Onions & Watermelon
Rinds, 227
Potato & Eggplant Skewers, 85
Roasted Fingerling Potatoes with
Caramelized Onions & Nuts, 120
Overnight Beet Oats, 62

P

papaya
Papaya Milkshakes, 191
Papaya Poke Stacks with Wasabi
Slaw, 169
Papaya Seed Powder, 231
peas
English
Chayote & Mango Slaw with
English Peas, 104
Pea Purée Toast, 71
split, Yellow Split Pea Hummus, 220
sugar snap, Cucumber, Pea & Daikon
Salad with Almond & Ginger
Dressing, 110
peppers
bell
Annatto Rice with Kidney Beans &
Romanesco Florets, 170
Black Bean Dip, 218
Braised Nopal Cactus Pads, 150
Cauliflower Ceviche with Coconut &
Passion Fruit Marinade, 157
Cauliflower Steaks with Herbed
Succotash, 176
Creamy Farro Casserole with
Broccoli & Butternut Squash,
164
Crispy Sprouted Tofu with Stir-Fried
Vegetables, 171
Domino Rice & Beans with Spicy
Adobo Seasoning, 115
Fava Bean & Zucchini Salad with
Apple Cider Dressing, 94
Guasacaca (Spicy Avocado Sauce),
215
Jackfruit & Leafstalk Tacos with
Avocado & Radish Greens Crema,
177
Mango Salsa, 225
Nopal Cactus Pad & Quinoa Salad,
93

Plantain Dumplings, 126
Quinoa-Stuffed Peppers, 175
Roasted Red Pepper Dip, 217
Spicy Chayote & Tomato Casserole, 143
Split Pea Soup, 135
chipotle, Corn Lollipops with Chipotle & Tofu Cream Sauce, 128
Fresno
Carrot-Top Chimichurri, 218
Jícama & Corn Salad with Aquafaba Mayonnaise Vinaigrette, 95
Persian cucumber, Amaranth Tabbouleh with Cucumber & Pomegranate Seeds, 105
Pickled Carrots, 227
pickling and fermenting (recipes), 226–227
pineapple
Oat Waffles with Mango Sauce, 72
Pineapple Frozen Yogurt, 204
pitaya (dragon fruit), Avocado Smoothie Bowl with Fresh Fruits, 67
plantains
Plantain Chips, 222
Plantain Cups, 80
Plantain Dumplings, 126
Plant-Based Meatball Soup, 141
pomegranate seeds
Amaranth Tabbouleh with Cucumber & Pomegranate Seeds, 105
Chunky Tropical Fruit Tizana, 183
Sweet Potato & Great Northern Bean Salad with Tahini Dressing, 96
potatoes. See also sweet potatoes
baby, Potato & Eggplant Skewers, 85
Garbanzo & Potato Stew, 151
Lentil Minestrone, 138
red
Black-Eyed Pea & Vegetable Stew, 142
Chayote Tagine with Prunes & Apricots, 149
Roasted Fingerling Potatoes with Caramelized Onions & Nuts, 120
prickly pears, Cantaloupe & Prickly Pear Ice Pops, 210
prunes, Quinoa Porridge with Stewed Bananas & Prunes, 66
pulses, 238–239
Black-Eyed Peas, 238
Black & White Beans, 238
Garbanzo Beans, 238
Green Lentils, 239
Kidney Beans, 238
Red Lentils, 239
Split Peas, 239
pumpkin, Spiced Pumpkin Soup, 139
purple cabbage
Chayote & Mango Slaw with English

Peas, 104
Sweet Potato & Great Northern Bean Salad with Tahini Dressing, 96
Sweet Potato Tacos with Collard Greens Shells, 178
Tostones Nachos with Crumbled Sprouted Tofu, 166
purple cauliflower
Millet & Okra Salad, 101
Savory Quinoa Beignets, 87
Purple Sweet Potato Gnocchi with Carrot-Top Pesto, 160

Q

quinoa
Coconut & Chia Bowl with Warm Ancient Grains, 69
Nopal Cactus Pad & Quinoa Salad, 93
Quinoa, 242
Quinoa Porridge with Stewed Bananas & Prunes, 66
Quinoa Pudding, 199
Quinoa-Stuffed Peppers, 175
Savory Quinoa Beignets, 87

R

radicchio
Vegetable Toast, 71
Zucchini Noodles & Grilled Portobello Steaks, 172
radishes, Roasted Radishes with Garlic & Parsley, 123
raspberries
Avocado Smoothie Bowl with Fresh Fruits, 67
Berry & Banana Sorbet, 201
Leguminous Chocolate Pudding, 209
red lentils
Mango Salsa, 225
Red Lentils, 239
Swiss Chard & Lentil Salad with Balsamic Dressing, 107
red potatoes
Black-Eyed Pea & Vegetable Stew, 142
Chayote Tagine with Prunes & Apricots, 149
rice
brown
Annatto Rice with Kidney Beans & Romanesco Florets, 170
Brown or Wild Rice, 242
Cinnamon-Spiced Brown Rice Smoothie, 186
Domino Rice & Beans with Spicy Adobo Seasoning, 115
wild
Brown or Wild Rice, 242
Edamame Pilaf with Ginger & Shaved Almonds, 125

Wild Rice & Tomato Salad with Balsamic & Maple Dressing, 109
Roasted Fingerling Potatoes with Caramelized Onions & Nuts, 120
Roasted Heirloom Carrots with Tahini Sauce, 117
Roasted Okra with Maple Butternut Squash, 119
Roasted Radishes with Garlic & Parsley, 123
Roasted Red Pepper Dip, 217

S

salads, 91–111
Amaranth Tabbouleh with Cucumber & Pomegranate Seeds, 105
Asparagus Salad with Avocado & Grape Tomatoes, 99
Chayote & Mango Slaw with English Peas, 104
Cucumber, Pea & Daikon Salad with Almond & Ginger Dressing, 110
Curried Cauliflower Salad with Apples & Celery, 108
Fava Bean & Zucchini Salad with Apple Cider Dressing, 94
Jícama & Corn Salad with Aquafaba Mayonnaise Vinaigrette, 95
Millet & Okra Salad, 101
Mushroom & String Bean Salad with Roasted Heirloom Carrots, 98
Nopal Cactus Pad & Quinoa Salad, 93
Shaved Fennel, Celery & Pink Grapefruit Salad with Dill & Yogurt Dressing, 102
Sweet Potato & Great Northern Bean Salad with Tahini Dressing, 96
Swiss Chard & Lentil Salad with Balsamic Dressing, 107
Wild Rice & Tomato Salad with Balsamic & Maple Dressing, 109
Salsa Verde, 215
sauces, dips, pickles & more, 213–227
Barbecue Sauce, 214
Black Bean Dip, 218
Carrot-Top Chimichurri, 218
Cauliflower Leafstalk Kimchi, 226
Creamy Garlic Sauce, 214
Crispy Millet Crackers, 223
Cucumber & Shallot Raita, 219
dippers, 222–223
Fava Bean Spread, 219
Guasacaca (Spicy Avocado Sauce), 215
Lime-Pickled Onions & Watermelon Rinds, 227
Mango Salsa, 225
Pickled Carrots, 227
pickling and fermenting, 226–227
Plantain Chips, 222

Roasted Red Pepper Dip, 217
Salsa Verde, 215
Yellow Split Pea Hummus, 220
Sautéed Beet Greens, 127
Savory Quinoa Beignets, 87
Savoy cabbage, Papaya Poke Stacks with Wasabi Slaw, 169
seasoning blends, 240
Furikake Seaweed Seasoning, 240
Homemade Curry Powder, 240
Spicy Adobo Seasoning, 240
Umami Mushroom Powder, 240
seed powders, 231
Avocado Seed Powder, 231
Papaya Seed Powder, 231
seeds
chia
Coconut & Chia Bowl with Warm Ancient Grains, 69
Crispy Millet Crackers, 223
Oat Waffles with Mango Sauce, 72
Tamarind Juice, 184
Watermelon Pizza, 64
flaxseeds
Amaranth Pancakes with Apple Compote, 61
Broccoli Stalk Cakes, 79
Buñuelos (Yuca Beignets) with Cacao Dipping Sauce, 207
Chocolate & Garbanzo Cookies, 205
Loaded Breakfast Smoothie, 188
Plant-Based Meatball Soup, 141
Yellow Split Pea Hummus, 220
hempseeds
Buñuelos (Yuca Beignets) with Cacao Dipping Sauce, 207
Cinnamon-Spiced Brown Rice Smoothie, 186
Coconut & Chia Bowl with Warm Ancient Grains, 69
Loaded Breakfast Smoothie, 188
pomegranate
Amaranth Tabbouleh with Cucumber & Pomegranate Seeds, 105
Chunky Tropical Fruit Tizana, 183
Sweet Potato & Great Northern Bean Salad with Tahini Dressing, 96
sesame
Crispy Millet Crackers, 223
Falafel Bites on Endive Boats, 88
Shaved Fennel, Celery & Pink Grapefruit Salad with Dill & Yogurt Dressing, 102
sides, 113–129
Acorn Squash with Wilted Kale, 118
Corn Lollipops with Chipotle & Tofu Cream Sauce, 128
Crookneck Squash with King Oyster

Mushrooms, 122
Domino Rice & Beans with Spicy
   Adobo Seasoning, 115
Edamame Pilaf with Ginger & Shaved
   Almonds, 125
Plantain Dumplings, 126
Roasted Fingerling Potatoes with
   Caramelized Onions & Nuts, 120
Roasted Heirloom Carrots with Tahini
   Sauce, 117
Roasted Okra with Maple Butternut
   Squash, 119
Roasted Radishes with Garlic &
   Parsley, 123
Sautéed Beet Greens, 127
Yuca with Leek Mojo Sauce, 114
small bites, 75–89
   Barbecue Cauliflower, 86
   Broccoli Stalk Cakes, 79
   Falafel Bites on Endive Boats, 88
   Fava Bean Pod Bollitos, 83
   Jackfruit Empanaditas, 77
   Plantain Cups, 80
   Potato & Eggplant Skewers, 85
   Savory Quinoa Beignets, 87
   Stuffed Shiitake Mushrooms, 82
   Stuffed Squash Blossoms, 78
smoothies
   Avocado Smoothie Bowl with Fresh
      Fruits, 67
   Cinnamon-Spiced Brown Rice
      Smoothie, 186
   Loaded Breakfast Smoothie, 188
soups and stews, 131–153
   Black Bean Chili, 147
   Black-Eyed Pea & Vegetable Stew,
      142
   Braised Nopal Cactus Pads, 150
   Broccoli Soup, 146
   Chayote Tagine with Prunes &
      Apricots, 149
   Creamy Butternut Soup, 136
   Eggplant & Sweet Potato Curry, 144
   Fava Bean & Avocado Soup, 134
   Garbanzo & Potato Stew, 151
   Lentil Minestrone, 138
   Mango & Ginger Gazpacho, 133
   Plant-Based Meatball Soup, 141
   Spiced Pumpkin Soup, 139
   Spicy Chayote & Tomato Casserole,
      143
   Split Pea Soup, 135
   White Bean & Kale Stew, 152
Spaghetti Squash with Plant-Based
   Bolognese, 165
Spiced Hibiscus Tea, 192
Spiced Pumpkin Soup, 139
Spicy Adobo Seasoning, 240
Spicy Chayote & Tomato Casserole,
   143

spinach
   Broccoli Soup, 146
   Stuffed Shiitake Mushrooms, 82
spinach (baby)
   Avocado Smoothie Bowl with Fresh
      Fruits, 67
   Loaded Breakfast Smoothie, 188
split peas
   Split Pea Soup, 135
   Split Peas, 239
   Yellow Split Pea Hummus, 220
squash
   Acorn Squash with Wilted Kale, 118
   butternut
      Creamy Butternut Soup, 136
      Creamy Farro Casserole with
         Broccoli & Butternut Squash,
         164
      Roasted Okra with Maple Butternut
         Squash, 119
      Stuffed Squash Blossoms, 78
   chayote
      Chayote & Mango Slaw with
         English Peas, 104
      Chayote Tagine with Prunes &
         Apricots, 149
      Lentil Minestrone, 138
      Spicy Chayote & Tomato Casserole,
         143
   Crookneck Squash with King Oyster
      Mushrooms, 122
   Spaghetti Squash with Plant-Based
      Bolognese, 165
   Spiced Pumpkin Soup, 139
stews. See soups and stews
Strawberry-Top Spritzer, 185
string beans, Mushroom & String Bean
   Salad with Roasted Heirloom Carrots,
   98
Stuffed Shiitake Mushrooms, 82
Stuffed Squash Blossoms, 78
sugar snap peas, Crispy Sprouted Tofu
   with Stir-Fried Vegetables, 171
sweet potatoes
   Cauliflower Ceviche with Coconut &
      Passion Fruit Marinade, 157
   Eggplant & Sweet Potato Curry, 144
   Purple Sweet Potato Gnocchi with
      Carrot-Top Pesto, 160
   Sweet Potato & Great Northern Bean
      Salad with Tahini Dressing, 96
   Sweet Potato Tacos with Collard
      Greens Shells, 178
Swiss chard
   Quinoa-Stuffed Peppers, 175
   Swiss Chard & Lentil Salad with
      Balsamic Dressing, 107

T
Tamarind Juice, 184

tea, Spiced Hibiscus Tea, 192
toasts, 70–71
   Avocado Toast, 70
   Hummus Toast, 70
   Pea Purée Toast, 71
   Vegetable Toast, 71
tofu
   Crispy Sprouted Tofu with Stir-Fried
      Vegetables, 171
   Leguminous Chocolate Pudding, 209
   Plant-Based Meatball Soup, 141
   Tofu Perico Scramble, 63
   Tostones Nachos with Crumbled
      Sprouted Tofu, 166
tomatillos, Nopal Cactus Pad & Quinoa
   Salad, 93
tomatoes
   Annatto Rice with Kidney Beans &
      Romanesco Florets, 170
   Asparagus Salad with Avocado &
      Grape Tomatoes, 99
   Barbecue Sauce, 214
   Braised Nopal Cactus Pads, 150
   Eggplant & Lentil Stacks, 158
   Eggplant & Sweet Potato Curry, 144
   Lentil Minestrone, 138
   Plantain Cups, 80
   Spicy Chayote & Tomato Casserole,
      143
   Tofu Perico Scramble, 63
   Tostones Nachos with Crumbled
      Sprouted Tofu, 166
   Wild Rice & Tomato Salad with
      Balsamic & Maple Dressing, 109
Tostones Nachos with Crumbled
   Sprouted Tofu, 166

U–V–W–X
Umami Mushroom Powder, 240

Vegetable Broth, 232
Vegetable Toast, 71

watermelon
   Cauliflower Ceviche with Coconut &
      Passion Fruit Marinade, 157
   Chunky Tropical Fruit Tizana, 183
   Lime-Pickled Onions & Watermelon
      Rinds, 227
   Watermelon Limeade, 193
   Watermelon Pizza, 64
White Bean & Kale Stew, 152
wild rice
   Brown or Wild Rice, 242
   Edamame Pilaf with Ginger & Shaved
      Almonds, 125
   Wild Rice & Tomato Salad with
      Balsamic & Maple Dressing, 109

Y

Yam & Maca Truffles, 208
Yellow Split Pea Hummus, 220
yogurt (plant-based)
   Cucumber & Shallot Raita, 219
   Cultured Cashew Yogurt, 235
   Pineapple Frozen Yogurt, 204
   Shaved Fennel, Celery & Pink
      Grapefruit Salad with Dill & Yogurt
      Dressing, 102
   Spiced Pumpkin Soup, 139
   Watermelon Pizza, 64
yuca
   Buñuelos (Yuca Beignets) with Cacao
      Dipping Sauce, 207
   Yuca with Leek Mojo Sauce, 114

Z
zucchini
   Crispy Sprouted Tofu with Stir-Fried
      Vegetables, 171
   Fava Bean & Zucchini Salad with
      Apple Cider Dressing, 94
   Vegetable Toast, 71
   Zucchini Noodles & Grilled Portobello
      Steaks, 172